A Jungian Perspective on the Therapist-Patient Relationship in Film

Within this book, Ruth Netzer explores the archetypal components of therapist-patient relations in cinema from the perspective of Jungian archetypal symbolism, and within the context of myth and ritual.

Film is a medium that is attracted to the extremes of this specific relationship, depicting the collapse of the accepted boundaries of therapy; though on the other hand, cinema also loves the fantasy of therapy as intimacy. Through the medium of film, and employing examples from over 45 well-known films, the author analyzes the successes and failures of therapists within film, and reviews the concepts of transference and counter-transference and their therapeutic and redemptive powers, in contrast to their potential for destruction and exploitation within the context of a patient-therapist relationship.

This book will be a fascinating read for Jungian analysts, psychologists, psychiatrists, and therapists with an interest in the link between cinema and therapy, as well as filmmakers and students and teachers of film studies.

Ruth Netzer is a clinical psychologist, Jungian analyst (senior lecturer and supervisor), poet, and painter, and does research in literature and cinema. She has published 12 non-fiction books on Jungian psychology and 12 books of poetry (which have won 5 literary awards), as well as scores of professional articles. She teaches at the School of Jungian Psychotherapy in Seminar HaKibbutzim College in Israel.

A Jungian Perspective on the Therapist-Patient Relationship in Film

Cinema As Our Therapist

Ruth Netzer

Translated by Batya Stein

LONDON AND NEW YORK

Designed cover image: *Feelings* by Ruth Netzer

First published 2024
by Routledge
4 Park Square, Milton Park, Abingdon, Oxon OX14 4RN

and by Routledge
605 Third Avenue, New York, NY 10158

Routledge is an imprint of the Taylor & Francis Group, an informa business

© 2024 Ruth Netzer

The right of Ruth Netzer to be identified as author of this work has been asserted in accordance with sections 77 and 78 of the Copyright, Designs and Patents Act 1988.

All rights reserved. No part of this book may be reprinted or reproduced or utilised in any form or by any electronic, mechanical, or other means, now known or hereafter invented, including photocopying and recording, or in any information storage or retrieval system, without permission in writing from the publishers.

Trademark notice: Product or corporate names may be trademarks or registered trademarks, and are used only for identification and explanation without intent to infringe.

British Library Cataloguing-in-Publication Data
A catalogue record for this book is available from the British Library

Library of Congress Cataloging-in-Publication Data
Names: Netzer, Ruth, author. | Stein, Batya, translator.
Title: A Jungian perspective on the therapist-patient relationship in film: cinema as our therapist / Ruth Netzer; translated by Batya Stein.
Other titles: Cinema as our therapist. English
Description: London ; New York : Routledge, 2024. | The original title is 'Cinema as our therapist'. | Includes bibliographical references and index. | Translated from Hebrew.
Identifiers: LCCN 2023055638 (print) | LCCN 2023055639 (ebook) | ISBN 9781032608372 (hardback) | ISBN 9781032608341 (paperback) | ISBN 9781003460688 (ebook)
Subjects: LCSH: Psychoanalysis and motion pictures. | Jungian psychology. | Motion pictures—Psychological aspects.
Classification: LCC PN1995.9.P783 C562513 2024 (print) | LCC PN1995.9.P783 (ebook) | DDC 791.43019—dc23/eng/20231221
LC record available at https://lccn.loc.gov/2023055638
LC ebook record available at https://lccn.loc.gov/2023055639

ISBN: 978-1-032-60837-2 (hbk)
ISBN: 978-1-032-60834-1 (pbk)
ISBN: 978-1-003-46068-8 (ebk)

DOI: 10.4324/9781003460688

Typeset in Times New Roman
by Apex CoVantage, LLC

To David Kadinsky, my first therapist

I'm writing to tell you what I didn't dare to tell you then.
I was young and you, a short, red-headed older "Yeke,"
heavy with years, sat in a small room
circled by pictures and statues, in the spirit of the place you came from.
My parents came from there too, but lost everything on the way.

You were a small god with a kindhearted smile,
and the smell of your pipe reminded me of mother's lover
and of father's pipe. Then, I didn't allow myself
to feel I loved the smell.
Now, I can sense it.

Your handshake was formal. All the meetings ended like that.
A table between us. Like my parents, you were taught to keep bounds.
When I showed you my drawings, you didn't manage to praise them.
Perhaps you even envied me.

I remember you fondly
because you believed I could be loved.
And because I managed to cry.

I was sick, even though I didn't know it.
After you died, I dreamt that I came to you in heaven.
You were a dentist. You said I didn't need treatment
and to go back down.

(Ruth Netzer)

Contents

Acknowledgements		*viii*
Preface		*ix*
	Personal Introduction	1
1	Psychological Aspects of Cinema	4
2	Therapist-Patient Relationships: Love and Death	30
3	Archetypes Activated in Therapist-Patient Relationships	37
4	Therapists as Mirrored in Cinema	67
5	Cinema as a "Chief Supervisor" for Therapists	96
6	Cinema, Madness, and Anti-psychiatry	118
7	Therapy and Redemption: Myth, Healing, and Religious Symbolism	123
8	Therapy in Cinema: The Wholeness of the Self, the Union of Opposites	131
	Glossary	*133*
	Index	*137*

Acknowledgements

Many thanks to Dr. Avi Goren-Bar for encouraging me to move forward with the translation process, and for his guidance and support along the way.

Many thanks to Batya Stein, translator, for her dedication and devotion, for investing so much time and effort in the thorough translation process.

Preface

This book reflects my recognition of the vast importance of cinema as a substitute for literature and ancient myths. Over time, I also became aware of the many films dealing with therapy and found that they focus mainly on its very core—the therapist-patient relationship.

The therapist is the psychologist, the psychiatrist, the doctor, the art therapist, the social worker, or alternative therapists using channeling, healing, shiatsu, and various body approaches. All sustain a unique relationship with patients, both hierarchical and reciprocal, which enables change and healing processes even though they may also involve power and exploitation.

The world of psychotherapy addresses this issue at length, and cinema reflects the importance of paying attention to these relationships, focusing on their emotional aspects rather than on interpretation and insight into the patient's inner world. The psychoanalytic theory of object relations is the basis for cinema's focus on the therapist-patient relationship. According to this theory, psychotherapy rests on insights into the patients' relations with significant figures in their lives and the connection that develops with the therapist when reconstructing and attempting to repair them. The therapist is a selfobject who lends himself to the patient. Heinz Kohut (1984) coined this non-hyphenated compound to imply that the therapist is the other, a self for the patient. He locates the need for fusion with the selfobject at the center of his theory on human existence and development and the healing powers of psychoanalysis. Films are mainly concerned with the transitional space between therapist and patient as a therapeutic field where, as in drama, the conflict and its solution unfold.

This book examines these relations from a symbolic Jungian perspective within a mythical context. The focus is on the essential archetypal aspects of therapist-patient relationships, bearing the positive dimensions and the difficulties, their healing power, and their destructive potential.

The therapist-patient relationship is already described in myths as the relation of individuals with a guide who is a selfobject god, a priest, a rabbi, or a spiritual master. From Jung's perspective, all myths deal with the voyage of the hero who overcomes obstacles in a search to constitute the self, and, in practice, these are also the myths of the psychotherapeutic journey. These myths serve as instructions for the voyage of both therapist and patient, providing knowledge about possible stations on the way, expected obstacles, and paths for coping with them. These myths show us that the healing processes, the change leading to growth, the dialogue one conducts with one's depths and with the guide that enables the process—have all existed for a very long time, as have the healing rituals.

After the era of myths, the human and therapeutic voyage shifted to legends and literature. In Jung's wake, Rollo May sees *The Divine Comedy* as the individuation myth common to pilgrim and guide, and as the model for the therapist-patient relationship (May 1991, 153). Today, cinema too deals with it. The fundamental perception of this book is that cinema grants the psyche expression, insight, and healing and thus becomes our therapist. The relation between cinema and the spectator conveys the therapist-patient one. Furthermore, just as every patient serves the therapist as a mirror, so do films focusing on the therapist-patient relationship, reflecting to them their problematic and ideal aspects, and enabling them to see how they are perceived.

Cinema tends to describe extreme relationships, breaking therapy's accepted boundaries and, at times, representing the therapist as questionable and even as sick. Cinema also conveys the fantasy of a deep and intimate tie between therapist and patient, including its erotic consummation, which is impossible. In all these aspects, cinema is like a collective dream and a guide meant to teach us how to be good therapists.

I will end this preface by giving thanks: thanks to the makers of cinema who taught me so much about therapeutic relations, thanks to my patients, from whom I learned what therapeutic relations are, and thanks to my students for their participation and their comments in the workshops on therapy and cinema.

References

Kohut, Heinz (1984) *How Does Analysis Cure?* ed. Arnold Goldberg (Chicago: University of Chicago Press).
May, Rollo (1991) *The Cry for Myth* (New York: Norton).

Personal Introduction

I have always preferred cinema to theater—at first because I could afford a movie ticket when a theater one was too expensive for me, and later because I was captivated by the magic of cinema's appeal to all the senses. Films felt to me more alive, true, and persuasive. Through cinema, I became acquainted with the lives of other people, in other countries and other circumstances, encountering plots, ways of expression and feeling, turmoil, and yearnings I had not known.

In the world of cinema, I could surrender without fear. I could forget myself entirely even though, unwittingly, I thereby met myself as I had not known till then, because—like all art—cinema reflects not only the world of the creator but also the world of the spectator. In the formulation of poet Agi Mishol, "It is then I understand that I'm the screen, and the only way to find out who I am is to guess what is projected on me" (Mishol 2008, 55).

For me, cinema is bound to the passion for life and for knowledge of the unknown that is reflected in another world. At times, I imagine that I go around the world filming a documentary with my gaze and everything around me is an event in it. The world then sharpens, and what happens from moment to moment takes place before me in a film in real time.

The more I encounter cinema in the dialogical space, the more it speaks to me with new insights. I feel it and it feels me. I interpret it and it interprets me and us to me (Stein 1988).

As every art at its best, cinema evokes in me a sense "as if the image launched desire beyond what it permits us to see" (Barthes 1981, 59). And as in every other art, in cinema, too, we sustain a dialogue with those we only look at, as it were, because when capturing the image of the other with our gaze we are also being captured with their gaze. As I once wrote:

> Clean black-and-white takes a picture
> of the stairwell.
> A Siamese cat paces lazily
> to a tranquil circle, punctuating
> my gaze with his eyes.
>
> (Netzer 1989, 24)

DOI: 10.4324/9781003460688-1

In the many movies dealing with psychotherapy, I noted that therapy is presented either extremely favorably or extremely critically, often distorting what I know happens in the clinic through my experience as both patient and therapist.

I wondered what attracts cinema, which began in the early twentieth century (very close to the birth of psychoanalysis), to deal with psychotherapy, the gift we received from Freud, Jung, and others. Artists and bohemian circles, including those involved in cinema, are well-known consumers of psychotherapy and many may have felt a need to convey their—good or bad—experiences of it. Over time, I came to think that cinema's intensive concern with therapy is significant and that the main focus of films dealing with this topic is on the dialogical relationships that are therapy's very core. Are not relationships the very core of life?

Curiosity led me on a fascinating voyage to many movies. Gradually, I understood that films are the collective dream of our era. Hence, like dreams generally, they purposefully mean to bring us to a new consciousness of human existence and to greater self-awareness, an assertion that applies to every spectator but even more so to spectators who are therapists. Films dealing with therapist-patient relationships are meant to raise our consciousness about "learning from the patient," as Patrick Casement titled his book (1985). We must learn from patients and therapists in films and from the way therapy is presented in cinema, from the yearnings it evokes, and from the opposition to it within the cinematic medium. That is how I understood that cinema is our therapist.

Before approaching the therapist-patient relationship in cinema, I will consider psychological aspects of cinema that, inadvertently, influence our psyche and thus "treat" spectators: mutual looks and their meaning; the viewer-viewed dialogue; the objective-subjective shift; the voyeuristic look; closeness/identification v. distancing; the dosage of feelings; self-awareness; contact with the wound, with unconscious depths, and with the dream; raising repressed contents; and healing processes.

Below is a poem I wrote about an expressionist painting from the early twentieth century, which gradually becomes a film shot:

> I think it's already midnight. The bar is almost empty.
> Humphrey Bogart's double, who bends over the counter
> in a suit and tie, wears Leonard Cohen's hat,
> men dressed like that then, in the early twentieth century.
> His face is steadfast. The cigarette between his fingers singes the dim counter.
> The redhead beside him cracks her fingers.
> Her long hair is pulled back, her neck bare, her face open.
> Her gaze is focused on a toothpick she's holding
> to disguise her unease. She's quiet.
> The man talks. The barman is the father confessor.
>
> (Netzer 2015, 92)

Then I understood. Cinema is our father confessor. But we, too, the spectators, are the father confessor of cinema's protagonists.

References

Barthes, Roland (1981) *Camera Lucida: Reflections on Photography* (New York: Hill and Wang).
Casement, Patrick (1985) *On Learning from the Patient* (London: Tavistock Publications).
Mishol, Agi (2008) "Across Me, Along the First Row." In *University of Darkness: Israeli Movie Poems*, eds. Moshe Dor and Raffi Weichert (Ra'anana, Israel: Even Hoshen) [Heb].
Netzer, Ruth (1989) *April Morning* (Tel Aviv: Sifriat Hapo'alim) [Heb].
Netzer, Ruth (2015) "American Painting." In *The Single Body* (Tel Aviv: Safra) [Heb].
Stein, Ruth (1988) "The Psychoanalytic Dialogue as a Written and Read Text," *Sihot/Dialogue: Israel Journal of Psychotherapy* 2 (3): 233–239 [Heb].

Chapter 1
Psychological Aspects of Cinema

Ancient cave paintings, picturesque hieroglyphics, and murals in age-old temples in all cultures attest that pictures preceded everything. We also experience dreams in pictures even though we report them in words, and cinema returns to the original images—the psyche's constitutive elements. Like any creation, cinema emerges from the unconscious of the writers-directors and the depths of their creative selves, which are rooted in a psychic substrate common to all humanity—the collective unconscious. The Jungian perspective on cinema addresses the archetypal human motifs conveyed through it.

Archetypes are fundamental models of thought constructs and psychic images. They are common to all humans beyond time and space (for example, the archetypes of mother, father, child, God, the way, the transition, the struggle, suffering, victory, death, and, in fact, every human characteristic). They can only be expressed through symbolic images. Archetypes, to reach our consciousness, need to be concretized-incarnated in a symbol, in a dream, in myth and legend, in the human story, and in the work of art. Archetypal images now come to life on the screen, which mediates between a person's consciousness on the one hand and the depths of the individual psyche and its underlying all-human substrate on the other.

The Gaze and the Possibility of Knowledge

Jung argues that, without the creative human gaze, the world would not exist (Jung 1989, 256). Paraphrasing Donald Winnicott, who claimed there is no such thing as a baby alone, we could say that a work of art, including in cinema, does not exist as such, and it is looking at it that redeems its potential for existence.

In films, we look at the world that, as it were, looks at us. Like the choir in ancient Greek plays, the character speaking from the screen addresses the spectator directly. The spectator and the screen image are partners in the cinematic event, eliminating the border between sender and receiver as if they were together in a shared space. The direct contact with the speaking figure enables a seemingly intimate encounter, sometimes as an alternative to an intimacy hard to attain in real life.

The gaze of the cinematographer, who is the one framing the cinematic look, turns what is captured in the shot from an objective into a subjective event and the event itself from an object into a subject. Then comes the next stage, where spectators look at the shot and endow the filmed object with their subjective gaze. Henckel von Donnersmarck says we have an inner window through which we can see the world, and although it becomes clouded, we must clean it up and see things as they are (Rotter 2011, 8). Cinema is that window. Are the clouds our subjective gaze?

Wim Wenders conveys a passion for a type of cinema that transcends subjectivity. In his film *Lisbon Story* (1994), he seeks a mystical fusion with the world and attempts to deny that a self is looking through the camera in order to reach a picture shot without a human eye. The camera he carries on his back shoots on its own. Wenders claims that the camera, so long as no eye pollutes it, is in a pure, complete, and perfect union with the world.

Building the moment in the shot frame and building the image in the sequence of images in the film convey the choices of the director-artist, who endows the shot image with meaning and uniqueness. As in any art, in cinema too, no detail is trivial. It is imbued with significance as soon as it is part of the work. And then, "the most ordinary things start becoming signs, and any sign may lead to another, with the desire to see and know that's inherent in photography, what Benjamin called the psychoanalysis of vision. This metamorphosis of random objects into signs is one of the foundations of cinema" (Godard and Ishaghpour 2005, 65).

Cinema, too, like psychoanalysis, creates the illusion that the gaze can see the invisible, discover and decipher the secrets of the unconscious. At the same time, it constantly confronts us with the limitations of the power to see and to know and with the deception that what is seen reflects actual truth. This deception is the same illusion we reencounter in Oedipus' hubris, which led him to believe he had solved the riddle of the Thebes Sphinx—the human riddle. The urge of Oedipus' hubris to know the truth of his life, later revealed as an unbearable sin, nurtures the illusion of consciousness seeking to know more and more in a naïve belief that, equipped with knowledge, it will vanquish life's perils. Wilfred Bion points to the danger posed by the hubris of knowledge and deciphering endorsed by Oedipus, which he claims is also present in psychotherapy (Bion 2018, 86–87).

Henry Unger sees the spectator's gaze as voyeurism and speaks of cinema's rhetorical influence on the consumer as the art of temptation to voyeurism (1991, 18, 38). He argues that, in *Rear View*, Hitchcock uses a corpse "to evoke in us remorse about our voyeurism. Our life of prying exposed us as aesthetic necrophiliacs" (ibid., 45), a rather negative formulation of the voyeuristic aspect.

The camera can be an actual mirror reflecting everything as is. True, the camera can change, conceal, and dim the original sight using the technical means currently available, except that cinema has become increasingly responsive to the voyeuristic impulse, breaching the privacy and intimacy boundaries of the filmed body-psyche. By coercing the exposure of reality and encroaching on it in a variation of "Big Brother," the camera highlights cinema's penetration-phallic powers. This invasiveness endangers the secretive, mysterious aspect of both external and psychic reality. Eros and Thanatos, sexuality and death, which had always been viewed as sacred mysteries of existence, are described in films in crude and blatant terms and, at times, in a violent and vulgar fashion bordering on pornography. Sexuality and death have been profaned in the cinema with the loss of the natural modesty intended to downplay the sacred foundation of human existence. In Greek mythology, Artemis punishes Actaeon and turns him into a stag because he looked at her nakedness, and Orpheus is forbidden to look back at Hades when trying to bring back Eurydice. Deep truth needs a cover. At its best, a work of art invariably entails disclosing what is hidden in honor of the mystery of existence and in recognition of our limited powers to decode the secret. Psychoanalyst Stephen A. Mitchell notes that "certain kinds of experiences . . . are difficult or impossible to risk displaying with others. It is as if they exist in secret, hidden recesses of being and they can feel as if they constitute a core or center of the self" (Mitchell 1993, 138). Although therapy seeks to deepen knowledge of the unconscious' most hidden recesses, it acknowledges the importance of the untold secret (Netzer 2004, Ch. 4). Mythology, religion, and mysticism limit the human license to gaze at the mystery of existence, knowing that we must separate what is forbidden to see from what is permitted, according to what human consciousness can contain and elaborate. They also describe the perils of the gaze, depicted in the myth that forbids Lot's wife to look back at the destruction of Sodom and in the myth that forbids Perseus to look at the Medusa's face. Moses wished to see God's face and was told he could not, "for man shall not see me and live" (Exodus 33:20), and only God's back could be seen.

Mythology, and in its way psychotherapy, suggest approaching the powerful mystery through its symbolic elaboration, which is always a partial revelation that points to the thing but does not reveal it directly. In the myth of Perseus, he is forbidden to look directly at the face of the Medusa, who would turn him to stone. Instead, he must kill her when looking at her reflection in the shield polished as a mirror that Athena had given him. This indirect glance, contemplating the reflection rather than the thing per se, is sustained through a symbol—the bridge regulating passage between the conscious and the unconscious.

Cinema, however, often disobeys these instructions. The cinematic gaze, seeking dramatic extremes, scorns the psyche. It excites the audience and, thus, at times, breaks the boundaries of both the film and the spectator. The camera neither spares the spectators nor cares about how much they can bear. Cinema can turn into an audiovisual provocation of spectators who are immature and as yet unable to protect themselves. At times, cinema raises powerful issues, terrifying and hard to digest, without taking into account the (relative) inability of spectators sitting in a closed hall to escape the sights before them. Given that cinema stresses unconscious materials, emotional and instinctive, the quantity and the suitable balance between the various elements require renewed attention.

The Mirror and Consciousness

Cinema speaks in the language of pictures, which also serve as mirrors that reflect us. Jacques Lacan argues that, at the mirroring stage, children identify themselves in the mirror, and the sight reflected shapes in them a consciousness of self. The observing eye and the mirror, therefore, are symbols of consciousness.

We look at the mirror to see how the other sees us. That is the social aspect of shaping the persona, which is the mask of our appearance in society. Self-knowledge also has a narcissistic quality since we look at the mirror to reproduce the mother's admiring look and reaffirm our positive features.

The narcissistic gaze, however, can be transformed into a look in the service of consciousness, as myths reveal. Japanese mythology tells us about the sun goddess who was offended, hid in a cave, and refused to bring light to humanity. The gods then outwitted her and set up a mirror at the cave's opening. When she could not hold back and went out to look at herself in it (her narcissistic need), the gods pulled her out, and ever since, she has returned to shine (in the service of human consciousness).

Like literature and myth, cinema at its best is a mirror that, for better or worse, reflects aspects of ourselves as we indeed are. The narcissistic gaze thus turns into a truth-loving and self-conscious one. The role of cinema is to bring the individual and society to awareness of contents it considers essential. In that sense, what inspires cinema is the collective unconscious, which propels humanity to processes of change and development. It promotes collective consciousness and thus drives personal and social changes. Hephaestus, the blacksmith, prepared for Achilles a shield that was as polished as a mirror and reflected the entire universe. This shield is perhaps a symbol of mythology that, like a mirror, reflects the psyche of all the world's dwellers and the world itself. Mythology arranges the chaotic multiplicity of human events into a structured, ordered plot that is purposeful and meaningful, enabling us to look at what threatens the world and at our own depths. Cinema, which sustains the camera's role as a mirror mediating between the cinematographer and the film and between the film and the spectator, now assumes the mediating role of the myth and Athena's shield/mirror. Psychotherapy, too, fulfills the mediating/arranging role of Athena's shield. Hamlet says that the purpose of playing "was and is, to hold, as 'twere, the mirror up to nature; to show virtue her own feature, scorn her own image, and the very age and body of the time his form and pressure" (Shakespeare 1923, 1147). With a group of wandering actors, Hamlet stages a play in the royal court that replicates his uncle's murder of his father. Through this play, Hamlet means to raise awareness of the murder and examine his uncle's reaction to a plot that, as it were, is imaginary but, in truth, describes his actions. Using a play to generate awareness of a person's hidden world is part of every story, play, and film.

Director Wim Wenders says: "When I started making films, I believed that cinema is the art of the revealed to the eye. As time passed, I've become increasingly convinced that cinema is the art of the hidden from the eye and has the strange power to transcend even beyond the revealed to the eye" (Klein 2009, 13). The hidden is in the facts unknown to the spectator and the hidden psychic truth.

Cinema sustains a time-space where the full spectrum of our unconscious world occurs in front of us. Thereby, it allows for a dual situation: to live while split off from ourselves without being aware that cinema reflects us, and also the opposite—to become aware of ourselves through it. Awareness becomes possible when the experience and its observation come together and when the proper connection links the experiencing unconscious and the observing consciousness. In our encounter with a world of sights and images, the dialogue between our conscious and unconscious is significant in the dream and in cinema. Dialogue after the viewing can lead to self-awareness. Genuine awareness bearing a potential for change is not a rational grasp but rather an insight that is part of the emotional experience—where cinema leaves its mark.

The fundamental role of the cinema is like that of literature and myth—to place a mirror in front of us so that we will know ourselves and to raise to consciousness unconscious parts of our psyche as well as contents of the collective unconscious that drive us and the whole of humanity and have yet to be worked through. Viewing a film enables us to strain psychic contents through the sieve of our consciousness, making them acceptable to serve as change agents.

In this process, cinema plays a significant role in promoting the development of individual consciousness and human consciousness in general. Writing about cinema from a psychological perspective could thus further awareness of archetypes and myths operating in the culture and in the individual from the depths of the collective unconscious, expanding collective insight and consciousness.

Cinema as Dream, the Unconscious, and Consciousness

Like all works of art, a film emerges through inspiration processes dictated by the unconscious without knowing a priori where they will lead to. That is the meaning of Federico Fellini's saying: "Once finished, the film is always busy contradicting me" (Kast 1965, 14), and "in a sense, everything is realistic. I see no border between the imagined and the real" (ibid., 18). In Lacanian terms, we could say that, in cinema, the realistic representation of the imagined, the symbolic, and the real is identical. Thus, as in the dream, they become one and hardly distinguishable. The spectator of a film becomes the temporary owner of the cinematic protagonist's consciousness and can now choose: either to surrender altogether to an experience that jumbles boundaries or to separate the real, the imagined, and the symbolic—what is reality, what is imagination, and what is a dream.

Jung claims that a great work of art is like a dream. It never explains itself and is never unequivocal. We must not expect artists to explain their creations. A dream never says, "This is the truth." Instead, it presents an image, as nature enables a plant to grow, and leaves us to draw conclusions (Jung 1984, 65–105). Jung's analogy between the work of art and the dream also applies to cinema. Various and contrasting meanings can come together when we allow the work of art to affect us as it affects the artist.

The analogy between art and dream rests on their shared origin in the unconscious. Already at the dawn of cinema, theorists pointed out its similarity to the dream, which is experienced as the visual observance of an event, as is a film.

Cinema emerges in the intermediate space, the transitional space (in Winnicot's terms) where art originates—the space between reality and imagination and between the conscious and the unconscious. Pier Paolo Pasolini, poet and filmmaker, thought that the dream is the material of the cinema and, indeed, many images of Fellini, Hitchcock, Bergman, and Tarkovsky seem to have sprung from dreams. Bergman claims that the role of cinema is to bring the dream back to life, thereby helping us to confront the hardships of existence (Unger 1991, 69). We could say that every film, like a dream, symbolically and concretely projects before us the contents of our unconscious and of the human psyche as a whole, which is part of us.

Over three decades, Fellini drew all his dreams. Following the advice of his Jungian analyst, Ernst Bernhard, he painted them in gouache or watercolors in his "book of dreams," a very personal notebook showing the process of creating his images and working them through in dreams. Fellini practiced as musicians do, creating an iconographic repertoire of images for future use. Sam Stourdzé, who curated Fellini's exhibition, writes: "He was interested in questions that Jung had posed because they were also the questions he was asking: he had to understand what we can gain from our dreams, how they can be used as inspiration . . . he had to understand himself and understand what, out of his private story, could be a universal image" (Bankir 2009, 2). Fellini used dream pictures to create archetypal cinematic images such as those of the large, exuberant, tender, and big-breasted women who appeared in his dreams. In other words, Fellini dealt with the experiential power of images rather than with their symbolic meaning, enabling their full visual concretization in the cinema.

In pre-digital cinematography, film negatives had to be developed in a *camera obscura*—a dark room—while producing a digital film no longer requires the laboratory ritual of developing film in the dark. When watching a movie, however, we return to the darkness that, from now on, is a *camera obscura*, where the film emerges within us while we watch it. The spectator in the dark does not move, as when neutralizing physical movement in the dream. The dream, too, emerges in the darkness of our souls.

Entering a movie house resembles entry into a world of darkness. As in the night's world of dream, from which we return, we also enter the theater's darkness and return to the outside light after awakening from the dream.

In a dream, images from the unconscious are projected as living pictures, part of a personal film shown before our closed eyes on the screen of the inner dream while the dreaming consciousness simultaneously experiences and observes. When we wake up, we project it again on the illumined screen of wakeful consciousness.

Many myths grew from the great dreams of private individuals that the tribe adopted as a constitutive story. Like a dream, the myth describes inner processes projected from the depths of the collective unconscious onto the screen of the collective consciousness layer assuming shape. As myths are expressions of dreams from humanity's childhood, so could cinema be viewed as the current expression of the collective unconscious, which is projected to us as humanity's dream.

Both cinema and dreams work on the spectator's pre-verbal and pre-conscious layers. In the cinema, as in the dream, what is projected before us, as in our consciousness, are reflections or images of things perceived as real even though they are virtual representations. And yet, by comparison with other arts, cinema, like the dream, is experienced as a concrete reality rather than a reproduction or a processed representation of it.

The dream is an inner reality that reaches us after undergoing processes of masking, concealment, metonymy, and symbolization. Activating the psyche are defenses and hidden goals that blot out, evoke, change, compress, and intensify the images and pictures of memory and create the dream. The psyche, then, is the director of its dreams. In cinema, too, there is a screenwriter-director who sends her truth from a set of masking and symbolization. This analogy between dream and cinema is present in Jung's reference to the dream: "A dream is a theatre in which the dreamer is himself the scene, the player, the prompter, the producer, the author, the public, and the critic" (Jung 1974, 52).

Like the cinema world, the dream world can take over reality to the point of blurring its borders. One expression of the dream taking over concrete reality is Borges' essay about a man who dreamt he had passed through Paradise and had a flower presented to him as a pledge that his soul had been there and found that flower in his hand when he awoke (Borges 1964, 11). This encroachment of dream into reality occurs in Woody Allen's film *The Purple Rose of Cairo* (1985). The cinematic character leaves the screen and enters the real life of the woman watching it, Cecilia, a hard-working waitress who runs away to the cinema from the harsh circumstances of her life. *The Purple Rose of Cairo* shows at the neighborhood movie house and Cecilia repeatedly goes back to see it until the film's protagonist, Tom Baxter, notices her and leaves the screen to meet her. Baxter thanks her for coming time after time to see the movie and Cecilia falls in love with him.

Cinema was born in the early twentieth century when psychoanalysis emerged, and Freud published *The Interpretation of Dreams* (Freud 1976 [1900]). Art, which discovered psychoanalysis, was enriched by images from the unconscious that influenced the rise of a surrealistic trend combining dreams, imagination, and reality. Artistic cinema, like Luis Buñuel's, uses the quasi-dream surrealistic dimension. Buñuel said that cinema is the superior way of expressing the world of dreams (Buñuel 1960, 41). The structure of the dream and of cinema is indeed similar in the leaps from scene to scene and the absence of any commitment to rational narrative. This understanding led cineastes to include dream fragments in their works, thereby adding a layer of mystery and the tension of the deciphering urge. Buñuel argued that enigma and mystery are fundamental elements of all artistic creation and are generally lacking on the screen (ibid.). However, in the post-Buñuel avant-garde and spiritual cinema, the dreamy, delusional, surrealist, associative dimension is dominant.

Cinema, like the dream, conveys the hidden yearnings, fears, and anxieties of both its protagonists and spectators, which could be the reason for cinema's multiple images of sex and violence that, according to Freud, are the main forces operating in dreams and in the psyche. From Jung's perspective, the role of dreams is to lead us to self-knowledge and self-awareness in all areas of our existence since the dream is the drama that plays out between parts of our psyche, which become manifest as characters in a dream. When a woman dreams that she is watching a film, she is watching the script of her inner psyche. Here is the potential for awareness. With the dreamer, we will examine what is her experience—to what extent is what appears to her as a film an enhanced experience? Or perhaps the opposite, to what extent is it distant and alienated? For instance, a young man dreamt he was watching a film and that his psychologist was beside him. In his dream, the young man panics and flees the movie house. The psychologist symbolizes the self-awareness that watching the film makes possible while the dreamer, who is not yet ready for the self-examination where he will come to know himself through the film's contents—flees. Edward Whitmont and Silvia Perera claim that such dreams point to crucially significant motifs in our lives (1989, 100).

Looking at our dream, like looking at a film, can expand our consciousness of self, but we can always elude consciousness. The following is the dream of a young man beginning a process of psychotherapy who used the cinema metaphor: "A spy was sent abroad on an important mission. It's unclear whether he is a spy or a charlatan who never performed the mission. It's unclear whether he is a real person or an actor." The dream raises doubts as to whether the impulse of psychic development operates correctly within him: has the dreamer assumed the task assigned to him—tour the unknown land of unconscious depths to develop self-consciousness—or is he merely a charlatan, pretending to cooperate with the therapy, playing an actor's role and detached from his true self?

Hidden (2005) describes, through a film within a film, the hide-and-seek game a man plays with the truth of his past and his life. George, a reputable television man, married and with a child, has a small secret he wishes to forget. When George was a child, his parents decided to adopt an Algerian orphan. Little George, however, had not liked this new figure in his life and told deceitful stories about him, which led to his eviction from their house. The Algerian boy was taken away to an orphanage, and from that point, his life became a constant struggle to survive. Mysterious videotapes begin arriving at George's home, bringing his past sin up to the surface. Director Michael Haneke uses the videotapes to send an accusing look, wordless and soundless, to the house and the life of smug George. He uses the camera to expose sin, pretense, cover-up, and repression. The mute gaze releases repressed secrets, bringing up the terrible past and its consequences. In the wake of the videotapes, George embarks on a journey to the past and meets Majid, who commits suicide in front of him. Yet, the director's attempts to evoke in him feelings of guilt, responsibility, humaneness, sorrow, compassion, or understanding fail. As in Oedipus, the discovery of the past leads to another calamity but, contrary to Oedipus, the awareness of evil, of the powers of the shadow that had animated him in the past, do not drive George to an internal process of guilt, repentance, atonement, and change.

The sender of the videotapes is not identified. They could represent flashes of repressed documentary contents rising to the surface in George, his repressed guilt urging him to reencounter his past, or they could be flashes of nightmares. One could claim that Haneke inserted the videotapes into the story from outside as a director's stunt. Traditional cinematic realism thus collapses, exposing Haneke's artistic intention to use the tools of documentary photography and film that, resembling a dream, bring back a deliberately forgotten memory to penetrate consciousness and cause change. And if the recipient, the story's protagonist, has not changed, we learn that the purpose of the change is meant for the spectator.

Identification, Separation, and the Emotional Element

Mordechai Geldman writes:

> The creative act is often an alternative to the primary symbiotic connection with the mother, enabling inseparable fusion with an object resembling the relationship of the infant and the child with the mother's physical and psychic reality. The creative act is a kind of mirror, or a realm of doubles, where the creator is reflected as the mother's world had been reflected in his childhood or as he had been reflected in her world.
>
> (Geldman 2006, 145)

Geldman notes that this is an absolute fusion that enables separation because the creator fuses with the created work but also defines himself through it and, in the end, allows it to exist by itself as a child separating from the mother. These remarks apply to all forms of creativity.

Geldman's assertion seems to apply to the consumer of the work as well. Readers of a written text or viewers of a plastic work experience their own "realm of doubles," alternatively shifting between fusion with the work and its observation. Cinema is a pictorial-sound reality of sensorial fullness that overwhelms spectators, who are absorbed into it as if fusing with it. Thus, as in the primary symbiosis with the mother, when the musical background acts almost as a lullaby meant to dim consciousness, the suggestiveness of the rhythmic sound prompts entry into another state of consciousness unique to cinema and intensifies it. In this state, the fusion of the spectator and the observed, of object and subject, takes place more closely than in any other medium. The spectator-observed relationship resembles the therapist-patient relationship: a drawing together up to immersion and dual naked fusion in an experiential bath, "the alchemic bath." The "alchemic bath" is the area common to the unconscious of both participants drawing closer and closer together until they are one, and their subsequent separation (Netzer 2004, 430–445). Cinema indeed facilitates complete emotional identification. Some people can cry when identifying with a film character while unable to cry over their own lives.

Due to cinema's strong emotional element, its emotive-cathartic and educational role is comparable to that of Greek tragedies. Karen Armstrong claims that Greek tragedies and dramas were staged within a ritual religious context and included a catharsis of compassion that represented a transition from personal sorrow to communal partnership. She argues that these plays fulfilled a vital role in the initiation of Athenian youth and their acceptance as full citizens: "Like any initiation, tragedy forced the audience to face the unspeakable and to experience extremity . . . the audience learned to feel the pain of another person as though it were their own, thereby enlarging the scope of their sympathy and humanity" (Armstrong 2005, 39).

Her claim is interesting. The research on initiation (usually of males in tribal cultures) has addressed the issue of strengthening the masculine dimension that disregards feelings. Armstrong describes a more developed stage of training for empathy. Cinema, then, can be used to initiate humanity into empathy.

Cinema derives from the creator's unconscious and affects the spectator's unconscious. Hence, driven by the urge to experience genuine feeling and create an emotional provocation, cinema brings up repressed contents in the spectator's psyche. Sitting in a dark hall, like in the darkness of night, lowers defenses and heightens the emotional identification that enables self-awareness. Significant self-awareness does not happen solely through rational interpretation but through the heart. In fact, this is the only possibility for us to encounter ourselves face to face, and this awareness also enables empathy with the other.

Terrill Gibson also addresses the initiation aspect of cinema. He views cinema as a potential medium for awakening and integrating the soul. In his view, cinema works on us as a dream, a vision, a trance, and a choreography of images. The soul awakens and changes through these images, making cinema an initiation ritual and an experience of transformation. Cinema is the experience of the living soul and initiation as transformation occurs through contact with the living soul of the world, the *anima mundi* (Gibson 2005, 73).

While fusing with it, cinema imposes on us a kind of trance experience of hypnotic invasion while oblivious to the surrounding reality. From this perspective, cinema is the therapist, and the spectator is the patient.

Lars von Trier's film *Zentropa* (1991) bluntly presents the hypnotic element triggered in the spectator. The film begins with a man's low, slow voice suggestively instructing the protagonist (and the spectator) to relax in order to imagine himself in the place and at the time the movie begins (post-World War II Germany). While hearing the suggestive voice, we see a fast-moving railway line on the screen, as the sight of the line when we look at it while traveling in a high-speed train. The uniform monotonous scenery also contributes to the hypnotic state. The movie's protagonist comes to Germany from the United States. His move to Germany fuses with the spectator's entry into the world of post-war Germany and with the entry into the film itself.

Myth, literature, and cinema fulfill the same role. They show us we are not alone in this story that is not ours, as it were, but is ours. As Bruno Schulz writes in "The Book": "For under the imaginary table that separates me from my readers, don't we secretly clasp each other's hands?" (Schulz 1988, 127).

Contrary to myth and literature, however, cinema works on sight and hearing and thus on the primary unconscious levels of the psyche. Its experiential-fusing influence, therefore, is vast and swift. The technological qualities of the cinematic medium enable it to breach the laws of time, place, and causality, describing a dreamlike delusional existence typical of the language of the unconscious. It thus breaches the borders of reality and the normative defenses of the ego's "three monkeys" that we build around ourselves—not to hear, not to see, and not to talk about what threatens us. An overlap is evident between the therapist's invasiveness, which exposes the patient's truth, and the cinema's invasiveness. Cinema invades the spectator's psyche as it tries to invade the patient's psyche. The preceding exposition highlights the suitability and appeal of cinema to the description of psychological problems to investigate their sources and their therapy while also treating us, the spectators, who share the feelings of the cinematic patient.

In the cinematic context, the spectator's inevitable involvement with the film fits with the therapist's involvement in the patient's psychic processes. According to Robert Segal, the spectator's involvement in the plot exists already in the myth. Segal argues that "the real victimizer [in the Oedipal myth] is the myth-maker and any reader of the myth grabbed by it. Here the myth is about the fulfillment of the Oedipus Complex in the male myth-maker or reader . . . At heart, the myth is not biography but autobiography" (Segal 2004, 93). He then notes: "Identifying himself with the named hero, the myth-maker or reader vicariously revels in the hero's triumph, which in fact is his own. *He* is the real hero of the myth" (ibid., 96–97). I will add that, according to this approach, the reader-spectator is not only the victorious hero but also the failing hero, the suffering sinner, and also the punished and the punisher. The hero in myth, in art, and in cinema lives our lives for us. The hero is our envoy, our psyche's proxy, a representation of aspects of our psyche and thus also our victim, the scapegoat of our aggression, the sacrifice we offer instead of ourselves. And when the hero is redeemed, we are, too. The plot's hero, like the shaman going away on his voyage for the community, leaves in order to heal us. Cinema deals with this desired and threatening involvement when it is drawn to deal with therapist-patient relationships.

On the spectator's involvement in Hitchcock's cinematic scenario, Ishaghpour's words accord with my concern with films about therapy. In his view,

> the editing of the film is formed by the logic of fantasy and involving the spectator's imagination and desires in the film . . . On one level the spectator projects into it his fears and desires, the hopes being realized bringing about their punishment with nightmare implacability; on this level most of his films work like models of myth, and owe their success to that. Hitchcock understood what might be called the underlying power of cinema and put it to work.
> (Godard and Ishaghpour 2005, 65)

Roland Barthes prefers the intensive ("mad") power of feeling that photography (hence also cinematography) evokes in us rather than the sense of restraint ("tame"):

> Mad or tame? Photography can be one or the other: tame if its realism remains relative . . . mad if this realism is absolute and, so to speak, original, obliging the

loving and terrified consciousness to return to the very letter of Time: a strictly revulsive movement which reverses the course of the thing, and which I shall call, in conclusion, the photographic *ecstasy.*

(Barthes 1981, 119, emphasis in original)

Barthes sees in the art of photography the possibility of expressing what is true, when he brings the photographed image "to that crazy point where affect (love, compassion, grief, enthusiasm, desire) is a guarantee of Being" (ibid., 113).

The poet Haim Nachman Bialik, too, emphasizes the importance of intensive feeling at the conclusion of his article "Revealment and Concealment in Language":

So much for the language of words. But, in addition, "there are yet to the Lord" languages without words: song, tears, and laughter. And the speaking creature has been found worthy of them all. These languages begin where words leave off, and their purpose is not to close but to open. They rise from the void. They are the rising up of the void. Therefore, at times they overflow and sweep us off in the irresistible multitude of their waves; therefore, at times they cost a man his wits, or even his life. Every creation of the spirit which lacks an echo of one of these three languages is not really alive, and it were best that it had never come into the world.

(Bialik 1975, 137)

His assertion on languages without words is also relevant to cinema, which often speaks in the language of music, feeling, and tears. In Martin Buber's terms, we could say that these pre-verbal languages enable us to create an intimate relationship of I-Thou with cinema and with ourselves.

Art researcher Suzi Gablik objects to modernism and postmodernism, and her quest is for meaningful art, which awakens the capability of enchantment (Gablik 1991, 53). The art of cinema indeed does this, but not in the sense of evoking excitement. Instead, it awakens the inner psyche, which lives its depths.

Fellini, as noted, was in Jungian therapy for many years. In *8 ½*, Fellini tells us about a director, Guido, who makes a film about a director making a film. He tries to make a "true" film that "will not tell a false story again." The search for truth, both in his personal life and his cinematic endeavor, takes over his entire being and fossilizes his creativity. Daumier, the intellectual critic, advises him to give up his art and write on a clean page. We thus learn that the shot at the director's head in the film is the murder of his psyche's intellectual element, which had paralyzed him. The artist is henceforth released to live out other psychic layers that will enable creativity. A scene in the film tells us that "the mantra for finding the valuable treasure is asa-nisi-masa." After we learn about the Italian children's game where an "s" is added to every syllable, we understand that the word, in this case, is anima (Levy 2008). Anima means soul; in mystic terms, *anima mundi* is the soul of the world. In the superb formulation of poet Czesław Miłosz: "If not for the secret of each singular anima/ Scoffers would have been right, the trace of a human vanishes" (Milosz 1995, 19). Anima is the feminine-emotional element in the soul, and Jung described it as the psychic function that bridges consciousness to the depths of feeling and the unconscious. It is also the basis for understanding all cinematic creativity because the key to an artwork, rather than intellectual-logical analysis, is the encounter of the heart, which cinema intensifies through its influence on the senses and mainly through music. The meeting of consciousness with the emotional-feminine element, the anima, enables us to engage in a genuine dialogue with ourselves and, thus, with the other. Cinema appears to fulfill the role of the anima as a bridge to the unconscious. Jung claimed that, in the twentieth century, the human soul leaned toward logos and rationality. At the same time, he saw a need to return to a feeling dimension, given that the irrational emotional aspect is what enables participation in transformation processes.

People genuinely wish to be emotionally stirred, and when a work of art moves us, we feel grateful to its creator for making this possible. I do not mean sentimentality or excitement but a sense of depth, of the power to touch our profound and hidden feeling point in a place infused with a sense of meaning about existence itself, even if we cannot formulate it. Cinema thus becomes a distilled container for our feelings, one we borrow so that we might meet them, live with them, and then return them to the cinematic container that keeps them and elaborates them for us, just like the therapist contains-elaborates the feelings of the patient. Perhaps that is Pessoa's intention when he writes: "Leave pain on the altar/ As an offering to the gods" (Pessoa 1998, 113).

We must remember that cinema, like myth, not only describes the psychic processes unfolding in its audience but also influences them, and the suggestive power of films is even more significant when the audience is made up of children and young people. In a review of the literature covering the 1966–1992 period, Snyder finds that films influence adolescents far more than any other age group (Snyder 1992). Cinema can thus contribute to the proper development of the adolescent's socialization process, but also to deviance. Films are a comprehensive and long-term source of ideas and approaches, especially for young people concerned with values and identity issues who identify with characters that resemble them (or with those they would like to resemble) and relate to them as imitation models. Watching films can thus be a source for social learning of positive and negative roles. Snyder illustrates how films like *Rambo* could lead to identification among adolescents struggling with issues of power, authority, and social pressure. Adolescents can also adopt the narcissistic features of film protagonists and make them part of their developing personalities.

Horror movies are popular among adolescents, reflecting their conscious and unconscious fears and anxieties. Films can also allow adolescents to escape tensions that affect them since they invariably offer solutions.

Snyder addresses a prominent research topic—the connection between films and violence. Data show disturbed adolescents are more vulnerable to the influence of films dealing with deviant patterns such as aggression and suicide. This finding, however, could apply to all age groups. Some individuals seek in films the strong, "greater than life" moments of excitement that, at times, are an alternative to the missing feeling and fail to identify the significant and potentially adverse effects of these films on them.

Cinema, however, also allows for an antithetical approach to identification and emotional involvement, stressing the separation that follows the watching of the film. Cinema is then the patient, who the spectator-therapist contains-listens to, looks at, reacts to with empathy, and interprets.

Another stance that film spectators can adopt is distance and defamiliarization. This reaction could reflect fatigue after encountering too many exciting and powerful elements, leading to imperviousness to, and alienation from, the human suffering described in it.

In Ingmar Bergman's *The Touch* (1971), Bergman creates deliberate distancing by interviewing his actors on their interpretation of the character they play in the film. The actors' turn to the spectators prevents them (and the spectators) from fusing with the character. According to Unger (1991, 69), Bergman urges us to distance ourselves from the character so that we do not sink into it and remember to observe it from the outside. He compares this to the device endorsed by Bertolt Brecht, who seeks to alienate the audience from the play and raise awareness of their status as spectators by keeping a reasonable distance.

The Wounding and Healing Cinema-Spectator Encounter

This distinction between cinema's two types of experience—identification and separation, closeness and distance—resembles Roland Barthes' distinction between two responses to photography, the *studium* and the *punctum*. In *Camera Lucida* (1988), Barthes distinguishes these two modes (to which he refers as "elements") that develop in the space between the spectator of the photograph and the photograph itself. The *studium* is a distant, matter-of-fact, rational observation, "as I invest the field of the *studium* with my sovereign consciousness" (ibid., 26), a vector of the spectator's consciousness to the picture. By contrast, regarding the *punctum*, "it is not I who seek it out . . . it is this element which rises from the scene, shoots out of it like an arrow, and pierces me . . . this wound, this prick, this mark made by a pointed instrument . . . *punctum* is also: sting, speck, cut, little hole—and also a cast of the dice" (ibid., 26–27). The *punctum* rises from the photograph and pierces us, touching the wound in our heart, the true self, creating an intimacy of identification with the photograph that is also wounding and leads us to meet unconscious psychic contents. No wonder, then, that looking at a photo of his mother after her death led Barthes to discover the *punctum*.

Punctum cinema breaks through the habitual, ordinary, comfortable, bourgeois, sleepy barrier of our consciousness. As Kafka says of a good book, it enables us to truly feel that it is like an axe for the frozen sea inside us.

In psychotherapy, all that patients are capable of is a distant, *studium*, conscious contemplation, while the therapy aims to bring them to the proper *punctum* meeting with their wounded sensibility. Cinema, like art in general, and even more intensely, can create this meeting.

The distinction here is between the *studium*—an observing gaze in a stance of consciousness moving from the spectator to the picture that I would call a masculine look or speech—and the *punctum*—an emotional gaze that raises from the picture itself and I would call a feminine look or speech.

I would generalize and say that the *studium* and *punctum* attitudes are at work all the time (though not always), not only in the relationship between the spectator and the visual or aural creation as well as in the reader-text one but also in the intersubjective and therapist-patient relationships. The power of the *punctum* that raises and enters us from the work, from the other, and from the patient enables a deeper and more authentic encounter that touches the spectator's and the observed's wounds. Contact with the wound is a must in our relationship with ourselves and in the therapist-patient one (Halifax 1982).

Barthes claims that, in the photographed image, he seeks the deepest self beyond the pose before the camera, the "zero degree" of the body only revealed by a look of extreme love. He wishes the photographed self not to be a ghost, a mummy, or an image but a private life. His passionate quest is for what is beyond the pose (the persona) of the people standing before the camera. And then, rising from the photograph is "an erotic or lacerating value buried in myself" (Barthes 1981, 16). That is the sense of emotional excitement. He explores photography "not as a question (a theme) but as a wound" (ibid., 21). Barthes' movement in photography and writing toward the authentic self, toward the wound, is like the passion in psychotherapy to discover the true self beyond the posing of the persona and the false self (of both therapist and patient). Psychotherapy is presently going through a crucial move toward discovering authentic therapist-patient relationships in the dialogical space, like authentic relationships of mutual *punctum* between the spectator and the photograph.

Because of its sensorial concreteness, the emotional wounding and healing *punctum* power of cinema at its best is far greater than that of all other arts. And indeed, what speaks to us and excites us so much in quality films is their *punctum* power.

Many artists acknowledge the link between the work and the wound. Sometimes, a work that touches the depth of a spectator's heart is touching their wound. The work exposes the wound of the creator and its spectator-reader in order to heal it, thereby turning the work into a "wounded healer." Federico García Lorca writes about the creative power, the *duende*: "The *duende* wounds, and in trying to heal that wound that never heals, lies the strangeness, the inventiveness of a man's work "(Lorca, 2007). The "strangeness" Lorca writes about is the unique human selfhood, and the thread of Ariadne that leads to it touches the wound of the soul. The wound becomes a key motif in the work of Joseph Beuys, and healing it was the challenge he faced in his life and his art: "Drawing was for him only a means to raise awareness, a 'tool' to unite the physical and spiritual worlds, a path to self-healing and a preparation for the role he set for his life and his work—the healing of society" (1996, 2). Seemingly, cinema assumes this role—to lead its spectators, all potential therapists-patients, to a meeting with the existential wound to be healed through it.

The Film as a Bridge to the Creator's True Self and as Self-Healing

When art is true art, it conveys its creator's true self. "Fellini defined the cinema as: 'The art in which man recognizes himself in the most direct way, the mirror in front of which we must have the courage to discover our souls'" (Solmi 1967, 18). Like every artistic activity, film making can serve its creator's psyche since it expresses both conscious and unconscious dimensions. Thus, cinema enables the spectator and the filmmaker to regress to wounded places in the psyche while suggesting healing options and reconnection of the I-self split.

The autobiographical materials of film creators and the dilemmas they grapple with at various times are consciously or unconsciously described in many films. Prominent examples are *Dreams* (1990), where Akira Kurosawa deals with the interpretation of eight dreams he had in the course of his life; *Fanny and Alexander* (1982), where Ingmar Bergman describes his childhood hardships; *Amarcord* (1973), based on Fellini's memories and events in his childhood village; the films of Theo Angelopoulos where he interweaves names of family members and traumatic biographic experiences; and Bertolucci's declaration that every one of his films is autobiographical.

Like autobiographies generally, the cinematic autobiographical look serves the comprehensive conscious perspective leading to a sense of cohesiveness and meaning by weaving life experiences together. A candid autobiography acts as a kind of therapeutic confession, touching a person's true self and allowing a process of awareness that involves introspection and an understanding look, forgiving and compassionate beyond all.

Several examples follow of how making a movie assists in the healing of the film's creator. Jim Sheridan's film *In America* (2002) follows a family, including parents and two daughters, who try to hide their grief and guilt for the death of their son, Frankie, who fell down the stairs and died from a cancerous tumor caused by the fall. The ten-year-old elder daughter ceaselessly videotapes the family, and the film describes events from her perspective, including pictures of her brother since she begins filming before his death and goes on shooting after it until the end of the film.

Sheridan dedicated the film to a younger brother who had died at an early age, and the girl in the movie seems to play Sheridan's role, coping with his grief by making this film. The film is not only an attempt to overcome death by preserving memory but also to create a new life instead of the one that was lost or never experienced. The sister's videotaping creates an experience of continuity and a family bond, preserving the family memory and her own psychic cohesion. Real-time cinematography allows her to be and not to be at the same time, that is, to simultaneously participate in life and assume the stance of a witness-distant spectator, which protects her from emotional drowning. At the film's end, the sister says that she assumed responsibility for treating the family and that her filming was meant to help her parents to hold on to life. Indeed, at the end of the film, her parents recover following the birth of a baby girl and after the father cries and grieves for his son, returning to life from his emotional paralysis. Only after this process can the sister go on with her life without the camera's help.

Similar changes occur in the animated autobiographical film *The Moon and the Son* (2005). In the film, director John Canemaker engages in a dialogue with his dead father—he asks questions, expresses anger at him, and his father "answers." The director enters into a painful account of the shame he had felt in his childhood for his father's involvement with the Mafia, and the film begins with a dream he tells his father: "The night you died, I dreamt that you are the man on the moon. My brother and I feed you as we did when you were ill in the hospital, and then, suddenly, as in our childhood, you lunge at us and attack us." In the film, the father tells the harrowing story of his life, frustrations, and suffering, leading to his offensive and insulting relationship with his family. At the end of the film, the director returns to the dream and says: "On the night you died, I dreamt that you are the man on the moon." This time, he does not describe the father's violent behavior he had spoken of in the dream that opened the film. The impression is that this is a new dream he had at the end of a course of therapy, conveying the process the dreamer underwent while making the film. This process diminishes and removes the destructive force of the aggressive father as he had been in his life and as reflected in the dream. He turns into a humane figure who can subsequently look at his son from his dwelling on the moon as a concerned and even benevolent character. The son is now also released from the paralyzing-castrating terror evoked by the father and redeems his creative power, expressed in the very act of making this film.

Coping with trauma is the theme of *Waltz with Bashir* (2008), an animated documentary film that follows director and screenwriter Ari Folman's journey through his consciousness. Folman goes in search of three days of the 1982 Israel-Lebanon War that were erased from his memory without a trace, particularly the Sabra and Shatila massacre. In interviews about his film, Folman was recurrently asked why he had chosen animation and answered that this was the only way he could have told his story. The specific animation technique chosen for *Waltz with Bashir* is deliberately anti-realistic. The film's use of animation illustrates a perception of the war as something surreal, reflecting an apparent inability to confront the concrete reality of it. Only the last scene, portraying the massacre's horrendous results, is realistic photography. The audience is shown authentic images of piled-up corpses, ruin, and devastation. The shock at the film's end is unimaginable. Folman is perhaps describing in this fashion the inevitability of his drawing closer to the memory of the trauma—distancing himself through animation, which has a symbolic dimension until, ultimately, the defenses of distance no longer work when the massacre's traumatic memory breaks through. Folman's is a classic therapeutic journey, and he attests right at the beginning that making it was a healing experience for him.

Myth and Ritual: Cinema as Ritual

Myths are ancient archetypal stories that describe potential basic models of a person's development in the course of life. I will claim here that cinema became the ritual expression of contemporaneous myths.

Ritual, by definition, is a reconstruction of the myth in the current reality. The ritual tells and presents the myth in experiential concrete action. For example, the ritual of the Passover Seder includes the Haggadah reading, eating symbolic foods, opening the door for the prophet Elijah, and singing songs that describe the meaning of the holiday. All are expressions of a ritual that, experientially, concretizes the myth of the exodus from Egypt. Lighting Hannukah candles and singing songs about the Maccabeans' victory is part of a ritual that reconstructs the myth of the Maccabeans' struggle against the Romans and the lighting of the candelabrum in the Temple. Tribal myths are part of the historical dialogue, passing the torch from generation to generation.

Every tribal ritual gathers its participants and empowers them through identification with its mythical contents, revived at the moment of the ritual. In the Passover Haggadah, this idea is expressed in the saying that "in every generation, a person is obligated to view himself as if he were the one who went out from Egypt." Thus, the ritual of reading at the synagogue the portion on the giving of the Torah during the Shavuot festival and all the congregation members stand up is a renewed acceptance of the Torah by the participants who hear this reading.

Contemporary individuals, who have lost the sense of being part of social and religious myths, are forced to search on their own for the meaning of their lives. This quest, described in the myths of the search for the philosopher's stone and the holy grail, has intensified and may have generated the psychotherapy that attained recognition at the time of Freud and Jung in the early twentieth century. Rollo May (1991) claims that the loss of myths in the modern world is the main reason for the birth of psychoanalysis, which is itself based on myths. Freud founded his theory mainly on the Oedipal myth as a central key to the understanding of the psyche, while Jung founded his on myths in general as fundamental constructs for the understanding of humans grappling with existence.

Most rituals reenact or express a myth significant to the community. Since most myths deal with the human stance against more powerful forces in nature, the divinity, and the psyche, and mainly with the hero's active contest with all obstacles, myths describe both the peril and the human victory. In this sense, the stories of the myth and their dramatization in ritual were a kind of group therapy enabling catharsis to the listener who, through them, lives the threat and the rescue from it. They were a kind of ancient bibliotherapy that supported the individual and the collective psyche sharing the common fate reflected in the myth and the potential solutions to the dilemmas of their lives. In this context, Freud argued in *Totem and Taboo* that collective neurosis saves us from personal neurosis.

Myths deal with the hero's struggle against obstacles, his victory, and his contest with his weaknesses, flaws, and sins. Thus, the listener to the myth or the participant in the ritual of its actualization identifies with the hero's powers and, briefly, becomes a hero too. The ritual is also a realization of myths that belong to the tribe as a whole and recurrently reaffirms its collective constitutive foundation. The ritual thus reinforces the identity of every individual member of the group and the group's identity. The ritual serves religion and plays a clear role in strengthening, preserving, and transmitting social institutions. Emil Durkheim, the scholar of religion, saw ritualism as an expression of shared consciousness. In his view, the object of the ritual is the community itself, whereas the "sacred" or the "divine" are merely other names for the collective spirit (Or 1996, 9–18). The ritual thus strengthens cohesion not only for the individual (like rituals of shamanic healing or exorcism) but also for the communal-tribal collective.

Segal says that cinemagoing also combines myth with ritual (Segal 2004, 142). Cinema is like a ritual that concretizes the mythical story within it. Cinema as ritual is a dramatic concretization of the film's story, which takes place in a collective event with many participants—the audience. It reifies the movie as the ritual reifies the myth in a recurrent projection-concretization and as a repeated presentation-action within a unique space meant for this purpose. This repeated reification grants it the mythical validity of a life truth.

Whitmont and Perera note:

The drama, at its best, depicts the ritualized, 'just so' of life. Hence its cathartic effect, as well as its attraction in all ages, from antiquity, when it represented the action of the gods or fates, to the present, secularized plays, movies, and TV productions. They all reveal the archetype of life as likened to a show, play, or dream of the deity . . . The motif of the life theatre (the Greek root word, *theathron*, meant the stage on which the witnessing audience beheld the spectacle of the gods and goddesses, the creative and destructive forces of life) is an archetypal ritual.

(1989, 100)

Walter Murch (2005) claims that cinema is founded on an eternal human impulse—to leave home. In the cinema, we gather together in the darkness with strangers who resemble us in spirit to listen to stories and reencounter the myth staged in the ritual around the fire of the movie screen. Gibson (2005) claims that the movie house is like a dark cave entered in silence, where we see pictures flickering on the walls in the light of burning torches—an ancestral human ritual in all cultures, from the Altamira caves up to the Indian shamanic rituals. The mystery of the holy cinematic caves is a response to a human need that will not end.

Cinema leads us to an encounter with experiences resembling ours and with the hardships of life's voyage and their possible solutions, which are the basic mythical constructs of humanity. Yet, since we have lost the myth, the ancient ritual, and the consolation of the human encounter around the fire, the cinematic ritual became a passive and lonely alternative. Rosario Castellanos formulates this notion when commenting on television: "The space which Homer permitted vacant/ the center which Scheherezade occupied/ . . . the place where the people of the tribe came together to listen to the fire/ is now occupied by the Grand Idiot Box" (Popma 1998, 23).

This gathering to watch cinema is a three-staged ritual, the same three stages characterizing the structure of the hero myth according to Joseph Campbell (1975, 35) as well as the structure of the initiation ritual according to van Gennep (Turner 2008, 58). In the first stage, the hero separates from the familiar surroundings and goes on his way. In the second stage, he reaches a strange place, where the experience of the encounter with the threatening splendor, unfamiliar and unknown, takes place. This is the stage that Turner calls liminal, the threshold stage that will be followed by a change in the hero. In the third stage, he returns, bringing the knowledge/treasure he acquired through his experience; that is, he internalizes the meaning of the experience and undergoes a change toward a more developed existential state.

Prometheus, for example, steals the fire from the gods and returns to earth. Jason, who sails to Colchis, overcomes the serpent guarding the golden fleece and returns with it. These are wandering journeys to other regions, far beyond the sea, to heaven, the underworld, the land of the spirits, and back.

Jungian psychologist Don Fredericksen (2005, 31–40) relates to filmmakers who delve into psychic depths as creators of liminal cinema. He argues that, given the current absence of group-collective initiation processes, cineastes who deal with psychic symbolic meanings use the making of the film to go through their own initiation process toward self-identity. Their films deal with the entry into depths and with the liminal experience.

Every experience of myth, ritual, creativity, and rites of passage requires an entry stage and an exit stage. Entry and exit are transitional stages that enable the psychic process of moving from ordinary life to the experiential event and the return from it to everyday life.

The triangular structure of the film-watching ritual includes the entry, the experience, and the exit from the film. Like the hero in the typical model of the myth, in the first stage we leave our familiar and protected home and enter the cinema, where the second stage of the experience—the other realm— takes place. In the end, we reach the third stage, where we are supposed to return home with new experiences and knowledge and absorb them.

Another ritual of entry and exit takes place within the film. The first stage is the beginning of the film, which always includes a section that leads us into it, as an introduction to a journey, presenting the names of the main actors and the director before entering the physical-psychic space where the film takes place. The living power of cinema is so strong that we need this preparation. In the second stage, the plot unfolds (the conflict and its resolution, the experience). Finally, in the third stage, the names of all the film's participants are projected, signaling the differentiation between the characters and the actors playing them (paralleling the stage in the theater when the actors come out front stage and bow to the clapping public). This stage serves as the separation from the film, the exit, and the return to ourselves. In that sense, the film as ritual illustrates a mythical element common to both the film's content and the spectator's experience as the hero leaving on a journey, entering the experience's locale, going through it, and leaving after being changed by it.

Maya Deren, a pioneer of avant-garde experimental cinema (Mor 2010), addresses the significance of these change processes in the spectators. She visualizes a cinematic art that creates an experience of techno-shamanic ritual in the spectators of her films, a transformative ritual experience transcending borders. Her films are based on wordless images, meant to exert a more substantial influence on the spectator's unconscious (Jackson 2002).

Jack Kornfield notes that Western psychology does not refer to rituals. In his view, rituals speak in a primary symbolic language, like dreams. They are the language of the heart and enable change and transformation in consciousness through basic life symbols: fire, water, earth, and air. Rituals help us in ways not always clear to us—they are means for containing our feelings and thus support us (Kornfield 2008, 305). By their very essence, rituals turn to emotional and unconscious aspects beyond the rational. They influence us through their symbolic, experiential, and irrational power and are meant to create the referred emotional involvement, enabling identification and change. Cinema works in the same fashion.

Cinema spectators are both spectators and participants in a group ritual. Jung notes that there is participation in a transformation process even without taking an active part in the drama of the ritual unfolding outside the individual, who is only a witness-spectator-present. At such times, too, the individual identifies with the ritual activity or participates in the ritual symbolically. Jung, however, notes that genuine transformation requires deep participation in the experience. When participating in a ritual or experiencing big mystical dreams without profound involvement, these great experiences will leave no trace in the individual (Jung 1970, 51).

Director David Mamet ascribes importance to the irrational aspect of ritual. He writes:

> "Is God dead?" and "Why are there no real movies any more?" are pretty much the same question. They both mean that our symbols and our myths have failed us—that we have begun to take them literally, and so judge them wanting. . . . When we demand a rational and immediately practical translation of rituals, we deny their unconscious purpose and power.
>
> (Mamet 1986, 35)

Mamet's films attempt to realize a ritual that reaches the unconscious.

The Cinema Ritual and the Psychotherapy Ritual

To explore the analogy between the cinema and psychotherapy rituals, let us sum up the meaning of ritual.

The ritual exists at the foundation of personal and group life and is limited to a time and a place. It is a significant recurring activity intended to strengthen existential certainty through the following features.

1) Repetition emphasizes the fixed, stable foundation and confirms the ceaseless recurrence of life, enabling changes in the outer and inner world to take place on this fixed platform.
2) Ritual activity actualizes a potential and is experienced as a human power influencing and controlling external and internal reality in magic, symbolic, and psychological terms, dispelling anxieties and fears while strengthening and building the ego.
3) The ritual has symbolic meaning for the individual or the group. It reifies a personal or group symbol, a personal or group myth.
4) The ritual is based on a defined set of activities, as a formal element that structures and organizes the chaos and strengthens the archetype of order at the basis of the individual's ego and self (the essential archetype that symbolizes the wholeness of the psyche) and at the foundation of the society. The symbolic activity aims to reaffirm existence and order, which overcome chaos and evil.
5) The ritual is emotionally meaningful to the participant.

Ordinary rituals have a place in our daily routine—like our arrangements when we get up, eat, sleep, meet others, host guests, and so forth. Some rituals are daily, and some are group-social and religious rituals anchored in tradition and at the core of the collective self. The mythical-symbolic source of the ritual can be heavenly or transcendent, and the ritual thereby becomes a ceremony seeking to influence and appease the gods.

In an analogy to therapy, the ritual seeks to influence the unconscious, mitigate its destructive sway and enable its positive power. The myth in therapy is the personal myth of the individuals' life stories, which is their individuation voyages. The recurring activity in therapy is dialogue.

The elements of set form, order, organization, continuity, action, and control emphasize the ritual's role as supporting the ego against the chaotic powers of the unconscious. Therapy, too, is defined by place, time, and the rules of the therapeutic contract. Hazan writes that ritual enables us to

> relate symbolically to existential problems of insecurity and uncertainty, creating order within disorder. It enables us to live with the problem as part of the world of events and experiences without necessarily finding solutions for it. . . . The ritual includes a distinct dimension of adaptation to the reality where it was created . . . thereby also facilitating cultural expressions that would be forbidden in ordinary contexts. For example, grappling with taboos, dirt, secretions, sex, and death.
>
> (Hazan 1992, 91–92)

Edward Casey adds a further dimension. He clarifies how, in every ritual, the ordinary, familiar, and secular encounters the other beyond us, the transcendent, the holy. In his view, the ritual is the threshold to the holy (Casey 1985, 20). If so, I would argue that the ritual is the threshold to the encounter between the overt and the covert, between the conscious and the unconscious, and between the ego and the sanctified root of the nuclear self. Whereas Hazan emphasizes in the ritual the expression of the threatening-forbidden and shadow elements of the psyche (which are considered inferior and negative), Casey argues that the ritual's role is to set the proper laws for action in the realm of the unconscious and the holy-covert, providing a bridge between them and the conscious and mundane.

The views of Hazan and Casey are also suited to aspects of therapy as a ritual since therapy allows expression to the forbidden and the holy that are both conscious and unconscious, which are the two sides of the psyche, thereby enabling the neutralization and regulation of their power.

The following dream is one of a patient's that supports Casey's position. She describes a psychic move resembling an initiation ritual of entry into the depths, which parallels entry into a room or some space where there is someone else (possibly the clinic and, the one present there, the therapist):

> A secret entry accesses some underground spot, and this is a subterranean journey to all kinds of strange places. The feeling is that these places are meaningful, and reaching them matters. Entering them is complicated, however, as in a war between good and evil. A transition to another reality, as it were. There is some room where all sorts of things need to be done to move to the next room, as if in some holy ritual. The underground journey begins, passing through stages and processes, and then there is a meeting with some woman who accompanies us. We must do something, and the feeling is threatening and also exciting.

May writes of modernity's loss of rituals that, in the past, had helped humans to grapple with life's hurdles. In our culture, when trying to get back after a failure or distressing circumstances of change and transition, we find no place to turn, no rituals providing safe ground, group belongingness, or some response, and all that is left is one's fragile self. This is a further reason, says May, for the swift growth of psychotherapy as a profession (1991, 153). Psychotherapy could be considered an alternative ritual to earlier (including religious) rituals. That is also one reason for the significance of defining the structural element of time and place in psychotherapy since rituals are characterized by time and place determinations.

Transition rituals denote transitions in life as, for example, rituals of birth, maturation-initiation, marriage, divorce, death, and burial. Other transition stages could be physical moves or changing workplaces. These junctures are also critical points, liable to lead to crises and, therefore, often the reason to turn to psychotherapy that serves, among other things, as an alternative transition ritual.

Seemingly, the construct that characterizes the structure of transition rituals and the structure of the myth described above also characterizes the psychotherapeutic process (depth therapy) as a transition ritual that realizes the stages of the myth in the individuation voyage. Therapy is separation from old constructs, entry into the mystery of the psyche's depths, and experiencing an encounter with its hidden possibilities. The return from there, equipped with new knowledge, enables change and integration into life and coping with transitional stages.

The patient thus goes through the psychic voyage protected by the ritual structure that is reenacted in every therapy session: the entry to the clinic, the meeting with the therapist and with the psychic contents, the exit from the clinic, and the internalization of the new contents that emerged. In addition, the ritual of psychotherapy rests on the meaning and the power of ancient healing rites.

The power of the recurring element in the ritual is described in the mythical story about marching around the walls of Jericho. The walls collapsed only after the seventh day of marching around them. Thus, in therapy, we must reencounter the same contents in a cyclical and recurring ritual process and connect to the sound of the ram's horn—the inner voice breaking through to the gates of heaven to bring down the defenses' psychic walls that turned into an inner jail.

Kornfield notes that, in Buddhist therapy, the session begins and ends with a ritual act, such as a gong or a bow. Entry and exit rituals matter because they enable the transition from the routine world to the inner world of therapy and the exit from it. Kornfield suggests the possibility of therapists creating their own ritual, praying to the assisting powers for help in containing the sorrow and the hardships they meet in their work because "we do not work alone for change; the power of life works with us" (Kornfield 2008, 286). When we look at the ritual of Western psychotherapy, he argues, we find that patients meet in sterile rooms and clinics lit by cold fluorescent lights, sitting in uncomfortable chairs unsupported by the language of ritual. In his view, we follow bizarre rituals that forbid touching, hugging, and asking how the therapist is doing while strictly keeping the rigorous "time's up" rule. This account is an obviously inadequate description of most therapists today.

In tribal cultures, the social ritual met the needs of the individual, whose psyche was anchored in collective social symbols and rites. At present, when people are meant to be self-aware and lead individual lives, they cannot make do with the symbols of the social ritual and need to work through their personal psychic contents by themselves. The psychotherapeutic ritual enables the individual's growth process.

Note that cinema, ritual, and therapy unfold in the transitional space between the conscious and the unconscious, between external and internal reality. In these liminal spaces are play, creativity, imagination, and symbols. We are free to move in them, to become through them and within them.

The analogy between the cinematic and the therapeutic rituals enables us to see the therapeutic aspect of the cinematic ritual and how cinema functions as our therapist. In this book, I attempt to set up a mirror in front of the therapist-patient relationships as reflected in films.

References

Armstrong, Karen (2005) *A Short History of Myth* (Edinburgh/New York: Canongate) (Digital Edition).
Bankir, Ariela (2009) "Fellini of the Spirits." *Haaretz,* July 20, *Galeria,* 2 [Heb].
Barthes, Roland (1981) *Camera Lucida: Reflections on Photography*, trans. Richard Howard (New York: Hill and Wang).
Beuys, Joseph (1996) *Objects and Drawings: Catalogue* (Tel Aviv: Tel Aviv Museum) [Heb].
Bialik, Haim Nahman (1975) "Revealment and Concealment in Language." In *Modern Hebrew Literature*, ed. Robert Alter, 130–137 (New York: Behrman House).
Bion, Wilfred R. (2018) *Second Thoughts: Selected Papers on Psychoanalysis* (London: Taylor and Francis).
Buñuel, Luis (1960) "A Statement." *Film Culture*, 21: 40–41.
Borges, Jorge Luis (1964) "The Flower of Coleridge." In *Other Inquisitions: 1937–1952*, trans. Ruth L. C. Simms (Austin: University of Texas Press).
Casey, Edward (1985) "Reflections on Ritual." *Spring*, 102–109.
Campbell, Joseph (1975) *The Hero with a Thousand Faces* (London: Abacus).
Fredericksen, Don (2005) "Why Should We Take Jungian Film Studies Seriously?" *Spring* 73: 31–40.
Freud, Sigmund (1976 [1900]) *The Interpretation of Dreams*, trans. James Strachey (London: Penguin Books).
Gablik, Suzi (1991) *The Reenchantment of Art* (London: Thames and Hudson).
Geldman, Mordechai (2006) *True Self and the Self of Truth: Psychoanalytic and Other Perspectives* (Bnei Brak: Hakibbutz Hameuchad) [Heb].
Gibson, L. Terrill (2005) "Cin-Imago Dei: Jungian Psychology and Images of the Soul in Contemporary Cinema." *Cinema and Psyche* 73: 71–89.
Godard, Jean-Luc and Youssef Ishaghpour (2005) *Cinema: The Archeology of Film and the Memory of a Century*, trans. John Howe (Oxford: Berg).
Halifax, James (1982) *Shaman: The Wounded Healer* (London: Thames and Hudson).
Jackson, Renata (2002) *The Modernist Poetics and Experimental Practice of Maya Deren* (New York: Edwin Mellen).
Hazan, Haim (1992) *The Anthropological Exchange* (Tel Aviv: The Broadcast University) [Heb].
Jung, C. G. (1970) *Four Archetypes: Mother, Rebirth, Spirit, Trickster*, trans. R. F. C. Hull (Princeton, NJ: Princeton University Press).
Jung, C. G. (1974) *Dreams*, trans. R. F. C. Hull (Princeton, NJ: Princeton University Press).
Jung, C. G. (1984) *The Spirit in Man, Art, and Literature, C. W. 15.* trans. R. F. C. Hull (London: Routledge and Kegan Paul).
Jung, C. G. (1989) *Memories, Dreams, Reflections*, trans. Richard and Clara Winston (New York: Vintage Books).
Kast, Pierre (1965) "Federico Fellini: Visites et entretiens." *Cahiers du Cinema* 164, March, 8–22.
Klein, Uri (2009) "The Loss of Simplicity." *Haaretz*, November 20, 13 [Heb].
Kornfield, Jack (2008) *The Wise Heart: A Guide to the Universal Teachings of Buddhist Psychology* (New York: Random House).
Levy, Asher (2008) "Fellini—His Life, His Work and His Musings." http://www.tv-il.com/articles-139.htm [Heb]
Lorca, Federico García (2007) *Theory and Play of the* Duende, trans. A. S. Kline, https://www.poetryintranslation.com/PITBR/Spanish/LorcaDuende.php
Mamet, David (1986) *Writing in Restaurants* (London: Penguin Books).
May, Rollo (1991) *The Cry for Myth* (New York: Norton).

Milosz, Czeslaw (1995) *Facing the River*, trans. Robert Haas (New York: Ecco Press).
Mitchell, Stephen A. (1993) *Hope and Dread in Psychoanalysis* (New York: Basic Books).
Mor, Lila (2010) Dr. Lila Mor's homepage http://www.screeningthespirit.com
Murch, Walter (1995) *In the Blink of an Eye: A Perspective on Film Editing* (Los Angeles: Silman-James).
Netzer, Ruth (2004) *Journey to the Self: The Alchemy of the Psyche—Symbols and Myths* (Ben Shemen, Israel: Modan) [Heb].
Or, Amir (1996) "Myth and Ritual." *Helicon* 17: 9–18 [Heb].
Pessoa, Fernando (1998) *Fernando Pessoa & Co*, trans. Richard Zenith (New York: Grove Press).
Popma, Rachel (1998) *Selected Poems of Rosario Castellanos in Translation* (Indiana).
Rotter, Larry (2011) "Poles Apart." *Haaretz*, November 6, *Galeria*, 8 [Heb].
Schulz, Bruno (1988), "The Book." In *The Street of Crocodiles and Sanatorium under the Sign of the Hourglass*, trans. Celina Wieniewska (London: Pan Books).
Segal, Robert (2004) *Myth: A Very Short Introduction* (Oxford: Oxford University Press).
Shakespeare, William (1923) *The Complete Works of William Shakespeare* (London: Collins).
Snyder, S. (1992) "Movies and the Adolescent: An Overview." *Adolescent Psychiatry* 18: 74–90.
Solmi, Angelo (1967) *Fellini* (London: Merlin Press).
Turner, Victor (2008) *The Ritual Process: Structure and Anti-Structure* (New York: de Gruyter).
Unger, Henry (1991) *Film and Philosophy* (Tel Aviv: Dvir) [Heb].
Whitmont, Edward C. and Sylvia Brinton Perera (1989) *Dreams: A Portal to the Source* (London: Routledge).

Chapter 2

Therapist-Patient Relationships
Love and Death

Questions touching on the patient's deep need, the skill/dedication of the therapist, and the therapist's committed involvement to help the patient are recurrent topics in films.

I will consider here the fundamental archetypal elements (and the complexes derived from them) linked to the archetypal essence of the therapist, the therapy, and the therapist-patient relationships as reflected in films. The archetypes to be examined include the mother, the father, the self, the guide, the redeemer-messiah-Jesus, the wounded healer, the magician, and the shaman. I will deal with the pull of love, hatred, overinvolvement, fascination, and closeness; with the archetypes of incest and the holy coupling; with the persona, the shadow, treason, doubt, and hope; with the search for the anima, the inner child, and the true self that takes place in the psyche of both therapist and patient. Tracing how therapist-patient relationships are reflected in many films will provide insights into their significance.

For this purpose, the following films will be considered: *Man Facing Southeast* (1984), *Persona* (1966), *One Flew Over the Cuckoo's Nest* (1975), *Holy Smoke* (1999), *Julie Walking Home* (2001), *The Soul Keeper* (2002), *A Dangerous Method* (2011), *Sybil* (1976), *The Three Faces of Eve* (1957), *Equus* (1977), *Good Will Hunting* (1997), *Ordinary People* (1980), *David and Lisa* (1962), *The Son's Room* (2001), *Lantana* (2001), *Analyze This* (1999), *Spellbound* (1945), *Zelig* (1983), *Intimate Strangers* (2004), *Marnie* (1964), *Don Juan De Marco* (1995), *K-Pax* (2001), *The Name of the Game* (1987), *Happiness* (1998), *Shrink* (2009), *The Silence of the Lambs* (1991), and *Dr. Pomerantz* (2011). In this chapter, I will focus on three: *The Soul Keeper*, *Julie Walking Home*, and *Man Facing Southeast*.

The name of this chapter, "Therapist-Patient Relationships: Love and Death," hints at its concern: cinema's tendency to endorse archetypal dichotomies—or-or, all or nothing, to be or not to be, to go to the brink, or—as a patient once defined this outlook—"to devour the world or be depressed."

From a psychic perspective, this is a problematic existential state of swinging between poles, splits, severe psychic disturbances, and borderline or even psychotic tendencies. Amos Oz once said that, were we to take the most outstanding literary heroes, we would probably find all of them should have been hospitalized: Raskolnikov in *Crime and Punishment*, Ahab in *Moby Dick*, the protagonists of

DOI: 10.4324/9781003460688-3

Hamlet, Dr. Jekyll and Mr. Hyde, Othello and more. Indeed, crazy people and those at emotional extremes are fascinating raw material for films. The psyche strives for balance and for a suitable equilibrium directed by the "self"—the psyche's center regulating opposites. The problem is that cinema loves drama and finds proper and balanced dosages boring. Consequently, it tends to radicalize opposites. But that is also the way of the dream! It is revealed in enhanced symbols and extreme situations in order to raise something to consciousness and to perturb us until we open up to it.

Reexamining the films discussed below raised fundamental questions for me. It enabled me to deepen insights into the archetypes involved in the healing processes and confronted me with the therapist in cinema as possibly a reflection of myself as a therapist. It also led me to face contents from these films in my dreams.

My discussion here is my subjective interpretation of my dialogical encounter with the films, my transference or countertransference vis-à-vis these films. I will relate to my encounter with the cinema as simultaneously an encounter with the patient and the therapist in me.

Focusing on Three Films

I open the discussion with two films dealing with therapist-patient relationships—*The Soul Keeper* and *Julie Walking Home*. Both films deal with going to extremes—extreme experience and extreme danger. Further on, I expand the discussion to *Man Facing Southeast*.

The keeping of the patient's soul in *The Soul Keeper*, which is entrusted to a therapist who does so devotedly, is indeed placed at risk when the roles are reversed: the therapist assigns to the patient the task of keeping a stone symbolizing his soul so that she may come to trust his desire to help her. The patient is a girl called Sabina whose parents forcibly hospitalized her because she suffered from a severe eating disorder, self-starvation, intense self-hatred, guilt for her sexual needs, and suicidal self-destruction, including actual suicide attempts.

The therapist's utmost devotion comes forth not only in listening, caring, and warmth but also in his telepathic connection with her. Even in his sleep, he can sense that she is in danger, and he awakens and rushes to save her. Even after they break off contact, he senses the moment she is in existential danger when the Nazis are about to execute her. He serves as father-mother to her and restores her dignity when he listens and understands, takes her from the hospital to an elegant coffee house, and feeds her, teaspoon after teaspoon. The patient, Sabina Spielrein, responds to the approach adopted by the therapist, the young Carl Gustav Jung. He was then beginning to seek ways of treating serious cases that therapists had, until then, dealt with only through restraint and punishment. His total devotion to the patient's needs almost destroys him, and her too.

Treating this patient—a talented, creative, passionate girl—poses a professional challenge to the young therapist. Gradually, he is drawn to her wild freedom, so antithetical to his frozen-ossified life with his wife (according to the movie version).

He enables the role reversal and gives in to her seductive request to interpret his dream, fulfilling his secret wish that she be his soul keeper. Sabina could be said to symbolize the anima figure for him—the feminine element in the man's soul, a muse that connects him to the instinctual, creative, and spiritual depths he had been barred from until then.

Jung the therapist had been an object of the patient's love and sexual yearnings from the start, when she projected onto him the figure of the good father—loving and caring—contrary to her father—bad, punishing, hostile, and killing. The therapist was not only an alternative to her father but he also symbolized the archetypal principle of the masculine *animus* that prepares the patient for responsible adult life. Furthermore, the therapist was for her what every therapist is for every patient—the guide leading her to the fulfillment of her personality and talents. As his inner guide to her own self, he also symbolized the inner redeemer.

All therapists represent for their patients the archetype of the *masculine* principle in the psyche and the *father archetype*, comprising borders, law, and order. In this film, the therapist breaches the boundaries of therapy as accepted today by always being available to the patient and allowing her to assume the role of his soul keeper and even interpreter of his dreams. He mixes up the roles and unwittingly asks her to treat him. An unconscious seduction thereby evolves, ultimately leading to an erotic relationship. In this sense, he did not fulfill his role as representing the borders-setting masculine fatherly archetype necessary for building the patient's ego. The affair between them marks the culmination of this breach of boundaries.

Consummating the love and the sexuality between them, even if—and it should be noted— it happened after the therapy ended, crushes both of them. When the therapist understands the danger to his marriage, he retreats, and she responds with destructive revenge. Her inner powers enable her to recover from the heartbreak of his betrayal of her.

The betrayal is twofold: the therapist first betrays the patient's trust and allows "therapeutic love" to turn into romantic-erotic love. When he later retreats from the affair, he betrays the patient by ending it, thereby forsaking her. The patient is thus deceived twice.

The Soul Keeper is based on Jung's relationship with Sabina Spielrein and was produced in the wake of her journals. According to her journals and the testimony of her therapists, the diagnoses of Sabina's character fluctuate between schizophrenia and a hysterical or borderline personality. After her recovery, Sabina became a leading child analyst and wrote extensively on the subject. She advanced the notion of life and death impulses endorsed in Freud's thinking. The film *A Dangerous Method* (2011) also deals with the relationship between Jung and Sabina.

In the second film, *Julie Walking Home*, we are told about the mother of a child who has cancer, who travels abroad to bring her son to a healer who saves sick people by laying hands on them. The child is cured, the mother and the healer fall in love, and, to consummate their relationship, he abandons his professional pursuits.

After their infatuation is realized in a romantic sexual relationship, the child becomes sick again. However, they then find he has lost his healing powers. The child is dying while his mother is now pregnant from her relationship with the healer. A new child will be born "in exchange" for the child who will die. Consummating the love between healer and patient is responsible for the loss of his powers and thus also for the child's death, but it also creates a new life in the body and soul of the mother. At the end of the film, the mother returns to her husband, even though their relationship had been close to ending.

Even though the film deals with alternative-miraculous-energetic healing rather than psychotherapy, it focuses on the same archetypal aspects of the therapist-patient relationship. The mother and the child appear as two aspects of the patient, whose absolute trust in the therapist enables a process of healing and change. The child experiences the energetic power that the healer transmits to his body, while the mother experiences a "therapeutic infatuation" with the healer.

Both films present special circumstances that expand the option of breaching the therapeutic borders and consummating therapeutic love in an extra-therapeutic connection. In both films, the therapist's figure is enhanced in the patient's perception from the outset, due to the mother's extreme distress when confronting death and to Sabina's enormous need for love, which will balance the death powers taking over (cancer and the suicide impulse). In both cases, the emotional-erotic love relationship outside the therapy was intended to deflect the power of death. In both films, the therapist seems to be pulled by the patient's intensive needs, which also answer his needs, and pays the price.

In both films, the therapy includes physical contact. The healer touches the sick child's body while Jung, Sabina's therapist, feeds her and, in another instance, carries her in his arms when he saves her from a suicide attempt. Physical contact is a response to primary, pre-verbal needs, hence the strong, seductive power inherent in it to gravitate toward physical-emotional involvement.

In both cases, the therapist develops a unique response to the patient—she is the *chosen* patient, like the parent's preferred child. Jung is the only one who listens to Sabina and rejects the harsh attitude toward her, both in her parents' home and at the hospital. Captivated by her rich and creative personality, he creates a special relationship with her. The healer confronts a line of people waiting for him and, from afar, envisages Julie carrying her son in her arms. He calls them in without waiting, which will also be his attitude toward them in the future. In the archetypal transference relationship between Julie and the healer, his projections on her are also discernible. She seems to symbolize the mother bearing her son, Mary and baby Jesus, which also appears in the Pietà—Mary holding the mortal Jesus. In his image of her, she comes to him as a mother carrying her sick son in her arms. The healer is also charmed by her singing, as Odysseus is attracted to the singing of the tempting siren, and as a man detached from his personal life who is drawn to the woman as anima, the feminine component of the psyche that can connect him to human feeling. The integration of mother and woman in her parallels his relationship with her as the Jesus-Mary relationship: Mary is the mother of Jesus and, later, his bride.

At the beginning of the film, we see the healer in his childhood, after a stay in a hospital for an operation without his parents. He heals other patients by laying his hands or his legs on them. His healing power flows from his inner wound, and his ability to experience his own wound is what allows for direct contact with the patient's wound. He is a healer through whom great powers cross, and he serves the needs of others while completely detached from his ordinary human needs. This healer symbolizes the archetypal quality of the wounded healer and the shaman.

We meet him at the start of the movie, as noted, as a lonely motherless child. This setting enhances Julie's meaning as an alternative to the missing mother and as the possible mother figure in the Pietà when he collapses into her arms, exhausted from the healing effort. In all these and in his colorless character, vague look, absolute commitment to self-sacrifice in the service of humanity, and covert-overt wound, he bears the symbolic meaning of Jesus the redeemer. In both films, the power of death and destruction wages a ceaseless struggle against the power of life and love. In both films, when the therapist consummates physical love with the patient as seducer and seduced, his therapeutic power is destroyed, and he himself is harmed. The patient's meeting with the therapist as he is after divesting himself from the therapist's persona and revealing his human flaws precludes any further projection on him of potentially healing archetypes. Like Samson (who abandoned his consecration to God when he gave in to a woman) whose hair, which had symbolized his unique power, was cut and then lost, so the healer who consummates his love for Julie loses his power.

Patients, too, are destroyed after erotic consummation with the therapist when they discover that the forces of death and annihilation, which love had been meant to heal, rise anew: Sabina confronts a deep crisis and launches a campaign of revenge and destruction against Jung. Julie's son dies.

And yet, despite the forces of destruction—and perhaps because the love relationship develops after the therapy has ended, building on the therapist's enormous altruistic investment in the therapeutic process—the love in both films is reciprocal, beautiful, profound, and ultimately bears new life. In both films, the removal of the healing projections from the therapist pushes the patient to recognize her powers and develop further on her own. Julie's marriage is restored and she will bring a child into the world, while Sabina grows into a healer.

Jung writes to Freud about his relationship with Sabina:

> Since I knew from experience that she would immediately relapse if I withdrew my support, I prolonged the relationship over the years and in the end found myself morally obliged, as it were, to devote a large measure of friendship to her, until I saw that an unintended wheel had started turning, whereupon I finally broke with her. . . . Like Gross [another Jung patient], she is a case of fight-the-father, which is the name of all that's wonderful I was trying to cure *gratissime* (!) with untold tons of patience, even abusing our friendship for that purpose.

On top of that, naturally, an amiable complex had to throw an outsize monkey wrench into the works. . . . Gross and Spielrein are bitter experiences. To none of my patients have I extended so much friendship and from none have I reaped so much sorrow.

(Freud 1979, 150–151)

He then notes: "Although not succumbing to helpless remorse, I nevertheless deplore the sins I have committed, for I am largely to blame for the high-flying hopes of my former patient" (ibid., 154). Freud's response conveys understanding of the situation's complexity and of the therapeutic failure that is often unavoidable:

To be slandered and scorched by the love with which we operate—such are the perils of our trade, which we are certainly not going to abandon on their account.

(Ibid., 141)

In view of the kind of matter we work with, it will never be possible to avoid little laboratory explosions. Maybe we didn't slant the test tube enough, or we heated it too quickly. In this way we learn what part of the danger lies in the matter and what part in our way of handling it.

(Ibid., 154)

Such experiences, though painful, are necessary and hard to avoid. Without them, we cannot really know life and what we are dealing with. I myself have never been taken in quite so badly, but I have come very close to it a number of times and had *a narrow escape*. . . . They help us to develop the thick skin we need and to dominate "countertransference," which is after all a permanent problem for us; they teach us to displace our own affects to best advantage.

(Ibid., 151–152)

Gadi Maoz writes on this issue:

Even when Jung and Spielrein no longer defined their relationship as therapeutic, it was actually still that. Possibly, we can learn from this that therapeutic relationships can never completely end. The therapy may have ended long ago but continues in the sense of transference that will forever be different from what we could call "real relationships."

And he adds:

Jung's confusion in the course of his relationship with Sabina is reminiscent of a similar process that Breuer underwent at about the same time when he was treating Anna O. Here, too, Freud was involved as a kind of guide, but Breuer, who also stumbled into erotic countertransference toward Anna O., disengaged from it in another way that ultimately led to his separation from Freud. In his case, Breuer's wife solved the problem for him by unequivocally informing him: "Either she or I." Breuer chose his wife and ended the therapy at once . . . Breuer, like Jung and Freud, did not know at that time how to grapple with erotic transference without hurting patients.

(Maoz 2010)

References

Freud, Sigmund (1979) *The Freud-Jung Letters: The Correspondence between Sigmund Freud and C. G. Jung*, trans. Ralph Manheim and R. F. C. Hull (London: Picador).

Maoz, Gadi (2010) "Sabina Spielrein: A Greek Tragedy or a Myth about the Development of Psychoanalysis." Website of The Israeli Jungian New Association—http://www.israjung.co.il [Heb]

Chapter 3

Archetypes Activated in Therapist-Patient Relationships

Jung made us aware that the patient's feelings toward the therapist are not only a transference of her feelings toward her parents in an attempt to restore and amend these early relationships but also projections of archetypal images of the mother and father present in the patient's psyche from the start, both in their positive and negative aspects. The therapist is the temporary substitute for many archetypal functions that have not yet developed properly in the patient or that the patient has not yet discovered in her psyche. The therapist is a substitute not only for the motherly and fatherly archetypes but also for the masculine, the feminine, the ego, and the redeeming self.

These archetypes are operative in therapist-patient relationships. Every archetype has both a positive and a negative-shadowy side. The Greek god Hermes (Mercury), who is considered the gods' emissary to humanity and the psyche's guide, and to whom I refer as the god of individuation and psychotherapy, is a deluding trickster who leads but also misleads the psyche (Netzer 2004, 237). Our constant task is to distinguish, every time anew, the good part from the bad part in the fruit of the tree of knowledge—what is the objective truth in the patient's perception of the therapist, and what are the projections derived from personal biographical experiences and from archaic archetypal ones.

The Mother and the Father

The patient's attitude toward the therapist includes projections of good and bad previous experiences with the personal parental figures. In addition, the good-loving-giving father-mother archetypes are activated in the expectations from the therapist. In contrast, present in the apprehensions and misgivings about the therapist are the archetypal figures of the bad-devouring-destructive father and mother. The patient's experiences with her parents and other parental figures join the archetypal parental images, thus creating complexes of parental figures in her psyche (a positive or negative mother complex, a positive or negative father complex).

The parental archetypes are first activated in the psyche of the baby or the child, and these are the primary archetypes in therapy. The *mother archetype* is the primary basic archetype, and the embryonic psyche grows under its cover. It is one of the fundamental archetypes operating in therapy (both in the patient's and the therapist's psyches), triggering an expectation of motherly love in the therapist-patient relationship. Erich Neumann (1955) distinguishes the *elementary mother*—containing, holding, listening, empathic, defending, protecting, caring, nurturing, and loving—from the *transformative mother*, who pushes the child and the patient to psychic development and, later, to separation from her. After the elementary stage of empathic containment comes the pressure to develop.

At the archetypal level, the motherhood experience is felt as complete, oceanic, infinite, symbiotic, paradise-like, one we long to go back to and recurrently search for in the therapeutic setting, but one we gradually separate from as the psyche gains strength and autonomy.

The *father archetype* appears in the evolving psyche at the next stage, the stage of consciousness-shaping, and its role is to give form, limits, law, order, organization, and conscious meaning to psychic life. In therapy, the father archetype is embodied in the formal elements of the therapeutic contract that determine borders of time, place, and payment rules.

The archetypal parental figures are projected onto the therapist. The motherly aspect is the emotional-containing aspect, nurturing and empathic, while the fatherly aspect defines, organizes, and interprets the therapeutic process and the psychic materials.

Discernible in the mother archetype is the feminine archetype, the emotional-intuitive aspect in the psyche that serves the relationships connecting us to ourselves and to others. Palpable in the father archetype is the masculine aspect—active, enterprising, rational, fighting, assertive, and implementing. Projected onto the therapist are the feminine and masculine aspects of the psyche. For the patient, the therapist serves as a model that incorporates an active function while still connected to his inner feelings and to others.

The parents' archetypes include their negative aspects as well. Contrary to the good mother archetype, there is also a bad mother archetype appearing in myths as a monster and in legends as a witch—the controlling, devouring, narcissistic mother who neither sustains the containing-protecting-defending-nurturing-empathic element nor enables the transformative developmental aspect, jeopardizing the existential autonomy of the child meant to separate from her.

Contrary to the good father archetype, there is also a bad father archetype—an authoritarian, despotic, controlling aspect representing the aggressive superego that punishes and castrates, demands obedience, and does not allow the child to listen to his individual voice.

Patterns of pleasing parents following an experience of "love on condition that I will be good" are transferred to the therapist, as is a fear of the parents' critical, judgmental, punitive stance. The archetypal images of the good and the bad mother and of the good and the bad father are alternatively projected onto the therapist according to the patient's early experiences. In turn, they influence givenness, trust, suspicion, expectations, anger, rebellion, and disappointment in the therapy. Parental projections are also present in the therapist's attitude toward the patient. The therapist may expect the patient to be the mother/father who affirms her worth, admires, and loves her. She may also fear the patient's criticism as a rigid and strict parent, suspects him, and pleases him by being overly kind.

Therapists who treat children and their parents, especially young therapists, often have difficulty confronting the child's parents as if they were their own. The therapist's emotional attitude toward the parents he is treating could be affected by his attitude toward his own parents, particularly in unresolved contexts such as anger with hurting, alienated, non-empathic, and controlling parents. Cinema spectators feel this way toward problematic and alienated parents of patients in films.

The Archetype of the Hero and the Detective

The therapist embodies for the patient the ego-self roles meant to regulate and coordinate between the id and the superego, between the unconscious and the conscious, and between the inner and outer worlds—between the individual and the society. This role includes the struggle against obstacles embodied in the *hero archetype* and the inquiry conducted by the interpretive consciousness embodied in the *detective archetype*.

The therapist embodies the mythical *archetype of the hero*, who departs to the realm of the unconscious and struggles with the patient's dragons—symbolic expressions of the unconscious' problematic aspects (anxiety, depression, obstructive defenses, and so forth). The purpose of this struggle is to help the patient overcome the dragons to discover the treasure they had been protecting—the positive, enriching, and fruitful aspect of the unconscious in the voyage for the truth of the self. In films, the therapist sometimes appears as the ideal ultimate hero and, at times, as an anti-hero when presented as flawed and blemished. Stephen Mitchell (1993, 43) claims that the analyst's self-portrait in Freud's case studies resembles that of super-detective Sherlock Holmes. In contrast, the therapist in current psychoanalytic literature more closely resembles television detective Colombo, who embodies the anti-hero in his seemingly confused remarks, careless appearance, and brilliant and insightful gaze.

Many films address the cause of the hero's psychic problem through the psychoanalytic narrative of "recovering the repressed." The assumption is that the biographic story is repressed and must be raised to consciousness, at times through hypnosis, or that the story is known to the patient but not to the therapist and the spectator, and the film then brings up this unknown story to their consciousness. The archetype of the detective who activates the therapist's psyche symbolizes the active consciousness of the ego that looks at the unconscious, investigates it, raises the contents to consciousness, and interprets them. The negative aspect of the detective-researcher therapist is prying intrusiveness and overemphasis on thought and intellect at the expense of feeling. The hero and the detective could become entrapped in a grandiose fantasy of their power.

The analogy between decoding the patient's psyche and the study of the dream on the one hand, and the detective inquiry on the other, has long been known.

Several films about therapy strengthen the script of the therapist's detective inquiry, among them *Equus* and *K-Pax*, and especially Hitchcock's films *Spellbound* and *Marnie*. Many of the films dealing with therapy are built as detective stories. The therapist who is identified with the detective archetype investigates the people tied to the patient's life, goes to their homes, looks into their life stories to track the patient's repressed secret, the trauma where the patient was a victim of violence or sexual violence (*Sybil, The Three Faces of Eve, K-Pax, Spellbound, Marnie, The Prince of Tides*) or where the patient committed a violent act (*Equus, Marnie, K-Pax, Persona*). During the film/ therapy, the crime/trauma is exposed through hypnosis or by confronting the location where the trauma occurred.

The detective narrative of these films assumes that the discovery of the crime, the trauma, and the repressed guilt lead to the patient's redemption, just as a detective's discovery of a crime leads to the punishment of the criminal. This approach preserves Freud's original belief that exposing the repressed unconscious conflict will remove the symptom, identifying the unconscious with the locus of the crime and with dark negative materials. When the entire unconscious is illuminated, triumphant consciousness will rule, and then, according to Freud, where the id had been, the self will now be. Films built in this pattern exalt the therapist as an omniscient decoder and researcher, strengthening his standing as an omnipotent savior. Hitchcock's *Spellbound* and *Marnie* are instances of this pattern.

Love

People who do not experience the full primary connection with the mother during infancy and childhood are basically deprived of love. A demand is often addressed to the therapist to fill this lack as a demand of primary fusion, be it with a parent who was experienced as a good mother or with a missing partner.

In *Moods*, Hoffmann ironically conveys our most basic need for motherly love: "Imagine that we could cradle ourselves like that and move from place to place like large babies carrying themselves. We'd calm ourselves down like mothers do when they rock their babies in the air and sing them lullabies" (2015, 119).

Another archetype is added to the primary archetype of *mother's love*: the *healing love* archetype. The primary experience is that love remedies all our wounds and pains. In *Crime and Punishment*, Sonia, who loves sinful Raskolnikov, enables him to undergo a healing change through her love for him, her belief in his goodness and in his chance at another life. Such love resembles that of the therapist, who believes in her patient's healing powers and loves him despite "his sins." In this spirit, contemporary neurologist Oliver Sacks writes, "The work of healing, of rendering whole, is, first and last, the business of love" (Sacks 1990, 273).

The holy grail everyone pursues as the aim and purpose of the psyche at times symbolizes the healing love potion. Plato says: "So you see how ancient is the mutual love implanted in mankind, bringing together the parts of the original body, and trying to make one out of two, and to heal the natural structure of man" (Plato 1956, 87 [191d]). And, in reference to the healing art, "one must be able to make loving friends of the greatest enemies in the body . . . our ancestor Asclepios . . . composed our art because he knew how to implant love and concord in these" (ibid., 83 [186d]).

Freud claimed that, essentially, we are healed through love. "Classic" psychoanalysis was trapped in an ideal and a delusion about the power and need of the therapist to remain neutral and objective, hence the recourse to seemingly objective means such as the couch, which preclude eye contact between analyst and patient. As a result, the therapist was not neutral and welcoming but distant and cold. By the second half of the twentieth century, however, it became clear that this detached therapeutic style perpetuates in the patient the loneliness and alienation that led him to therapy in the first place.

Psychoanalysts Heinz Kohut, Stephen Mitchell, and Thomas Ogden place at the center the empathic dialogic attention sustained in a face-to-face encounter. This approach coincided with the shift of psychotherapy from the emphasis on interpretation (ruled by the father archetype) toward containing, mirroring, and holding, based on recognition of the intersubjective therapeutic encounter as a mutual[1] encounter between therapist and patient. This deep empathy (ruled by the mother archetype), which Kohut sees as the cornerstone of the creation and healing of the self, is the basis of therapeutic love (Kohut 1984).

Carlo Strenger deals with the therapist's dilemma concerning the suitable response to the patient's love and whether such love heals. He distinguishes the classic, emotionally distant stance from the romantic stance that encourages emotional closeness (1998, 187). In many films, cinema also believes in healing through love—a romantic approach. From *As Good as It Gets*, we understand that what heals Jack Nicholson, rather than psychiatric drugs, is Helen Hunt's love. Hunt is not his therapist but a loved-loving woman.

So, what is proper therapeutic love (of the therapist for the patient)? Ellen Siegelman (2002) considers this question and cites Kenneth Lambert, who describes charity as depicted by Paul the Apostle: "If I speak in the tongues of men and of angels, but have not love, I am a noisy gong or a clanging cymbal. And if I have prophetic powers, and understand all mysteries and all knowledge, and if I have all faith, so as to remove mountains, but have not love, I am nothing" (I Corinthians 13:1–2). "So faith, hope, love abide, these three; but the greatest of these is love" (ibid., 13:13). What love is at stake here? "Love is patient and kind; love is not jealous or boastful; it is not arrogant or rude. Love does not insist on its own way; it is not irritable or resentful; it does not rejoice at wrong, but rejoices in the right. Love bears all things, believes all things, hopes all things, endures all things" (ibid., 13:4–7). Rather than a description of unconditional personal love, this is perhaps the love of the fairy in legends, a virtual archetypal good mother without a physical dimension and a personal ego before it became flesh and blood, possibly an idealization of absolute motherly love at the elementary containing stage.

For Siegelman, proper therapeutic love is neither absolute Christian charity, impersonal and clean of any shadow or personal needs, nor the infatuation based on the needs of a Dionysian erotic dimension for reciprocal admiration lacking realization.

In I Corinthians, love appears in the trinity of faith, hope, and love. Siegelman claims that therapeutic love is an act of faith and hope toward what the patient can be and what the patient already is. Faith and hope derive from faith in the healing potential of the self that exists in the patient from the start and in the healing power of therapeutic love (2002, 30). In fact, every therapeutic approach rests on faith, hope, and love (see also, for example, Mitchell 1993; Eigen 1981).

In the spirit of Siegelman's approach, I would say that proper therapeutic love is good-enough love (along the lines of Winnicott's "good-enough mother") rather than good-great-absolute love, in the Christian model of I Corinthians and of the holy mother. The feeling of love in human relationships and in therapeutic relations also includes problematic-shadowy aspects. Part of therapeutic love is also the needs and the longings of both the therapist and the patient, which could promote dependent love or controlling-demanding, narcissistic love. Recall that every love is deluding when it seeks to be total, eternal, and devoid of shadows and conflicts.

Moreover, in life and in therapy, love is deluding when projected onto purported "redeemers." These are charismatic, narcissistic figures allegedly bringing love and perfection. What they seek, however, is the love of their admirers for the hurt child inside them, who was deprived of love and is now incapable of giving love to others. Deluding love offers the goal of redemption only in the other and in the other's love.

The lack of love, so frequent in human relations, is perhaps the explanation for the equation of love with God as the source of the supreme total love that is missing and in whom we may find shelter. God's love is the absolute answer to experiences and fears of abandonment: "Cast me not off, forsake me not, O God of my salvation! For my father and my mother have forsaken me, but the Lord will take me up" (Psalms 27:9–10). The male therapist, at times, becomes an object of projections as the father-loving God, while the female therapist turns into an object of projections as the mother-loving goddess.

Judaism, Christianity, and Buddhism include pity and compassion as components of love. In *The Monk and the Philosopher* (conversations between a father and his son, who became a Tibetan monk), the son answers his father's question—"What's the difference between compassion and love?"—as follows: "Love is the necessary complement to compassion. Compassion can't live, or even less develop, without love" (Revel and Ricard, 2000, 167).

When loving the patient is hard, in cases with negative characteristics ranging from intense narcissism to a psychotic shadow, the only potential empathic bridge is the compassion awakened in the encounter with the patient's hidden wound and suffering. Compassion is sometimes the sole viable love, which can transcend the rejection evoked by the patient's disturbing shadow.

In psychoanalysis, the dimension of compassion appears in Kohut's empathy. The essence of therapy today is unquestionably human relations, closeness, and intimacy. Therapeutic love comprises emotional and ethical aspects: compassion, empathy, warmth, care, respect, altruism, devotion, and concern, as well as responsibility, commitment, and willingness to help (Levinas 1985).

In the context of the importance usually assigned to therapeutic love, Siegelman (2002, 30) notes that therapists who think they will heal the patient's wound/break through their love are in the realm of hubris. She claims that the Scylla and Charybdis of therapy are the inability to love enough and loving too much. In therapy, as in life, proper love gives space and is ready to let go to enable the patient's future separation.

Some films show proper love, with a therapist who is involved but not excessively—an involvement with broad and largely unrestricted borders that is expressed in deep personal giving, a touching hand or a hug, and, when necessary, accessibility beyond reception hours.

In *Good Will Hunting*, the therapist tries to create relationships of trust, intimacy, closeness, and love with the patient. He teaches him that love is the center of the world, as had been true of his own love for his wife, and he considers the therapy successful when the patient prefers to renounce a high position for the sake of a relationship with a girl. In the film *Don Juan de Marco*, the patient asks the doctor: "What is worth living and dying for? The answer is identical—only for love."

The Genesis story tells us that Adam knew his wife, implying sexual knowledge. The wording reveals that eroticism is tied to emotional closeness, which is also deep knowledge of the other. This closeness between knowledge and love and the many archetypal forces active in the therapist-patient relationship bestow on it its unique power and special appeal. They promote the proper "therapeutic infatuation"—a sense of love mixed with admiration for and idealization of the therapist. Freud spoke of the Eros-Thanatos oppositions at the basis of the psyche. Therapeutic love as Eros in its broad meaning (not as sexual eroticism), which is the antithesis of Thanatos (death), could be viewed as a critical factor in therapy. When it awakens between therapist and patient, it leads to change, to a weakening of the death-destruction forces, and even to healing (as we saw in *The Soul Keeper* and in *Julie Walking Home*). The problem emerges, as in these two films, when the Eros in the therapy translates into sexuality.

In every person's life, the child's initial symbiotic aspiration of fusion with the parent in early life is transformed in adulthood into mature and egalitarian love relationships and into finding a partner as a psychic complement. This incestual aspiration of fusion with the mother or the father translates in adult life into an attempt to unite with a partner. Many patients and therapists who experienced a primary injury in childhood in their relationships with their parents come to therapy because of their inability to love and, at the same time, due to an enormous need to receive unconditional love. Sometimes they imagine that therapeutic relationships involving unreserved closeness and a primary-symbiotic fusion, like that between mother and child, will amend their primary injury and emotional deprivation and serve as a compensatory amendment to their destructive feelings. The fusion aspiration could easily turn into sexual longings for the therapist.

Even when therapists believe they are fulfilling the needs of their patients and acting for their benefit, romantic-sexual relationships ex post facto exploit the patient's incestual desires. Practically, these relationships resemble parents' exploitation of their children's feelings and sexuality for their own satisfaction. Hence, the sin of sexuality between therapist and patient is equal to the sin of incest (Netzer 2004, 328; 435–437). The therapist can sometimes unwittingly hurt a patient who had already been hurt by a parent exploiting her for his own needs. In the therapeutic reality, every professional code bans such love. The therapist's awareness of the high frequency of parental exploitation, including sexual abuse, is necessary for avoiding ensnarement in the trap of therapeutic seduction-abuse, which could reconstruct parental abuse (Stein 1973). Full realization of the patient's needs for unconditional love, psychic or physical, is not the goal of therapy. Therapy aims to enable patients to experience and contain their feelings and needs and understand their source and meaning. Therapy is meant to allow patients to realize their feelings in real life, outside the therapy, not to make them emotionally dependent on therapists who will fulfill all their needs better than their disappointing parents and partners. The ability to delay primary gratification and the transition from a demanding need for immediate satisfaction of concrete needs to an understanding of their symbolic meaning (the transition from the concrete to the symbolic) are part of the strengthening and development of a consciousness of self in every person, and so also in therapy. Breaching therapeutic borders by satisfying sexuality transforms the relationship's symbolic meaning through concrete regressive fulfillment.

Romantic infatuation, which tends to be infatuation with infatuation itself more than with a particular person, is particularly problematic in the therapeutic relationship. Infatuation is activated by the archetype of Cupid, who is the son of Aphrodite, the love goddess. Cupid is her childish aspect, shooting addictive infatuation arrows at his victims. Unconscious forces rule the addiction, and infatuation is not a conscious adult capability to engage in human relationships and I-thou love.

Frequent in therapist-patient films are longings for healing through love, a love that is total and symbiotic as well as romantic and sexual. The Gabbard brothers claim that a female therapist who falls in love with a male patient is a recurrent cinematic character (*Spellbound, The Prince of Tides*), whereas, in reality, infatuations usually occur between a female patient and a male therapist. In their view, cinema thereby preserves the erroneous perception that the woman's salvation is the love of the proper man. The idea that love is the salvation of the feminine psyche's afflictions is applied in cinema not only to the female patient who falls in love with a male therapist but also to the female therapist who falls in love with a male patient (Gabbard and Gabbard 1989).

Irvin Yalom says that romantic love and psychotherapy are incompatible: "The good therapist fights darkness and seeks illumination, while romantic love is sustained by mystery and crumbles upon inspection" (Yalom 2002, 201). He notes:

> Strong sexual feelings haunt the therapy situation. How could they not, given the extraordinary intimacy between patient and therapist? Patients regularly develop feelings of love and/or sexual feelings for their therapist. The dynamics of such positive transference are often overdetermined. For one thing, patients are exposed to a very rare, gratifying, and delicious situation. Their every utterance is examined with interest . . . they are nurtured, cared for, and unconditionally accepted and supported.
>
> Some individuals do not know how to respond to such generosity. What can they offer in return? Many women, especially those with low self-regard, believe that the only real gift they have to offer is a sexual gift. Without sex — a commodity they may have depended upon in past relationships — they can only foresee a loss of interest and ultimate abandonment by the therapist. For others, who elevate the therapist to an unrealistic, lofty, larger-than-life position, there may also be the wish to merge with something greater than themselves. Still others may compete for love with the unknown patients in the therapist's practice.
> (Ibid., 192–193)

The desperate need for love provides fertile ground for turning therapeutic love into erotic-sexual infatuation with the therapist. The need of both the patient and the therapist are present here, concretely attesting to one or the other's need to be *chosen*, preferred, and most beloved (in a version of the biblical "Your only son, whom you love"). This quest often translates into longings for the romantic-erotic realization of therapeutic love. At times, the male patient imagines himself as an ugly duckling that the therapist's love will transform into a swan, and the female patient imagines herself as Cinderella, whom the therapist's love will turn into a princess. The opposite is also true—the therapist needs the patient's love as a duckling or as Cinderella. We should also add situations where a woman/man therapist/patient seeks in sex the alternative to the intimacy they cannot create. In any event, the diversion of therapeutic love to a sexual channel urging realization conveys opposition to the therapeutic process and is a way of evading it.

Archetypes and complexes exist among therapists, too, as noted, and may tempt them to realize their romantic-erotic yearnings as people in need of their patients' love and admiration, when in fact they are fulfilling their own needs as people who have not dealt with their emotional and narcissistic issues. Such a connection is never egalitarian, and patients find it hard to resist the wishes and desires of the therapist. Yalom warns therapists: "Keep in mind that the feelings arising in the therapy situation generally belong more to the role than the person: Do not mistake the transferential adoration as a sign of your irresistible personal attractiveness or charm" (Yalom 2002, 193).

Heinrich Racker develops the motif of the therapist who needs the patient's love. He describes a situation where the therapist's transference to the patient of his feelings toward his mother may raise in him a hidden desire to be loved by the patient, which will become manifest in his infatuation with her. The frustration of this desire could evoke his rejection and hate for her, a wish that the patient should not develop new relationships outside the therapy and jealousy of her sexual-erotic relationship with her partner. An immature therapist could view any man loved by the patient as a competitor. Moreover, such a therapist could develop feelings of inferiority when the patient does not fall in love with him, turning her into a bad mean mother in his eyes (Racker 2018, Ch. 5).

The problem of the therapist swept into a relationship of infatuation and sexuality with the patient appears in all the films dealing with this motif. Probably, these films are close to a reality where erotic bounds-breaking ties develop in the therapy. In this context, I will mention Phillys Chesler, who deals with the personality of a therapist engaged in sexual exploitation. She cites the description of Charles Dahlberg, who notes the features of the seductive therapist as a man who chose to practice as a psychotherapist between 1930 and 1945 and was withdrawn and introspective, studious, passive, shy, more intellectually than physically adventurous, power-drunk, and not great in bed (Chesler 1989, 142).

The film *The Soul Keeper* describes the therapist's unawareness of the required limits between patient and therapist. No pre-defined borders had yet been set between therapist and patient, guaranteeing to the patient that the therapy was solely focused on attention to her needs. On the one hand, Freud conducted his therapeutic sessions at the beginning of the twentieth century sitting distantly and invisibly behind the couch where the patient lies. On the other, therapists attempted new forms of bounds-breaking therapies, such as Swiss psychoanalyst Marguerite Sechehaye, who brought a patient to her home and attempted to meet all her immediate needs, including feeding her. Another example is Hungarian psychoanalyst Sandor Ferenczi, who tried a method where the patient treats the therapist. This idea, which failed as a therapeutic system, is the basis of Irvin Yalom's book *When Nietzsche Wept* (1992). In this book, the therapist induces the patient to treat him through a manipulation meant to create a therapeutic relationship, and patient Nietzsche then "treats" the therapist. Note that Ferenczi fell in love and had an affair with a patient (Alma), the daughter of a woman (Gisela) with whom he had also had an affair and then married. Films describing fulfilled erotic relationships in psychotherapy—such as *The Prince of Tides*, *Zelig*, and *Holy Smoke!*—were made in the late twentieth century, when clear rules forbidding them were already known.

Yalom again warns:

Sexual transgression is also destructive for therapists. Offending therapists, once they examine themselves honestly, understand that they are acting for their own satisfaction rather than in the service of their patient. Therapists who have made a deep commitment to a life of service do great violence to themselves and to their innermost moral precepts. They ultimately pay a devastatingly high price not only to the external world in the form of civil censure and punishment and widespread disapprobation, but internally as well, in the form of pervasive and persistent shame and guilt.

(Yalom 2002, 194)

In some situations, infatuation in the therapy could result from the usual causes, such as attraction to certain qualities in one of the parties, and not from the projection of aspects that may not be there at all. In the television series *The Sopranos*, therapist Jennifer Melfi falls in love with patient Tony Soprano and is severely tested in her professional relationship with him. The patient is a brutal Mafia criminal and a sensitive family man. His sensitivity is evident both in his guilt feelings and in his attitude toward animals. Her infatuation with him seemingly reflects her attraction to his blatant and shadowy-aggressive masculinity, which also includes vulnerability. *The Sopranos* brings us a fortunate model where both patient and therapist fall in love, but the relationship remains professional and does not develop into an affair. The therapeutic neutrality they upheld at the beginning of psychotherapy was meant, among other things, to enable a safe distance from temptation. Mitchell compares the analyst, who must cautiously beware of the patient's seduction, to Ulysses, who avoids the sirens' allure by tying himself to the neutral mast while listening to their song. He thus succeeds in preserving the proper distance (1993, 144).

Jung drew his insights into therapist-patient relationships from the *Rosarium*. This ancient alchemical text describes the process of brother-sister or king-queen drawing closer, from being fully clothed to nakedness and copulating in an alchemic bath (Jung 1983, 74–84). Jung viewed this symbolic text, originally meant to describe chemical materials drawing together and blending, as a symbol of the convergence between various psychic elements and thus also as symbolizing the confluence between psychic elements in the therapist and the patient. He did not, however, view them as legitimizing sexual relationships between them. Quite the contrary. Jung found in this text insights into intimacy, through which we seek our spiritual-psychic complement, and relied on it as the basis for insights into the potential dangers of excessive therapeutic closeness (Netzer 2004, 430–445). The ancient text's description of deep psychic attachment as sexual intercourse demonstrates that the erotic-sexual archetype is inevitable in therapeutic contexts, and therapy seeks to channel sexual energy to its psychic-spiritual aim—the psyche's symbolic coupling with the psyche of the other and with itself.

The yearning for the romantic-erotic realization of therapeutic love could thus convey the basis of romantic love—the psyche's longing for its lost partner as described in the Platonic myth: the first human was split into a man and a woman and, ever since, each half seeks the lost other. The union of man and woman in sexual intercourse symbolizes the hierogamia (the archetype of the psyche's holy wedding), the renewed melding of the masculine-feminine in each one's psyche, the I-thou union as the merger of the psyche's opposites within itself. In addition, the psyche longs to unite with something greater, with the spiritual, the divine, the transcendent. Thus, the symbolism of the Indian tantra, alchemy, and Kabbalah.

This longing is recurrently renewed in the therapeutic connection. It is sometimes projected onto the therapist as a figure that mixes father-god, mother-goddess, and the omniscient God of whom it is said in the Jewish daily prayers, "May you never remove your love from us."

Ever since, psychotherapy has cast about for a proper way of empathy and giving, insight and feeling, which make up the therapeutic love enabling the connection between therapist and patient—a unique, asymmetrical encounter without parallel in other relationships. This connection sustains the proper distance-closeness between therapist and patient, allowing the patient to set the borders of his personality from the clear and safe borders set by therapeutic rules, to grow and carve out from it his unique path and his consciousness of self. This stage is the adult stage of therapeutic love, the I-thou love relationship based on the empathy activated by the anima, which developed from the motherly archetype and enables understanding of the other's feelings. The adult stage of therapeutic love is also the patient's ability to love the therapist, not out of infatuation and idealization but out of knowledge and acceptance of her flaws. Such love also enables the patient to love himself, with his own flaws and shadows. Samuel Shem writes: "These patients become aware that they can love—without being laughed at or having their love batted away—and be loved, and they open up, and heal" (Shem 1954, xiv).

Hate

To write about love in therapy without writing about the opposite feeling is impossible. Patients need a therapist not only as someone who can bear and accept their love but also as someone who can bear and accept their hate and aggressiveness. Patients evoke a broad spectrum of feelings in therapists. At times, the patient projects onto the therapist the bad father and mother (according to his experience of his own parents) or the negative aspect of the father/mother archetype, blaming, attacking, and being hostile to the therapist and evoking in her negative feelings toward the patient, leading her to experience herself as a bad parent.

The therapist's commitment is to acknowledge his own feelings, thereby assuming an emotional distance that enables him to examine their source in his personal biography as well. The commitment is to refrain from identifying with his own feelings and from acting on them unless such action serves the patient. The therapist must clarify to himself whether his negative feelings derive from the patient's objective characteristics and behavior or from his projections onto the patient, seeking to transform them into positive feelings while understanding the patient's difficulties. Mitchell notes that patients can come to love and hate through involvement with a therapist who has feelings of his own, including love and hate. The therapist, however, endeavors to mobilize the feelings on both sides in the service of analytical work to achieve constructive growth and development (Mitchell and Black 1995, Ch. 9). Winnicott, too, explicitly refers to hate in countertransference: "However much he [the analyst] loves his patients he cannot avoid hating them, and fearing them, and the better he knows this the less will hate and fear be the motive determining what he does to his patients" (Winnicott 1949, 69). He even considered the possibility of the therapist directly expressing hatred toward the patient as a therapeutic tool. This puzzling issue will become clearer when we see that Winnicott said this regarding the treatment of psychotics, who at times convey hate directly and view the therapist's revelation of negative feelings as an authentic expression that enables them to place trust in him because "if a psychotic is in a 'coincident love-hate' state of feeling he experiences a deep conviction that the analyst is also only capable of the same crude and dangerous state of coincident love-hate relationship. Should the analyst show love he will surely at the same moment kill the patient" (ibid., 70). Winnicott points out that, in some analyses, the patient seeks the analyst's hate, and objective hate is then required. "If the patient seeks objective or justified hate he must be able to reach it, else he cannot feel he can reach objective love" (ibid., 72). He also notes that psychotic anxiety and hate arise among those who work with severely ill psychiatric patients.

The crude and denied hate of therapists toward psychotic patients, added to fear of them, may explain the use of injections and ruinous electric shocks in the treatment of psychotics and those who were considered law-breakers (*One Flew Over the Cuckoo's Nest*, *Man Facing Southeast*).

The Therapist and the Archetype of the Self

Jung referred to the bridging-connective function between the unconscious and the conscious as transcendent. This function enables change processes toward a consciousness of self, a connection of opposites in the psyche, and the integration of the self, which is the psyche's wholeness. The therapist is the guide to the self.

I will relate here to several archetypes that come forth in the archetype of the therapist as a symbol of the self: Jesus-messiah-redeemer, the wounded healer, the shaman, and the omnipotent magician.

These archetypes, which closely resemble one another, are generally projected onto therapists, work in them, and are a priori present at the very foundation of the therapeutic system. The archetypes of Jesus-the redeemer and the magician appear more intensely in energetic therapy.

Archetypes: Redeemer-Messiah-Jesus, Treason, and Wounded Healer

The redeemer-messiah of the end of days in Judaism and Christianity symbolizes the realization of the psyche's wholeness, whose opposites join together for a peaceful existence symbolizing the realization of the self, which is the center of the personality. The messiah symbolizes healing and harmonious redemption. Jesus is one of its embodiments, and the therapist archetype expresses many aspects of Jesus as the purported redeemer of the patient's suffering.

Jesus bears the cross of suffering for his loyalty to an inner truth. He embodies the individual committed to his unique fate, even at the cost of misunderstanding the collective stance, and pays the price of loyalty to his true mission. He goes through his journey of anguish—the passion (which means both sorrow and desire) that ultimately brings redemption.

As the son of God, Jesus mediates between the supreme divine entity and humans, that is, between the psyche's divine potential and its realization in the consciousness of the self. He is the element aspiring to bring redemption to the soul, standing for the self and the way to the self. The need for redemption, for healing the suffering soul, led to the appearance of the Jesus figure in the world and to our projections of the *archetype of Jesus the redeemer* onto specific individuals. Jesus within us is the transcendent function in the psyche urging realization of the ego's dialogue with its complete self, which touches the divine-transcendent source, and he is the internal redeemer. Usually, the redeemer-savior archetype is projected onto the therapist when the belief in her power to lead the psyche to wholeness enables these forces to be gradually realized in the patient's psyche.

The patient's difficulties and suffering tend to evoke rescue fantasies in the therapist and could also awaken wishes to be an omnipotent redeemer. A therapist overly identified with the redeemer-Jesus archetype could be drawn into an involvement lacking emotional and practical limits in his efforts to heal the patient at his own expense. Over-identification then leads the therapist to bear the patient's suffering ("He has borne our sicknesses and carried our pains" [Isaiah 53:4]) and to sacrifice himself (by devoting exaggerated time and feelings), as Jesus sacrificed himself to redeem others.

Simultaneously, the reverse process unfolds when the therapist encounters the patient's shadow and suffering. The patient then becomes a symbolic substitute of Jesus by, as it were, bearing the therapist's pain-sins—once evil and suffering are projected onto the patient, the therapist can feel cleansed. Taking on the projections of Jesus, the patient atones for the therapist's pain.[2] The Jesus archetype, then, splits between the patient (the bearer of evil, the scapegoat, the sufferer, the sacrificed/punished atoning for us) and the therapist (the compassionate savior redeemer, the Pietà mother who bears/contains the sufferer in her arms).[3] It is important for the therapist to acknowledge the tendency toward this split between him and the patient in order to unite the suffering and its containment-salvation in both of them—in each one's psyche are both the anguish and the possibility of salvation.

The therapist is identified with the redeemer, but she, like Jesus, is also betrayed and sacrificed by the patient. At times, the patient experiences the weaknesses or mistakes of the therapist as a betrayal. The patient's aggressive response could then be experienced as ingratitude by the therapist, who also feels betrayed. Betrayal is an inseparable part of the Jesus archetype, as devaluation is a product of idealization.

In paranoia, the patient identifies with Jesus-the Messiah-the redeemer. The Jungian psychiatrist John Perry claims that, in messianic psychosis, when a person believes he is the messiah meant to bring justice, great love, and the heavenly kingdom to the world, the emphasis is on great love. This love comes to amend and compensate him for his grave deprivation of love and for personal injustice. According to Perry, the self-image is damaged in psychosis due to a childhood without love and its replacement with the child's condemnation as a scapegoat and as evil. The mother projects negative characteristics onto the child, which the child assumes and develops into a negative self-image—worthless, unloved, and undeserving. The psychosis compensates for the low self-image. The omnipotent archetype of the redeemer absorbs increasing amounts of energy from the person's libido, leaving consciousness split, fragmented, and disorganized. Perry also notes that, when we miss love and warmth in childhood, an urge to rule, power, and greatness develops later as compensation (Perry 1976).

When the ego fails to establish and sustain itself through proper defense mechanisms, an alternative archetypal figure takes its place—a powerful figure that will save it from helplessness, inner emptiness, and the anxiety it is gripped by. Thus, in paranoia, in megalomania, an omnipotent ego appears, an inflated, controlling, and aggressive figure, a kind of king warrior such as Napoleon. Even an inflated ego figure such as a king is insufficient in severe cases. The figure that invades the ego from the unconscious symbolizes the archetype of the self: the redeeming messiah (Neumann 1955, 88–89).

Identification with the messiah is seemingly the way for humans to save themselves from the fear of disintegration when the absence of a sense of center leads to identification with this alternative super-personality. The redeeming messiah is the ultimate center, enabling a mythical narrative foundation that provides internal cohesion and meaning. In states of paranoia, identification with the redeemer is concrete and shows no insight into this figure's symbolic meaning. The anxious, unstable person could identify with the super-archetype of the redeeming god who provides security and absolute certainty. Indeed, personality disorders or psychosis may involve rigid thinking and unwavering faith in the archetypal idea once the archetype takes control of the psyche, leading to a kind of existential safety. Paradoxically, then, paranoic fears also become the foundation of existential certainty. In paranoia, the patient is the chosen one, the redeemer messiah, and, consequently, also the persecuted and thus the sacrificed and betrayed sufferer.

Aldo Carotenuto writes about the *betrayal archetype*. He argues that every betrayal reproduces the original parental betrayal, whether it had indeed been blatantly so or only experienced as such. The reason is that, although the natural separation from the parents may be experienced as their betrayal and abandonment, the fear of losing love is often the fear of losing the parents' love, which we have already lost. Even in the case of a true betrayal, we confront the insight that not only has a lover betrayed us but so has the notion of absolute loyalty since the possibility of realizing absolute notions is rare. Whenever we trust, we open up an option of a betrayal experience. In his view, betrayal is often how a person seeks release from an over-constraining relationship, and the unconscious purpose of the betrayal experience is to be freed from it. Carotenuto says that the proper way of contending with betrayal is for the betrayed to acknowledge situations where they were the traitors (Carotenuto 1989, 77–87). At times, the therapist is experienced as a traitor-leaver when the patient, in her connection with the therapist, seeks to reconstruct a full and impossible love relationship and is betrayed by a reality that prevents this. In this sense, the patient seeks to turn the therapist into a redeemer. When the therapist does not become the redeemer-Jesus for the patient and does not totally sacrifice himself for the patient, she may experience this as a betrayal.

The healing aspect of the self is linked to the natural healing power in the psyche, as in the body, and to the natural human tendency toward homeostasis, balance, and wholeness. Every person's psyche contains the archetype of the inner healer, which is projected onto the therapist in the course of the treatment. The therapeutic process aims to connect the patient to the inner healer in his own psyche and return the projection of the healing power from the therapist back to himself. Healing is enabled through the therapist's contact with his wound, which helps the patient make contact with his own wound and activates his healing power.

Jung notes: "The doctor is effective only when he himself is affected. 'Only the wounded physician heals.' But when the doctor wears his personality like a coat of armour, he has no effect" (1989, 155). Therefore, the therapist's unhealed wound is not only not harmful to the therapist's powers but also enables her to heal others. Hence the *archetype of the wounded healer*. One example is the Talmudic story (BT Berakhot 5b) of R. Yohanan, who, in his pain for the loss of ten children, could heal the suffering of others (Netzer 2012). Another example is the cure of Dr. Langsam, who heals Hirschl in S. Y. Agnon's *A Simple Story* (1985). This doctor is a wounded healer who mixes his and Hirschl's emotional worlds when he gives Hirschl the romantic novels that his wife, who committed suicide, had read. Perhaps due to his own unresolved problems, the doctor may have identified with the distress of Hirschl, whose parents had prevented him from marrying his beloved Blume (Netzer 2009).

The myth of the wounded healer is based on the myth of Chiron, the legendary centaur, the ancestral first healer known as wise and good-hearted. He taught Aesculapius, the god of medicine, and also Achilles and Hercules, but Hercules accidentally hurt Chiron's knee, and the wound could not be healed. In that sense, the therapist is the healer wounded by his patient, who also betrays him, as Jesus was betrayed by his disciple. This betrayal is archetypal, inevitable by the very relationship between them. Chiron offered to die in exchange for the release of Prometheus, who stole the fire from the gods to give it to humanity. According to the sentence issued by Zeus, Prometheus could only be released from his fetters and his punishment if an immortal consented to die for him. Chiron, who was wounded and immortal, agreed to die to release Prometheus and release himself from his pain, in an early version of the archetype of Jesus, the wounded healer, who is betrayed and sacrifices himself to ease the suffering of others. In the Christian myth, Jesus is the wounded redeemer whose blood turned into the wine of the holy grail, which became a healing potion.

The Jewish messiah, too, is a wounded redeemer-healer. We are told that the messiah sits at the gates of Rome, opens his bandages, and redresses his wounds

(BT Sanhedrin 98a). Therapists treating their patients' wounds, also treat their own. The Jesus archetype is carried out in the patient-therapist dyad (Netzer 2004, 396–399). In the poem "If you'll give me my share," which Leah Goldberg (1960) addresses to her beloved, she asks him to unload his burden on her shoulders so that she might feel lighter and to bring to her the coldness of his loneliness so that she might feel warmer, promising to bear them willingly and not to fall. Goldberg's words lyrically describe how the patient's distress eases that of the therapist, thus turning the patient's pain into a gift to her. In that sense, the patient embodies for the therapist the wounded healer. The shared fate and the healing power of the wound are the alchemic bath therapists and patients have in common.

When reflected in the patient's wound, a therapist frightened by his own wound will not be able to fulfill his task, just as Kafka's country doctor runs away when he sees the patient's wound (Kafka 1945; Netzer 2009, 91–95). In the Midrash, God is a wounded healer:

> Rabbi Alexandri said: "If a person uses broken vessels, it is considered an embarrassment. But God seeks out broken vessels for His use, as it says, The Lord is near to the brokenhearted, the healer of shattered hearts. He is with that of a contrite and humble spirit. The sacrifices of God are a broken spirit, a broken heart."
> (Leviticus Rabbah 7:2)

The Jewish-kabbalistic myth about broken vessels and their mending (Kahane 2010), also an ancient myth about therapy, probably drew from this source in the Midrash.

In the field of philosophy, too, there is a call to touch the human wound. Emannuel Levinas objects to a philosophy dealing with the essence of existence, like Heidegger's ontology, which is indifferent to human suffering. Levinas argues that, in such a philosophy, there is not "one true tear, one warm drop of blood, any trace of human pain," and prefers the "wounded philosophers." A wounded philosopher, rather than looking at life as an objective spectator, is "chased by the vital need to grapple with the anguish of life" (Epstein 2005, 42). Levinas' philosophy, then, grew from the stance of the wounded healer, which is also his own life experience. As someone who lived through Nazi forced labor camps in the Second World War, he argues that assuming responsibility for the other is a way of amending the wound of alienation.

The archetype of Jesus appears in the film *Man Facing Southeast*. In this film, it is not the doctor but Rantés, the patient at the psychiatric hospital, who emerges as Jesus. Rantés appears in the hospital from nowhere, in some wondrous and unexplained way, like Jesus' miraculous birth. He appears as patient thirty-three in the ward, like Jesus, who was killed at age thirty-three. He helps the needy when he places his jacket on a patient, pats patients who wait in line to be touched by him, and in a restaurant, with church music playing in the background, telekinetically moves a plate full of food to a poor, needy woman thus reproducing, as it were, Jesus' miracle of the loaves and fishes. The patients touch him, and he touches them, fully identifying him with the savior. He tells the therapist: "If God is inside every one of you, you kill God every day," meaning that Jesus is killed every time anew. Dr. Denis, the psychiatrist, tells him: "The only thing missing is for you to say 'Blessed are the poor in spirit.' You shouldn't have said that you're from another planet. You should have said that you're Jesus." And the doctor wonders: "Insofar as Rantés gets closer to Jesus, his end won't be different." An unidentified female character who also appears in the film, and we gradually understand is his sister, is the feminine complement of Jesus, like Mary.

Rantés' delusion is that he comes from a heavenly world that sends him messages. He lives in a rich fantasy world, has a good rapport with children, and music is an intensive component of his life, but his body movements and his conduct in the world are robotic. Seemingly, he can satisfy his own denied need for human contact through his role as a redeemer of needy people. In the concert scene, he suddenly climbs onto the conductor's podium, leads the orchestra, and seems full of charisma as he intensifies the music's effect. The music is Beethoven's Ninth Symphony and the choir's call for universal brotherhood activates the audience, who begins to dance. It also affects the patients, who hear the music from afar and react with an ecstatic carnivalesque joy that leads them to break the hospital's gates. In this scene, Rantés is like the mythological Orpheus, whose playing affected the whole of nature. The hospital board is terrified by his supernatural power, blind to the positive aspect of the music, and threatened by it as if he were the flutist of Hamelin, leading the children (the patients) to chaotic loss.

Helping children and patients, Rantés brings a humane message, as he does when he says to the doctor that the psychiatric establishment ignores those who suffer and jails them. Hypocrisy and madness are in the establishment, not in those who are ostensibly patients—the "sad are poor in spirit."

Rantés seems detached from feelings, devoid of a personal ego and a personal biography. He is drawn into the collective and archetypal existence of his role as redeemer that fills the space of his inner world, emptied of feelings and personal identity. He frequently uses the first-person plural, saying "we" instead of "I," thereby identifying with a collective entity.

The absolute split between archetypal and personal existence (noted above in the healer character in *Julie Walking Home* as a split that prevents integration into real life) appears in Rantés as an expression of a psychotic state. The lack of information about Rantés' denied biography enables the patients, the therapist, and us, the spectators, to experience him as a creature from another world who plays the archetypal redeemer role. Similarly, the lack of information about the therapist's personal life enables patients to project onto him the healer-redeemer archetype.

Because he cannot trust the world, the therapist, and the therapy, the psychotic patient cannot project the redeemer on the therapist and, instead, identifies himself in grandiose-exaggerated ways with the redeemer archetype. He can thereby refrain from a transference relationship with the therapist that includes closeness, dependence, and human communication, which he is incapable of and finds threatening. Rantés thus appears as one who needs no help from others and cannot be helped by therapy.

In Rantés, the inflationary identification with the redeemer archetype serves the split between the human and the archetypal rather than their integration, which I see as the appropriate goal of the psyche's "redemption." The disturbing side of the redeemer as a false messiah lying to himself and to others is thereby exposed.

Nevertheless, the film constantly oscillates between our perception of Rantés as ill and our admiration for him as possessing superpowers, as a humane moral character giving hope to both the patients and the therapist and awakening faith, healing powers, and joy in them. By contrast, the institutional establishment depresses and destroys the psyche with medications and electric shocks. We watch the film from the therapist's perspective, who sees Rantés' illness but is also captivated by his charm and needs Rantés' presence as a healing power and a redeemer who may awaken his blocked psychic powers.

The film opens with a marginal episode that, at first glance, does not belong at all in the plot that precedes the main protagonist's story. The therapist, who will become Rantés' therapist, speaks with a new patient who tells him he had a suicide pact with his wife but killed her and not himself. He says, "I betrayed her." This story is the metaphorical gun that appears in the first act to end up shooting in the last one. The therapist, too, will betray his patients. Indeed, he betrays them from the start when he tells this patient, "We will help you," while thinking, "You will not be saved, my friend. Welcome to hell." At the film's end, the therapist, who does not stop the psychiatric injections that kill Rantés' body and soul, betrays him. After Rantés is given an injection that causes his total regression, he shouts—"Doctor, why have you forsaken me," echoing Jesus' cry on the cross—"My God, my God, why have you forsaken me?" The background music is frightful, and Rantés stands in the yard, limp, with another patient bearing him on his back in a crucified pose. Beatriz, his sister, wipes his face with a handkerchief, and he is in her arms, replicating the crucifixion scene. Here—his sister is as a mother, as Mary, a Pietà figure who holds Jesus in her arms after he is taken off the cross, and she is also as Veronica, who wipes his face.

The patients do not believe he is dead and say he will return in a spaceship.

If the patient Rantés is Jesus, the therapist is Judas Iscariot, who betrays him. The doctor allows the treatment of Rantés with anti-psychotic injections, which destroy the psychotic fantasy that is the source of his identity and his life and lead him to depression, catatonia, and death. Jesus the redeemer is executed by the Roman regime (the therapist calls himself Pontius Pilate)—the aggressive regime of materialistic collective consciousness that bans and kills individual spiritual development and the new knowledge that is transmitted from the collective unconscious through unique individuals. Totalitarian regimes endorse this approach toward artists and intellectuals, and also toward psychotherapy. This is also the establishment's stance toward people who expose its flaws and injustices, and that is what happened to Rantés. After the anti-psychotic injections bring him down to reality, Rantés channels his cosmic redemption impulse into care for the patients' living conditions. Yet, not only does the establishment at the hospital fail to welcome this initiative, but they even punish him by administering a more severe treatment, which worsens his situation.

Jesus is betrayed by an anti-Christ threesome antithetical to the holy trinity, uniting Judas Iscariot, the Roman rulers, and God, who enables it all. Indeed, more challenging than the human betrayal is the betrayal of God, who does not back the choice and the mission of the redeemer. Hence, Jesus cries out—"My God, my God, why have you forsaken me?" like Rantés at his end. Rantés, however, cries to the doctor who was supposed to redeem him.

The first two aspects of the betrayal originate in the ego's consciousness. Judas Iscariot, who betrays for money, embodies the monetary interest, the power interest, or another prestige interest of the personal or establishment ego. The Roman government embodies the opposition of institutionalized social consciousness, which also represents the opposition of the therapeutic establishment's consciousness to change and to new development whose source is in the collective unconscious.

But what is the meaning of God's betrayal?

The core of the self, which is God's image in humans, directs us in our mission. The self thus symbolizes God, who chose his only son, who is Everyman, for his mission. Jesus is the archetype of the divine, who assumed human form and was betrayed by God when he understood that he is not only divine but mortal. When we identify with the divine aspect in ourselves (when the ego inflates through identification with the self), we end up betrayed by the grandiose archetypal images of ourselves when we find we cannot escape human fate. In that sense, Rantés is betrayed by the (divine) inflated self inside him, which grew beyond human dimensions and guided him to live as redeemer-sufferer-victim.

Faith in the self—the inner guide that directs us to our mission and to the realization of the divine image—is projected onto faith and trust in the therapist. Rantés is loyal to himself in his way, and, nevertheless, he is betrayed not only by his self-images but also by the therapist. Therefore, the therapist's betrayal is hard to bear.

This film is an incisive critique of psychiatric treatment (before it acknowledged the importance of the soul in the version of Jung and R. D. Laing of the anti-psychiatry movement), which killed not only the psychosis but also the spark of authentic life in some of its symbolic expressions—poetic, prophetic, or psychotic.

One Flew Over the Cuckoo's Nest is another instance of this critique. The head nurse in the psychiatric hospital causes the lobotomy that kills the cheeky psychic life of the wild patient (played by Jack Nicholson), who refuses to obey the hospital's strict rules and brings some *joi de vivre* to the ward, inciting all the other patients. Again—the therapist betrays the patient and the renewal of psychic life that the patient suggests to him and the other patients.

In Ingmar Bergman's film *Face to Face*, the friend acting as therapist spends an entire day with the patient who is going through a psychotic breakdown, accompanying her in her private hell. In the evening, he tells her he must leave that day for another country and will remain there. The sudden separation, absolute and immediate, is a betrayal that becomes one more link in a chain of abandonments by her parents, grandfather, and grandmother. After she is suddenly betrayed, she musters all her powers to return, far too early, to her ordinary life. And indeed, it is questionable whether she ultimately did undergo change processes following the breakdown. I discussed above the manifestations of the betrayal motif when dealing with *The Soul Keeper*.

The story the film *K-Pax* tells resembles that of Rantés. Prot is a hospital patient, and he, too, is detached from any personal biography and lives a split life. He is identified with the redeemer—the patients seem to project this image on him, and he consents to it. He tells patients who turn to him that people can heal themselves and, for this purpose, assigns them three tasks—find the bluebird, experience death and resurrection and stay here, and be ready for anything. Prot, who claims he is from another planet and can see ultraviolet light, is ultimately betrayed by the grandiose images of his psychosis. Instead of returning him to his planet when he had been meant to according to his faith, the psychosis crumbles him at that critical moment into catatonia. The catatonic state is the patient's self-violence.[4]

Both in *Man Facing Southeast* and in *K-Pax*, the patient needs the inflationary identification with the redeemer's archetype as a compensatory defense from internal disintegration. Yet, he is a false redeemer-messiah because he cannot realize the redemption archetype as the integration of his psyche. The patient who "sacrifices" himself on the altar of the psychosis is the "emissary," the guide sent to the therapist. The patient serves as the therapist's "redeemer" and "wounded healer" by helping her (in the best case) to discover in her psyche the missing parts highlighted in the encounter with the patient's open and creative psyche and, at times, even to change through it. Hence, when the doctor in *K-Pax* asks the therapist why he is so involved in this case—"Why did you choose him?" she asks—the therapist tells her—"He chose me." In *Man Facing Southeast*, Rantés' therapist discovers how alienated and uncommunicative he had been, even with his children, contrary to the direct relationship that Rantés creates with them. These films are reminiscent of a case described by Lindner (1954) dealing with a patient who lives a split life. A scientist in his daily pursuits, he also lives a biographical identity he adopted from science fiction books. In voyages he undertakes in this virtual identity, he reaches distant interplanetary locations where he goes through fascinating experiences. The doctor's participation in these fantasy voyages enriched the therapist's life.

In both films, the identification and the projection of the redeemer occur on both sides of the therapist-patient equation. The patients in these films claim to be from another planet. Science fiction and films dealing with creatures from another world who reach Planet Earth convey both the anxiety about unknown powers and the longing for them. These powers can invade from the archetypal unconscious located in heaven, onto which psychic forces and the existence of the gods are projected. The power of astrology will attest to this. Jung noted that reported sightings of UFOs in the twentieth century conveyed the yearning for spiritual redemption directed at astral entities (Jung 1981, 328, 382). This Jungian assertion explains the redemption impulse that, in both films, holds patients (and to some extent also therapists) captive. The intense enchantment with creatures from the planetary world is wondrously described in the movie *Close Encounters of the Third Kind* (1977), when several individuals are magnetized by a mysterious radiation that projects from and draws them into a UFO as if calling them up to a spiritual mission. Seemingly, it conveys a need to join up with archetypal energy, enchantment, or even a spiritual dimension.

But the case of patients Rantés and Prot in *Man Facing Southeast* and *K-Pax* is different. They believe they are in touch with another planet since they split themselves off from their psychic life, their inner unconscious life, their biographical existence, and their urges and feelings, all of which were thrown far away into space. From their perspective, they are now in a distant territory beyond any human domain. The sense that new knowledge, a new message, or new life will come from another planet (Rantés) or that the person came from space (Prot) conveys the compensatory search for personal and existential unconscious materials, which were placed so far away. These repressed-distant contents wish to return to consciousness, and the psyche will be redeemed when it comes back together. However, the enormous distance between our planet and the other points to the distance between the conscious and the unconscious in them, and the difficulty of bridging them. The wish to reach a place (a spiritual, religious, moral world) that will bring redemption and is symbolized by the other planet must be distinguished from the absolute, concrete, and psychotic identification with this content, which they cannot see symbolically. The patients in both these films, considered redeemers, create alternative psychic constructs to the proper psychic structure for themselves and project not only the unconscious but also their own self onto the other planet. Through their virtual connection with the other planet, they experience a connection with the distant guiding center of the archetypal redeeming self. This is an interesting example of split and self-projection.

Expressions of the Jesus-redeemer archetype are also evident in *Equus*. The film's plot centers on a psychotic teenager who experiences passionate, ecstatic thrills with his horse. The boy, Martin, is hospitalized after an attack where he fatally injures and blinds his favorite horse. The lonely and bizarre adolescent, unable to establish human relationships, had worked as a stable boy and, at night, would ride his horse naked, whispering to it and reaching intense sexual ecstasy. The horse symbolized for him virility and sexuality, as well as the father and Jesus. In Martin's delusion, the horse says, "I see you, I will save you," symbolizing for him redeeming masculinity and Jesus the redeemer. The horse also symbolized for him the sacrificed Jesus. The boy castrates the horse after failing to consummate a sexual relationship with a girl at the stable, an event that the horse witnessed. Martin then blinds the horse, punishing it as if the horse had been the father who had banned his sexuality. At the same time, Martin feels he betrayed his beloved horse through his sexuality with the girl.

The sick boy identifies with the horse and with Jesus, punishes and sacrifices the horse, and whips himself as the one tortured and sacrificed. The therapist, played by Richard Burton, is riveted by the deep passion of the boy, who is thus as a redeemer breaking into the therapist's life.

The horse serves the boy as an alternative object to a person who can be trusted, project the self onto, and create otherself relationships with. The horse serves the boy as an otherself, just as the planetary entity is not only the self but also an otherself for Rantés and Prot. The difference is that the planetary entity is abstract and distant, whereas the horse is earthy and sensual, allowing for a social, comforting, and healing relationship, as animals serve humans in certain situations. The psychic disturbance rooted in the projection onto a spatial self conveys severe dissociation from the self. In contrast, the disorder where the animal becomes the object of the projection still leaves room for contact.

The patients in *Man Facing Southeast* and *K-Pax* identify themselves as redeemers, leading others to worship them. People's need to worship others, usually as an alternative to love and affirmation of their own self-value or even their very existence, may lead them to identify with the omnipotent super-archetype of the redeemer. *Equus* presents the boy's need to worship and identify with the redeemer.

The therapist in *Equus* senses that, when treating the sick boy to take away his psychosis and heal him, he also takes away his vitality. He thereby sacrifices him and betrays him, as if he were sacrificing the archetype of Jesus (as self) both in his and the patient's psyche.

Every identification with an archetype is identification with one extreme pole, which later pushes to the opposite one. Latent in absolute goodness is absolute evil. Latent in redemption is betrayal and sacrifice; in grandiosity is depression; in muteness (catatonic closure) is violence; in unconditional love is exclusion; in perfection is deceit. Roberto Calasso writes about this when he speaks of Ariadne, who was betrayed by both Dionysus and Theseus:

> Those two opposite figures were both manifestations of the same man who went on betraying her, while she went on letting herself be betrayed . . . Dionysus offered Ariadne the crown as a gift on the occasion of this, their first embrace . . . The crown is the perfection of deceit, it is the deceit that circles in on itself, it is that perfection which includes deceit within it.
>
> (Calasso 1993, 20)

The archetype of the redeemer, Jesus, described as the shadowless absolute good, is the perfection that contains deceit and betrayal by the very denial of the shadow within him. Jung notes that Jesus, presented as entirely positive, is a partial archetype of the self. But precisely because of his luminous perfection, the shadow appears as a necessary part of Jesus' fate to those who cruelly sacrifice him. Jesus, who is identified with the absolute good, draws the complementary pole of evil to him and becomes its victim.

People who live in an inflation of the good or in a spirituality identified with absolute good and negation of the shadow bring upon themselves the fate of violent harm by others. These are the terms of Rantés' story—he, who helps those in need, is sacrificed by the medical establishment.[5] Thus, people who deny their shadow and aggression can end up internalizing violence and directing it to themselves, hence the masochism of those who, like Jesus, take it upon themselves to be the victims of the world and of others' violence. Violence toward others also follows from denying one's shadow, as in the Crusades or the Inquisition, and I see this as the sadomasochistic shadow side of the Jesus archetype. According to José Saramago in *The Gospel According to Jesus Christ*, the one revealed as God is Satan. When Jesus asks, "What do You want with me?" God answers, "For the moment nothing, but the day will come when I will want everything" (Saramago 1994, 220), a statement denoting absolute identification with the Jesus archetype. When God demands from humans that they should fully identify with Jesus the good and the victim, God becomes Satan because he dooms him to die. Again, the archetypal identification is to the end and to death. Seemingly, this representation of God betrays humans because God is interested in humans only insofar as they serve the idea of God. God has no interest in living individuals and sees neither them nor their suffering. This God only sees God.

Consider Ingmar Bergman's film *Persona*, which takes place in a summer beach house in Sweden. Elisabet (played by Liv Ullmann), an actress who plays Electra, is sent there by her psychiatrist to recover from a nervous breakdown and self-imposed mutism. Alma (Bibi Andersson) is a professional nurse who has no psychotherapeutic training, and she accompanies her to take care of her. The two women spend long summer days together. Elisabet says nothing while Alma spends the time telling stories about her life. From the start, Elisabet is the patient. Her silence, however, leads to a reversal of roles between them: Alma, the therapist, feels grievously betrayed by Elisabet (the patient, who becomes her therapist) when she reads Elisabet's letter to her doctor telling him that Alma has childishly and charmingly fallen in love with her and that she finds it interesting to learn about Alma. Alma is deeply offended by Elisabet's distant, patronizing, and arrogant attitude. She finds that the warm intimacy she sensed when Elisabet listened to her reproduced her basic life experience—she does not truly exist to the significant other. She shouts at Elisabet: "You used me, and now you're throwing me away, hurt me, laughed at me behind my back, did research on me." But does not Alma betray Elisabet when she later sleeps with Elisabet's husband?

Indeed, at the beginning of *Persona*, we see a nail hammered into a hand, and at the end, we see a sculpted head with a bleeding hole. These are clear associations to the suffering of the betrayed Jesus bleeding on the cross and to the necessary betrayal we experience by the archetypal images of perfection—we expect their realization in us and in the other, and we discover, as Calasso notes, that perfection includes deceit. In other words, one who lives the archetype as a principle, as an idea, does not truly see the individual and betrays the human. The sobering up that follows from the betrayal of the images, says Carotenuto (1989), is necessary for the individuation process in general and the therapeutic process in particular. The encounter with the therapist's shadow and with our own, however painful and paradoxical, leads us to greater acceptance of ourselves when we are ready to accept our imperfections.

The Shaman Archetype

Mircea Eliade defines shamanism as "a system of ecstatic and therapeutic methods whose purpose is to obtain contact with the parallel yet invisible universe of the spirits and win its support in dealing with human affairs" (Eliade and Couliano 1991, 214). In tribal societies, the shaman is the key personality, fulfilling the all-containing role of the wise possessor of spiritual and medical knowledge, the religious figure who communicates with the spirits and the gods, heals the body and the soul, and is in charge of the religious-medical rituals of the tribe and of the individuals within it. The shaman is in a liminal space, between the human world and the world of the spirits, the gods, and nature, holding the powers and the skills to communicate with the forces beyond (Megged 1998, 27–31). Hence, he establishes direct experiential contact with the unconscious and retrieves from the depths and the heights of the collective psyche, from psychic and spiritual depths and heights, what is there waiting to be discovered. In that sense, he is like artists and mystics who go through symbolic all-human experiences, meaning contents flowing from the collective unconscious, and is compelled to pass on to the whole tribe the significant knowledge that has been delivered to him.

The shaman's role is to mediate between the cosmic and human orders. For society, he embodies an archetypal role found in the psyche of every individual—healing, and mediating between its parts. He implements the healing and integration potential inspired and guided by the self. He thereby realizes the archetype of Hermes, the emissary of the gods, who mediates between the gods and humans, between the various layers of the psyche, between the conscious and the unconscious, to promote the healing dialogue between them. The choice and training of the shaman for his post are tied to a critical event of illness or wounding and his recovery from it. The shaman is both the wounded healer and the redeemer, and he is the substitute or the social driving force of the redeemer archetype.

The shaman must be extremely modest to avoid entrapment in an illusion of megalomanic omnipotent power and exaggerated pride for his achievements and his choice for the role. Hence the importance of understanding that he was not chosen for the gratification of his ego but out of an inner impulse to realize his psyche's aim (the self) and for a social goal (the tribal self).

The Hassidic rabbi-*zaddiq* is also described as a shaman (Idel 1995, 75, 105, 214) and as having therapeutic qualities. Baruch Kahane (2010) describes the Hassid's direct personal connection to the rabbi as of vast therapeutic importance, as an event enabling the Hassid to connect to the root of his hidden self, draw from it, and amend himself.

The shaman archetype comes forth in the therapist, who delves into the unconscious—her own and the collective—when accompanying patients in their journey to the depths. The shaman, however, occupies a critical social-religious position for the tribe, while the therapist fulfills a mediating role for individuals.

In several of his writings, Jung refers to the therapist as a shamanic healer. Jungian psychologist Murray Stein (1984) describes the shamanic healer as one who "catches" the patient's disease, heals it within himself, and passes on the remedy to the patient, a stance that collapses the distance between therapist and patient. It leads to psychological identification with the patient, be it depression, anxiety, schizophrenic withdrawal, infiltration of characters or impulses from the unconscious, and so forth. Like the shamanic healer, not only does the therapist "take on" the patient's problem but also seeks the cure within himself (possibly by using symbols of healing related to the wound) and then transfers it back to the patient. In this form of therapy, the therapist's unconscious influences the patient's unconscious through *participation mystique* (parallel to projective identification). The tribal shaman "flies" to heights to bring remedy to those approaching him, such as a ritual where healing symbols appear. A contemporary healer knows he is going through an inner process of entry into the depths of his soul with the depths of the patient's soul to bring insights and symbols that can lead to healing, perhaps suggesting a mythical story of grappling with difficulties resembling the patient's.

The shaman, like the Hassidic *zaddiq* (Idel 1995, 75, 105, 214), must possess unique powers that enable him to meet experiences and powerful delusions without breaking apart or going mad. He must have powers and psychic forces as well as great openness to unconscious materials and must be able to control entry to and exit from these situations of super-consciousness. The paradox is that the shaman's ego borders must be both fluid and manageable. In the past, a shaman entering a trance through which he created direct experiential contact with the unconscious was considered psychotic. In contrast, today, there is recognition of a psychic-spiritual category of people able to cross borders who are not insane but super-sane.

The doctor in *Equus* cannot play the role of the shamanic healer and catches the illness of his teenage patient without finding a cure for him within himself. Several films show that some therapists are not fit for the shamanic role—their ego is weak, and the psychotic materials they meet in their patients carry them beyond the borders of sanity or morality.

In the films discussed so far, it is not the therapists but Rantés and Prot who are identified with the shamanic aspect of journeys to other worlds in order to bring healing to society. They can do so because the authority of shamans in society follows from their personal psychological experience and not from social ordination (Campbell 1988, 100). Unlike the tribal shaman, however, Rantés and Prot have weak egos and do not choose the time to enter the delusional state that controls them. A powerful combination of archetypes—the redeemer, Jesus, the shaman, the omnipotent magician—absorbs them into a super-archetype meant to fill the gap in the proper functioning of the ego, the self, and the ego-self axis. They went too far into the realm of archetypes and both films end in the patients' regressive withdrawal.

In *Julie Walking Home*, the healer lives the redeemer-shaman archetype that serves as a channel to the healing energies. His ego, seemingly weak, is a shamanic conduit for archetypal healing forces in the service of people in need of them. He, however, cannot regulate them and keep himself safe. He is unfamiliar with practical life and does not seek to satisfy natural ego needs such as material rewards and honor. He lacks self-awareness and is activated by greater omnipotent forces. In that sense, his mental existence is fragile, he is not mature enough for the shaman role, and the people surrounding him fulfill ego and reality roles for him.

When drawn to realize his emotional and instinctual world through his love for Julie, the patient, he responds to a vital need to realize parts of his personality so far denied. For this purpose, he learns, he must renounce his energetic archetypal power, sacrificing his shamanic role and his identification with Jesus in order to be a person. But since the ego's personality is undeveloped and he lacks self-awareness, he behaves like a helpless innocent child when acting in the real world. The sacrifice of his spiritual power is related to his turning into the son-lover of the woman (Netzer 2011, 140). In his relationship with her, he functions as a lover who impregnates the Great Mother and cannot be a real partner.

The Archetype of the Omnipotent Magician

The archetype of the magician and the omnipotence archetype comprise grandiose images that flow from unconscious mythical thinking lacking borders of time, place, cause, and reality, where anything can be imagined and performed. The need and the inclination to glorify the parent are transferred to the therapist, on whom these superpowers are projected.

The magician symbolizes "mana" powers—unconscious powers that influence like magic and wondrously create change (Netzer 2009, 209–218). Great spiritual leaders are described as possessing magic powers, famous as healers and miracle workers. Moses performs miracles, like Jesus, the Baal-Shem-Tov, and others. The immediate connection with the energies of the unconscious and with supreme psychic forces grants these exceptional individuals knowledge and powers of sight and healing beyond the ordinary laws of physics, time, space, and causality. Alternatively, they may be charismatic figures who suggestively influence the believers. Faith in magic superpowers sometimes enables patients to awaken such healing powers within themselves. The magician's power, then, may not be within the therapist-magician but in his glorification through the patient's projections.

Unwittingly, the patient tends to project on the therapist and mainly on the energetic healer, the qualities of an omnipotent magician. The risk for the therapist who identifies with the magician archetype lies in relating to healing as a single miraculous act ascribed to herself and her miraculous power while diverting attention from the true healing that should unfold through processes in the patient's psyche.

The therapeutic process compels the therapist to undergo a prolonged training process related to a conscious confrontation with her own depths. She is required to avoid becoming a healer endowed with unique magical skills and superpowers, who uses them for the needs of her ego to charm or manipulate the patient's symptoms, never meeting the patient's psyche or her own. That is the magician's charlatan shadow.

Yalom cites Dostoyevsky in *The Brothers Karamazov* when the Great Inquisitor proclaims that people always seek "magic, mystery, and authority." Yalom claims that healers throughout history are aware of this and, therefore, wrap their actions and their training in a cover of secrecy. The mystery of secrecy glorifies the honor and the awe rendered to them and creates a placebo effect of healing through the very faith in the doctor's healing power. According to Yalom, "The establishment of an authentic relationship with patients, by its very nature, demands that we forgo the power of the triumvirate of magic, mystery, and authority" (Yalom 2002, 84).

Yet, like Dorothy in *The Wizard of Oz*, when a patient is thrown into the land of distress by the tornado of a crisis, he needs faith in a therapist as a redeemer-magician endowed with superpowers. Dorothy, therefore, goes out to look for the magician who will save her. Yalom comments on this:

> Those who desire magic, mystery, and authority are loath to look beneath the trappings of the therapist. . . . More than one of my patients have invoked the metaphor of the Wizard of Oz to describe their preference for the happy belief that the therapist knows the way home . . . By no means do they want to look behind the curtain and see a lost and confused faux-wizard.
>
> (Ibid., 99)

But we must remember that, without faith in the Wizard of Oz, Dorothy would not have left on her developmental voyage. Without the archetypal images of the therapist as a redeemer, as an omnipotent magician able to show us the way home and help us overcome the obstacles, we will find it hard to muster the faith needed to depart. Against the power of distress, we require the archetypal force of redemption images.

Toward the end of Dorothy's voyage, her dog moves the curtain and, behind it, the Wizard of Oz is revealed as an ordinary man. When the patient has completed his journey and found his power within himself, he allows himself to discover that the therapist is merely an ordinary person. Cinema, which shows therapists in all their human aspects, flaws, and emotional wounds, is sometimes the dog who draws the curtain of the magician's persona that the therapist had been hiding behind. At times, it is the therapist who had previously set off impressive charismatic fireworks to persuade others and himself of his special powers (for example, in the film *The Soul Keeper*), and at times, the patient construes the therapist as possessing charismatic superpowers.

The tendency to project onto the therapist the archetypes of the redeemer-Jesus-shaman-omnipotent magician, which is meant to promote the therapist's healing influence, can also intensify dependence on her and fear of the therapist exploiting this dependence due to her own needs for dependency, love, self-worth, prestige, and money.

The therapist, too, can—or must—go through a process of renouncing fascination with the charismatic patient, as in *K-Pax*, *Man Facing Southeast*, and *Don Juan*. Fascination with the patient, too, derives from the magician's archetype.

Notes

1 The transition from objective alienated distance to the empathy of human togetherness occurred in philosophy as well. For Martin Buber, Franz Rosenzweig, and Emmanuel Levinas, to be in the world is to be in a relationship: "Not striving to attain the thing itself is what characterizes their philosophy but striving to be in a relationship" (Meir 2004, 91), both with the human and with the transcendent.
2 For similar ideas, see the Bionian therapist James Grotstein (Grotstein 2000, 219–253).
3 Laing and Esterson (1970) corroborate this idea.
4 An interesting parallel between violence and catatonia emerges in Hebrew, given the shared root (*i-l-m*) of these two terms.
5 This is also true of Job. He is blameless and upright and, therefore, awakens Satan's wrath, as in some of Patrick White's books—*The Aunt's Story*, *Riders in the Chariot*, and *The Solid Mandala*—and in Lars von Trier's films, where the evil ones sacrifice the blameless and upright.

References

Agnon, S. Y. (1985) *A Simple Story*, trans. Hillel Halkin (New York: Schocken Books).
Calasso, Roberto (1993) *The Marriage of Cadmus and Harmony* (Toronto: A. A. Knopf Canada).
Campbell, Joseph John, with Bill Myers (1988) *The Power of Myth* (New York: Doubleday).
Carotenuto, Aldo (1989) *Eros and Pathos: Shades of Love and Suffering* (Toronto: Inner City Books).
Chesler, Phyllis (1989) *Women and Madness* (San Diego, CA: Harcourt Brace Jovanovich).
Eliade, Mircea and Ioan P. Couliano (1991) *The Eliade Guide to World Religions* (San Francisco: Harper).
Epstein, Daniel (2005) *Near and Far: On the Thought of Emmanuel Levinas* (Tel Aviv: Broadcast University Series) [Heb].
Gabbard, Krin, and Glen Gabbard (1989) *Psychiatry and the Cinema*, second edn. (American Psychiatric Press).
Goldberg, Leah (1960) *Early and Later* (Tel Aviv: Sifriat Poalim) [Heb].
Grotstein, James S. (2000) *Who Is the Dreamer, Who Dreams the Dream? A Study of Psychic Presences* (Hillsdale, NJ: The Analytic Press).
Hoffmann, Yoel (2015) *Moods*, trans. Peter Cole (New York: New Directions).
Idel, Moshe (1995) *Hasidism: Between Ecstasy and Magic* (Albany, NY: SUNY Press).
Jung, C. G. (1981) *Civilization in Transition*, *C. W.* 10, trans. R. F. C. Hull (Princeton, NJ: Princeton University Press).
Jung, C. G. (1983) *The Psychology of the Transference*, trans. R. F. C. Hull, (London: Routledge & Kegan Paul).
Jung, C. G. (1989) *Memories, Dreams, Reflections*, trans. Richard and Clara Winston (New York: Vintage Books).
Kahane, Baruch (2010) *Breaking and Mending: A Hassidic Model for Clinical Psychology* (Jerusalem: Rubin Mass) [Heb].
Kafka, Franz (1945) *The Country Doctor*, trans. Vera Leslie (Oxford: Counterpoint Publications).
Kohut, Heinz (1984) *How Does Analysis Cure?* ed. Arnold Goldberg (Chicago: University of Chicago Press).

Laing, R. D. and Aaron Esterson (1970) *Sanity, Madness, and the Family: Families of Schizophrenics* (Harmondsworth: Penguin).
Levinas, Emmanuel (1985) *Ethics and Infinity: Conversations with Philippe Nemo*, trans. Richard A. Cohen (Pittsburgh, PA: Duquesne University Press).
Lindner, Robert (1954) *The Fifty-Minute Hour: A Collection of True Psychoanalytic Tales* (London: Transworld).
Megged, Nahum (1998) *Gates of Hope and Gates of Fear: Shamanism, Magic, and Witchcraft in Central and South America* (Tel Aviv: Modan) [Heb].
Meir, Ephraim (2004) *Jewish Existential Philosophers in Dialogue* (Jerusalem: Magnes Press) [Heb].
Mitchell, Stephen A. (1993) *Hope and Dread in Psychoanalysis* (New York: Basic Books).
Mitchell, Stephen A. and Margaret J. Black (1995) *Freud and Beyond: A History of Modern Psychoanalytic Thought* (New York: Basic Books).
Netzer, Ruth (2004) *Journey to the Self: The Alchemy of the Psyche—Symbols and Myths* (Ben Shemen, Israel: Modan) [Heb].
Netzer, Ruth (2009) *The Whole, the Fragment, and Its Repetition—Symbol- Literature-Poetry: A Collection of Articles from a Jungian Perspective* (Jerusalem: Carmel) [Heb].
Netzer, Ruth (2011) *A Hero's Journey* (Tel Aviv: Modan) [Heb].
Netzer, Ruth (2012) "On R. Yohanan's Healing." *Betipulnet* website http://www.betipulnet.co.il/articles [Heb].
Neumann, Erich (1955) *The Great Mother*, trans. Ralph Manheim (New York: Princeton University Press).
Perry, John Weir (1976). *Roots of Renewal in Myth and Madness: The Meaning of Psychotic Episodes* (London: Jossey-Bass).
Plato (1956) *Great Dialogues of Plato*, trans. W. H. D. Rouse (New York: New American Library).
Racker, Heinrich (2018) *Transference and Countertransference* (Boca Raton, FL: Routledge).
Revel, Jean Francois, and Matthiew Ricard (2000) *The Monk and the Philosopher: A Father and Son Discuss the Meaning of Life*, trans. John Canti (New York: Schocken).
Sacks, Oliver (1990) *Awakenings* (New York: Harper Perennials).
Saramago, José (1994) *The Gospel According to Jesus Christ*, trans. Giovanni Pontiero (New York: Harcourt Brace).
Siegelman, Ellen (2002) "The Analyst's Love: An Exploration." *Journal of Jungian Theory and Practice* 4: 19–34.
Shem, Samuel (1954) Introduction to *The Fifty-Minute Hour: A Collection of True Psychoanalytic Tales*, by Robert Lindner (New York: Delta).
Stein, Murray (1984) "Power, Shamanism, and Maieutics in the Countertransference." In Nathan Schwartz-Salant and Murray Stein, eds., *Transference/Countertransference*, 67–87 (Wilmette, IL: Chiron Publications).
Stein, Robert (1973) *Incest and Human Love* (Dallas: Spring Publications).
Strenger, Carlo (1998) *Individuality, the Impossible Project: Psychoanalysis and Self-Creation* (Madison, CT: International Universities Press).
Winnicott, D. W. (1949) "Hate in the Counter-Transference." *The International Journal of Psycho-Analysis* 30: 69–74.
Yalom, Irvin D. (1992) *When Nietzsche Wept: A Novel of Obsession* (New York: Harper Perennial).
Yalom, Irvin D. (2002) *The Gift of Therapy: An Open Letter to a New Generation of Therapists and Their Patients* (New York: Harper).

Chapter 4

Therapists as Mirrored in Cinema

Optimal Description of the Therapist-Patient Relationship

Some films dealing with therapist-patient relationships show therapists at their best—devoted, caring, humane, attentive, understanding, and helping as far as they can with the proper therapeutic love. The television series *The Sopranos* and the films *David and Lisa*, *Equus*, *Sybil*, *Good Will Hunting*, *Man Facing Southeast*, *K-Pax*, and *Ordinary People* are examples of this approach.

David and Lisa describes the treatment of David, a young patient in a residential therapeutic center. David's father died suddenly, and his mother seems caring but distant and inaccessible. The boy has nightmares and anxieties about physical contact because he feels that anyone touching him hates him and wishes him dead. He is detached and compulsively draws clocks and clock-looking machines that convey his alienation. In his nightmares, he sees the clock hand moving around and decapitating all the people that David is angry with. He is also anxious about the passing time that draws him closer to his death.

The clock symbolizes the division of infinite time into intelligible units that order, define, and limit human time, enabling the conscious activity of the ego—planning, production, and organization. The clock is thus a symbol of consciousness. About Hirschl, who goes mad in *A Simple Story*, Agnon tells us: "Father in heaven, wondered Hirshl, glancing up at the sky, what time can it be? He took out his stopped watch and studied it, then lay down in the grass with it hanging out of his pocket, one shoe off and one shoe on, happily laughing and ga-ga-ing to himself" (Agnon 1985, 172). The stopped watch is the human consciousness that ceased working: it is a time without time, like the timelessness of the unconscious territory, like the dream where there is no early and late, and like the timelessness of death and of the divinity, which are beyond ordinary consciousness.

The clock's cessation of human time symbolizes death or madness, and both convey the death of consciousness. Agnon tells us that, in his madness, Hirschl "lay in bed like a broken watch" (1985, 192). Hirschl's hanging watch is reminiscent of the liquid clock in Salvador Dali's famous surrealistic painting. Surrealism, as we know, tried to express pre-conscious existence, as that in the dream. The return to a dreamlike unconscious life beyond the consciousness of human time may express regressive qualities of unconscious and insane existence.

The stopped clock in the therapist's consulting room makes David restless. It seems to reflect the stillness of his psychic life, his psychic death, and his anxiety about physical death. The clock was sent for repair only after David broke it in a fit of anger. Here the film accords with the Freudian spirit, which views the obstruction of Eros and Thanatos (Eros as love and Thanatos as aggression) as the blocking of life. For David, who is blocked from expressing love and anger, the legitimation granted to his release of anger enables his petrified psyche to move and live again. Note that the therapist's meetings with David are not limited to a specific time and are not scheduled according to the clock! He comes and goes as he wishes, when he is interested, without the limits of therapy time. Nor are the accepted place borders kept: the therapist comes to his room, and they walk together in the garden of the residential center, an arrangement that may not fit conventional therapy but could be appropriate in an institutional setting.

The therapist, an extremely positive person, does keep other borders—he does not talk about himself and does not touch David, unlike other therapists at the center who often touch and hug the patients. In this case, the therapist must obviously avoid physical contact with David, who is so anxious about any form of it.

When the therapist repairs the stopped clock in his consulting room, David also goes through a repair experience organizing his consciousness and his attitude to reality. The clock's repair symbolizes the borders of the ego, which can break and be fixed. Respecting the boundaries of the laws of treatment is part of restoring the ego's borders.

Healing in the film occurs mainly through the relationship between David and Lisa, a patient who speaks in rhymed lines as if in poetry, creating intelligible formal borders for her chaotic reality. She has two identities—Lisa and Muriel. She asks David to tell her who she is. When he answers in rhyme, he conveys his insight that one must speak to her in her language and become part of her world. In time, he learns to create relationships of trust with both the therapist and Lisa, who expresses for him (and instead of him) longings for motherly warmth. Lisa directs these longings, which are also David's repressed needs, to a sculpture of the woman/mother at the museum, which she embraces and refuses to let go of.

David and Lisa are finally healed when Lisa turns to David, and he responds. He overcomes his anxiety about human touch when he stretches out a hand to her and holds her. When she asks, "Who am I?" David answers by saying, "Lisa is a pearl!" She is excited by her comparison with a pearl—not only an expression of beauty but also of the psyche's precious core (the self). She discovers that, henceforth, her identity will no longer be split.

The film enables David to encounter a male figure (the therapist) and a female one (Lisa) as therapeutic agents. The film does not grant full credit for the healing only to the therapist and points to healing factors in dyadic interpersonal relationships between patients.

Lisa is childish, skips, and behaves like a little girl, embodying for David the archetype of the impulsive and spontaneous child open to the experience of life as an authentic self and also the archetype of the *anima*, the female mediator to the psyche and its feelings.

The doctor-therapist in the film epitomizes the optimal therapist—warm, restrained, patient, and insightful. He becomes a parental figure replacing the missing father and an ideal identification model for David, who wants to study medicine like him.

Healing here is not a result of self-awareness and inquiry into past causes but of empathic warmth, acceptance, love, and a genuine emotional experience of the events in the therapy. All of them are healing agents, together with the physical human touch of Lisa's hand and perhaps also with the cohesive rhythmical power of the rhymed poetry sentences.

Breaking Boundaries

Contrary to the basic prescription of all psychotherapeutic methods about keeping boundaries in therapy, in most films (including those presenting therapists at their best), they are broken either temporarily or consistently:

Breaking contact borders—when the therapist touches and hugs.
Breaking place borders—when the therapist meets the patient outside the consulting room, be it in the patient's home and with his family or at the therapist's home.
Breaking time borders—when the therapist meets the patient whenever the patient requires and beyond the defined time.
Breaking borders of privacy and expression of feelings—when the therapist talks about herself and past situations of crisis and distress.

One example of this pattern is the film *Good Will Hunting*, where the young patient resists the therapeutic relationship imposed on him. The therapist speaking of his wife's death and of his ensuing crisis enables the patient, after many meetings, to trust the therapist. Trust is further enhanced when the therapist speaks of his anger and even shows rage against the patient who brazenly encroaches on his world. And yet, it is precisely the impropriety of breaking borders that enables the patient to come out and feel his common fate with the therapist. The boy can trust the therapist only after identifying him as a suffering, anguished person. Only then can the therapist become a wounded healer.

We saw the breaking of boundaries and the role reversal in *Persona* when the therapist became a patient. In *The Soul Keeper*, as mentioned above, Sabina prompts a role reversal when she suggests to the therapist that he should tell her his dream, which she will interpret.

In some films (*Good Will Hunting* and *Equus*), a hostile patient who refuses to cooperate agrees to talk about himself only after the therapist is ready to answer personal questions about his life. These questions convey the patient's will to break borders, to know whether the therapist can be trusted, or to control the situation and be equal to the therapist by breaking the built-in asymmetry typical of the therapeutic situation.

Although this book deals almost exclusively with films, my discussion fits television series too. The Israeli series *In Therapy* recurrently emphasizes how the therapist breaks boundaries by talking with patients about his family and in his infatuation with a patient and its sexual consummation. The physical conditions of his clinic are a priori without any borders separating the family lounge from the consulting room and without a waiting area that prevents patients from meeting one another. The therapist is presented with all his problematic human aspects. The inclination to focus on the therapist's weaknesses also characterizes Amy Bloom, the American novelist who writes *State of Mind*, the television series about a clinic. She explicitly notes that the topic that interests her touches on the vulnerabilities of therapists.

Romantic-Sexual Involvement

Some films (*The Soul Keeper*, *Julie Walking Home*) hold that consummating a therapist-patient romantic-sexual involvement, though breaking borders, is healing. But even if romantic involvement in these films occurs after the therapy, it has a destructive aspect.

Nathan Schwartz-Salant describes the meaning of erotic seduction for the therapist in a therapeutic process:

> The interactive field creates a wide spectrum of states that can range from experiences of an intense erotic current and desire for literalization to states of emotional and mental deadness and a total lack of connection. Since these latter states are so problematic for the pain they create and the wounding they inflict—especially upon the analyst's narcissism—their opposite, in which erotic currents can appear to create intense fields of union and a deep knowing of the other, become extremely seductive.
> (Schwartz-Salant 1998, 65)

In the film *The Prince of Tides*, a football coach seeks help for his sister, who has suicidal tendencies. When meeting his sister's psychiatrist, however, he becomes a patient, telling his life story and sharing traumatic events that he experienced. The therapeutic situation where the therapist gathers the crying patient in her arms opens the door to the breaking of borders that occurs later: the psychiatrist speaks about herself, therapeutic love translates into erotic love, they have an affair, and at the end of the film he returns to his wife. However, contrary to the two previous films, the affair occurs during therapy.

In Hitchcock's film *Spellbound*, the doctor in charge (Ingrid Bergman) devotes herself entirely to the patient and goes with him on a voyage to discover the meaning of his dream at the place where he dreamt it. The patient is a new doctor at a psychiatric hospital who suffers from amnesia. To the therapist, it is clear that an important clue about his past is hidden in this dream, which might explain the guilt that accompanies him. The voyage is meant to bring back from oblivion the traumatic event hinted at in the dream, which led the patient to forget his identity. The therapist, who falls in love, devotes herself without time and place borders, intermingling therapy and their romantic relationship. Doctor and patient meld here in all senses, and the therapy becomes a detective inquiry. In this voyage, the therapist (unlike the patient) is the one who forgets the proper borders.

Hitchcock's film *Marnie* also projects a mixture of therapy and romantic love. The film tells the story of a man (Sean Connery) who meets a beautiful woman (Tippi Hedren) and falls in love with her. Although he discovers she is a kleptomaniac, a compulsive liar, frigid, and sex-averse, he marries her. He coerces her to marry him to save her from jail for her thieving and becomes her omnipotent savior-redeemer. He also redeems her by saving her from a suicidal drowning attempt, by hiding her crimes from the police, and by covering her debts. He gives her the horse she loves to ride as a present, shows her enduring love, and tries to persuade her to go to therapy. Since she refuses, he assumes the role of therapist. He weaves into the "treatment" a detective inquiry into the sources of her childhood trauma, which causes her nightmares and threatening flashbacks. One night, he awakens her from a nightmare and tries to question her about its background. He suggests to her reading a book that includes a chapter titled "The undiscovered self," and she tells him that he is playing Freud. They enter a kind of therapist-patient game when he says a word, and she free-associates until she suffers a panic attack from an association related to the color red. He then hugs her, and, for the first time, she cries and asks him for help.

This film, like others, presents faith in the redeeming power of the therapist's boundless love, unlike the therapeutic love that remains within borders. Like the therapist in *Spellbound*, this film, too, realizes the fantasy of total one-sided devotion, of giving by a lover-therapist who does not need any emotional return or even any wish for economic and sexual compensation. His love is romantic sexless love. A narcissistic-childish-primary fantasy is realized, where the therapist is the ultimate parent who gives himself over entirely and utterly renounces his own needs. In *Marnie*, this love can compensate for what is revealed at the film's end—that her mother could not love her. At the end of the film, we learn that the source of the trauma underlying Marnie's kleptomania and frigidity is a murder that she committed in her childhood when she killed a man who had attacked her and her mother. Because of the trauma, she forgot the event and developed problematic symptoms.

Both films show an unquestionable and naïve faith dating back to the beginning of psychotherapy, i.e., its power to solve psychic problems by revealing the repressed critical event constitutive of the disturbance. Furthermore, both films convey the belief that only exposing the traumatic event together with total and boundless loving devotion will bring healing. In both films, the therapist, the detective, the lover, and the omnipotent redeemer are the same.

In the comedy *Zelig*, the therapist (Mia Farrow) devotes her time and her life to patient Zelig (Woody Allen), who frequently changes his identity up to a split personality. She brings him to her home, and day-to-day therapy culminates in a relationship and marriage. The therapist, Dr. Fletcher, is presented as a lonely woman facing problems in her interactions, a naïve person who does not grasp the patient's psychopathic shadow side. The entire film is a parody of therapist-patient relationships and presents a therapist who is clueless about therapy. The film's voiceover claims that the healing of the patient, who turns from a color-changing chameleon into "an individual with ideas of his own," is "not the victory of psychiatry but the victory of instincts, because Dr. Fletcher's methods did not follow what was then accepted in the profession. Instead, she felt a need and answered it, which is a great achievement." "In the end, what changed his life was not the social acceptance that he had so much wanted but the love of one woman." All that both the patient and the therapist needed in the film was the therapist's boundless love and devotion, not a genuine therapeutic engagement.

The irony is that acting as the therapist in the film is Mia Farrow, who, after years of a relationship and shared parenthood with Woody Allen, discovered him as a deceitful chameleon who had an affair with her adopted daughter. Allen thereby refuted his thesis in *Zelig* about recovery through love and without a therapeutic process. Did he indeed recover?

Archetypal Identification and Its Fascination

The energetic healer in *Julie Walking Home* and the patients in *Man Facing Southeast*, *K-Pax*, and *Equus* all live the grandiose archetypal existence of the redeemer. They are detached from their world and their ego consciousness, not planted in reality. When they lose the sense of their absolute archetypal power, they break apart. Total identification with archetypal life is dangerous. It creates a seesaw of power poles— omnipotent divinity v. suicidal weakness. Is that what happened to R. Nachman of Bratslav? This identification, which swallows up the ego of the one caught in it, is both a cause and a consequence of a weak ego.

In this fascination with impersonal archetypes (in ourselves or others), we are nurtured by their energetic power and can open up and develop. Development becomes possible when consciousness resists the fascination and permits a proper distance from these forces without being swallowed up. We also meet the archetypal power in big dreams that resemble myth and legend and are impressive, exciting, and sometimes extremely frightening. The therapist may meet the archetypal power in a patient's big dreams or in an actual power that overwhelms the patient and takes control of his behavior.

In some films, the therapist is attracted to the patient to the point of breaching borders and mixing identities, lured by the patient's primal, creative, emotional, and social powers as well as their vibrant imagination. This fascination is made possible by the therapist's concealed identity, the patient's problems, the heavy shadow behind the forgetting of his identity, and an enchanting grandiose inflation that fills the existential space created in the wake of this repression. These are the circumstances in *The Soul Keeper, Man Facing Southeast, K-Pax, Don Juan DeMarco, Persona, Intimate Strangers*, and *Equus*. In some films, the impulse to fuse with the patient's energy translates, as noted, into erotic infatuation.

A therapist fascinated with a patient is drawn to the vitality of the archetypal force the patient is caught in (as Don Juan, as a being from another planet, as a redeemer, as Jesus, as a criminal, as a sexual-pagan creature). The danger is that the therapist will act to preserve this force as is, forgetting that she is not only confronting an archetypal magnetic power but a suffering being swallowed up within his own myth. From the start, to be swallowed up by the archetype was meant to enable the patient to hide his suffering from himself and the world and be forgotten. In these circumstances, the therapist may also ignore the patient's pain and become absorbed in her own needs without seeing the patient's needs.

The intensiveness of the patient's psyche could become a fascinating life source for a therapist who feels blocked, detached, and yearning for contact with this vitality, as was true of Robert Lindner in his spatial journeys with a patient. Lindner was entirely captivated by their shared spatial delusion. Its control of him was dangerous in that, although he was aware of what was happening to him, he could not stop it: "We all of us possess areas of lessened resistance, and somewhere on the psychic armor of the strongest there is a vulnerable place. In this case it happened that the materials of Kirk's psychosis and the Achilles heel of my personality met and meshed like the gears of a clock" (Lindner 1962, 199). "I employed the rationalization of clinical altruism for personal ends and thus fell into a trap that awaits all unwary therapists of the mind" (ibid., 201). Fascination is not identical to emotional empathy and compassion. Nevertheless, as in Lindner's experience, fascination can pull the therapist toward the greater involvement and devotion that often provide the impetus to help a patient. The fascination is conveyed in the therapist's admiring look at the patient, who is the object of her enthralled gaze. The patient is thus granted the glowing look of an appreciative mother, which he had been missing, and the sense of being the special and preferred one, a substitute for the love he so much needs.

Often, this power of fascination operating between therapist and patient is also directed from the patient to the therapist and touches on the same emotional needs. The therapist, who is glorified by the patient and experienced as charismatic when the redeemer-magician aspects are projected onto her, is also the object of the patient's admiring look, which is a substitute for the love that the therapist needs from the patient.

The cinematic look's enchantment with the film's protagonist also captures the spectators in its seductive web. Cinema itself is indeed fascinated with psychotic and pathological materials.

In the film *Don Juan DeMarco*, Marlon Brando plays a psychiatrist whose personal and emotional life has declined and withered. He is in charge of diagnosing and treating a mysterious young man (Johnny Depp), convinced he is Don Juan, the legendary lover and adventurer. The young patient is swallowed up in the archetype of Don Juan, the attractive and faithless lover known as a seducer of women. The therapist (Brando, himself a symbol of passion in his youth), an older man about to retire, is riveted by the patient's fantasies, whose stories lead to a renewal of his sexual and romantic life with his wife (Faye Dunaway). The patient is released after merely ten days without undergoing treatment or changing. He does take off his Don Juan cape and the mask he had donned when he appeared as a Don Juan lover. He now wears ordinary clothes and, as it were, knows who he is, yet goes on living the fantasy of the great lover when he is, in truth, incapable of a real relationship with a woman. The patient, who identifies with the great lover and compensates for the absence of love and his experiences of rejection, imagines he has the power of love inside him and does not need it from the outside. In reality, no emotional connection emerges in his relationship with the therapist. As an inflationary lover, the patient was seemingly able to deny his need for emotional contact. If the patient gained anything from his conversations with the therapist, it is the therapist's enchanted "infatuation" with him.

In *Man Facing Southeast*, the therapist is captivated by Rantés, a patient who identifies with the archetype of the emissary from another world as a Jesus figure. This fascination, which reflects the gap between the powerful contents of the patient's life and the wasteland of the therapist's, leads the therapist to track Rantés as the preferred patient—"the chosen one." There is a parallel between the alienated patient and the isolated therapist. A further similarity is discernible between the therapist's relationship with his son (sustained through taped messages) and the patient's "reception" of messages from another world. Both are trying "to research the human brain" from a distance lacking empathy. The therapist attempts to study the patient's psyche, and Rantés asks to work in the hospital laboratory and study the brain's physical structure. The therapist speaks to the patient logically, "from the brain," and does not try to enter the patient's world. Neither one believes in therapy, but the patient cares about people and is willing to help those in need, a caring attitude less evident in the therapist. The therapist plays the saxophone alone while the patient plays for people in the church. Although both therapist and patient have similar difficulties in creating intimate ties, the patient is endowed with other human qualities that are part of his charm for the therapist.

So who is sane, and who is sick? Who lives the true reality of the psyche? At the beginning of their therapeutic sessions, the therapist leans backward, and the patient, Rantés, remarks that he appears as one who is trying to prevent contagion. The therapist then breaks borders, takes his children and Rantés to the circus, and is captivated by Rantés' ideas. He takes Rantés and his sister to a concert. His enchantment with Rantés is extended to his sister, becoming later an infatuation with her. His attraction to her conveys the impulse to merge with the values of the self that Rantés draws on—humaneness, the desire to be good to others, and the belief in a great power that guides him. The sister symbolizes the *anima*, the female-emotional bridge of the male to the depths of his soul. The therapist is detached from the *anima* as he is generally detached from relationships with women and, therefore, is attracted to Beatriz. Blue blood comes out of her mouth when the therapist sleeps with her. The therapist panics when faced with this hallucinatory reality, fears losing his sanity when dragged into over-involvement with the patient, and pushes her out. Blue blood is a characteristic of aristocrats and royals. In the film, blue blood symbolizes the aristocratic, royal, and irrational qualities that characterize the out-of-this-world existence of Rantés and his sister.

Within the cinematic fascination with madness, visible in this film (as in *Don Juan DeMarco*, *K-Pax*, and *One Flew Over the Cuckoo's Nest*) is the idealization of madness, contrasting with the therapist's presentation as lacking skills and psychic understanding. In this film, as in *K-Pax*, and *One Flew Over the Cuckoo's Nest*, the patients are good and humane, and their psychiatric treatment is ultimately cruel.

In *K-Pax*, too, the therapist is beguiled by the patient. A parallel prevails here: the patient says he is from a planet where there are no emotional ties, and the therapist is alienated from his wife and children. The therapist's fascination with the patient leads him to explore the latter's erased past. In a hypnotic and detective inquiry, he discovers the denied secret of the patient, who lost his wife and daughter in a violent event. This event emerges as the source of the patient's psychotic split—he has forgotten what happened and his true identity. When they part from one another, the therapist says he would like to know more about the planet of the patient, who replies—"It may be worth your while to become better acquainted with your family." The therapist does indeed go through a change and devotes himself to his family. In this case, the fascination serves the therapist's processes of change and self-awareness, but the patient pays the price for it. The hypnotic process where the clue to the terrible story is revealed leads to the patient's psychotic-catatonic collapse at the film's end. Hypnosis is forbidden in psychotic situations. Rather than a therapeutic necessity, the decision to hypnotize the patient to confront him with his traumatic past may have reflected the therapist's fascination with it and his commitment to the detective impulse while disregarding the patient's needs.

In *Equus*, too, the therapist strives to find out the truth about the traumatic event affecting his young patient through the invasive intrusion of hypnosis. Here too, the therapist is lured by the energetic primal power of madness. Enthralled by the boy's nightly nude rides and the sexual, ecstatic, and ritual excitement, the therapist begins to doubt whether it is proper to cure the boy's sickness and forgets that he is suffering.

Fascination with the patient may also be related to envy, which leads to the admiration and idealization of the complexes that activate him. In *Equus*, the therapist explicitly states he envies the boy. The film is accompanied by the monologues of the therapist who, like the patient, is also alone, detached from possible ties with women (his wife is estranged from him, and he has no friendly-emotional-spiritual or sexual contact with her). Like his young patient, he too is captivated by the charm of archetypal powers: he is attracted to the Greek gods but not truly capable of drawing sustenance from his intellectual curiosity and tourist visits to Greece.

At the very opening of the film, after the first session with the boy who refuses to cooperate, the therapist tells (the spectators) one of his dreams:

> I am a High Priest in ancient Greece. I wear a gold mask like Agamemnon and stand next to a stone holding a sharp knife, participating in a very important ritual that determines the fate of the crops or of a military campaign. The sacrifice is a herd of five-hundred boys and girls. On both sides of me are two more priests wearing masks. They are enormously strong and expertly catch each child and lay him on the stone. I cut the child's body from the throat to the navel, pull out the inner blood tubes and throw them steaming on to the floor. My two colleagues read them as if they were hieroglyphics. It's obvious to me that I am above everyone. My unique cutting skills have granted me this standing. Although the others do not know, I am nauseated by all this. The problem is that, if they find out that I am distressed and doubt the usefulness of this task—I will be the next on the stone. And then the mask begins to slip. The other priests look at me. Their protruding gold eyes fill up with blood. They tear the knife out of my hand . . . and I wake up.

The therapist's voice is harsh, and his dream describes vile cruelty comparable to the youth's.

Instead of a patient's first dream, a first (and only) dream of the therapist is cited here, which I will approach as if it were the first dream in the therapy that, according to Jung, is to be seen as a diagnosis and a prognosis. As a diagnosis, the dream describes the therapist killing the child inside him and his child patients. And indeed, the therapist later says that he cures his patients from their authentic primal madness toward a pointless dreary life, thus killing the children in their souls.

The dreaming therapist doubts whether it is right to identify with the priestly mask, which is the therapeutic mask/persona, and wants to rebel against his task—sacrificing children to the Moloch of the archetype-god/father symbolized by Agamemnon. The archetype of the father that symbolizes the culture and the law (the social values we must adapt to as well as the values and laws of therapy) is the archetype for whose sake the therapist sacrificed his inner child, who is the symbol of his authentic inner self. In his dream, the sacrifice is performed as a plea for the success of the army or the crops, meaning that the individual is sacrificed for the sake of the collective. Greek mythology says that Agamemnon offered up his daughter, imploring the gods to send winds and move his ships to fight in the Trojan War. He sacrificed his daughter for the pride of his ego, which pursued power and success. The therapist, who operates skillfully and successfully at the beginning of the dream, is busy with the pride of his ego and his superior standing. The turnabout in the dream is conveyed in his refusal to be like Agamemnon, who sacrificed his daughter (the emotional element of the psyche) to the gods for the supremacy of the father-patriarchate archetype—the order principle of the social establishment.

But then—and here is the problematical prognosis of the dream—the priests (representing other parts of the personality that do not renounce the complexes that had so far guided him) oppose him in order to destroy him. The aggression directed against the young patient and his inner child is now directed against him. The terrible ending is, from the start, rooted in what we know about the myth of Agamemnon—his wife murdered him.

And indeed, when the therapist ultimately equates healing with the killing of his young patient's authentic inner child, his doubts about his right to treat and heal lead him to a fierce identification with the boy. His psyche rebels against itself, and his consciousness is sacrificed. His fascination with the patient leads him astray to the point of losing his reality, testing and pathologically identifying with the sick patient.

The therapist's doubts about his right and his option of transcending his professional therapeutic stance, including the power it accords him, prevent him from changing and internalizing something from the primal instinct he encounters in the horse and in the boy. Rather than serving as an inspiration, the boy's primal force leads him to madness. The problem is that, from the start, what captivates him is the mad sexuality rather than a positive life energy. The therapist has a pre-psychotic dream that identifies with the destructive archetypal forces, and he cannot be saved from them.

The children's sacrifice in the dream is also reminiscent of the binding of Isaac. In the binding, we see the impulse (embodied in the divine command) to sacrifice the child so that God might command, "Do not lay your hand on the lad" (Genesis 22:12), opposing the urge to sacrifice. Contrary to Abraham, however, the dreamer appears as the sacrificing priest and, rather than being a passive commanded agent, he is identified with fierce ego pride. In Joseph Campbell's terms, "the dragon is one's own binding of oneself to one's ego" (1988, 184). The therapist is bound by the hubris of the power-hungry ego, the violence, and the victory (Agamemnon), as well as by the ego blocked from the primal-emotional world.

The therapist says: "I've assisted children and helped them in their pain and healed them, but I have also—beyond question—cut from them parts of personality that the normal God in all its aspects finds repugnant . . . I hear the voice [of Equus] calling me from the dark caves of the psyche . . . The big-headed figure asks questions that I've avoided all my professional life . . . What do I do in the consulting room, who has answers? I cannot find my place . . . The terrible thing is to take someone's worship away from them." And the wise friend who listens tells him: "Worship isn't destructive." Such worship (the boy's worship of the horse and the therapist's worship of the boy) is a fascination that, without consciousness, submits to a great power. And he answers: "Many men are less excited with their wives than he is with Equus." She: "And they blind their wives? The boy is in pain most of his life! And you can take away the pain!" He replies:

> "You know what passion is, that is passion and pain . . . A pain he chose and created. He created a desperate ritual of his own only to light one flame of ecstasy in the dreariness that enwrapped him. He destroyed and almost

destroyed himself, but he has known a passion wilder than I have ever known. And I envy him. That is what his stare says all the time: I galloped, and you? I envy him . . . I shrank and chose to live my life pale and provincial, because I'm a coward . . . I speak of Argos and he is trying to become a centaur. I haven't kissed my wife in six years and he stands in the dark suckling the sweat of God."

She replies: "The boy is in pain . . . he's not accusing you. He wants help from you."

Later, after the boy, in an attack of crying and choking, reconstructs the trauma of his failed sexual experience and the terrible attack against the horse, the doctor soothes him with a tranquilizer and says, "He'll go away now. You'll never see him [the horse] again. You'll have no more bad dreams. I'm going to make you well, you'll be fine. Trust me." He then remembers his friend's words: "The boy is in pain. And you can take it away and that is enough." The doctor goes on:

"He'll feel himself acceptable! . . . My desire might be to make him a caring husband and citizen . . . My achievement, however, is more likely to make a ghost! . . . Passion, you see, can be destroyed by a doctor. It cannot be created . . . You will, however, be without pain. More or less completely without pain. And now for me it never stops."

The emotional foundation in the psyche enables us to sense the pain of the other and prevent the sacrifice of the inner child. By contrast, the fascination blinds us and precludes compassion for the suffering boy.

Involvement Up to the Loss of Separation and Identity

Breaking boundaries, or their absence from the start, sometimes leads to a level of involvement whereby the therapist (who in films is not always a trained professional) loses the certainty of his identity, which is trapped in the patient's plight. So it is in *Persona, Man Facing Southeast, Holy Smoke,* and *Equus* where, to some extent, therapists lose their reality judgment.

The therapist sometimes loses her boundaries and is carried away by her weakness and her inability to draw borders. The reason could be the therapist's needs for symbiosis and for controlling and controlled dependence, which lead her to consent to the childish demandingness of an anxious patient, be constantly at his service, and visit him at his home, as in the comedy *Analyze This*. The patient in the film (Robert De Niro), a Mafia man suffering from anxiety and crying attacks, takes control of an ineffectual therapist (Billy Cristal). Therapists and patients mirror one another—both suffer from communication problems, are in authoritative social roles, and are presented in their shame and helplessness.

A process involving a lack of borders and complete role reversal occurs in *Persona* when the "therapist" talks and exposes the dark parts of her psyche, paralleling the silent patient's dark and repressed parts.

Excessive involvement and a lack of time-place limits result in confusion between therapist and patient, leading to violent outbursts. They mix into one another in neediness, violent aggression, anxiety about their separate identity, confusion between reality and fantasy, and their rambling and psychotic speech. Who do these contents belong to, and who uses the other? Who draws on the other's disturbed state? Alma scratches her hand, and Elisabet sucks her blood in an act resembling both a vampire feeding on its victim and a blood pact that exposes their lack of separation. The faces of the two women fuse on the screen. The confusion and the merger between them are also evident when Alma sleeps with Elisabet's husband, who appears not to differentiate between them.

The film begins with two burning lights melting into one another. It ends when they separate, presenting an alchemic metaphor of the therapeutic session, of the symbiotic moments that, in the best case, will enable the required adult separation, as attested by the pictures of the *Rosarium* where the king and queen separate after their sexual union (Jung 1978). The film ends with a separation, but there is no evidence that their fusion resulted in proper separation.

In *Face to Face*, too, Bergman deals with the collapse of identity borders between the therapist and her patients. This time, the therapist (Liv Ullmann) is a psychiatrist named Jenny. In one of her dreams, she sees one of her patients with a mask. When Jenny removes it, horrible wounds are exposed, and she hurries to put it back. The dream reveals an involvement without consciousness and borders in the psychiatrist's attitude toward the patient, reflecting the wounds of her own psyche.

Another patient she meets in her dream tells her that doctors had operated on her head to remove her anxiety, but when they closed her up, they forgot about day-to-day anxiety. This patient, too, mirrors her predicament to the therapist—her untreated concerns. The dream is also critical of Jenny for treating her patients at the physical level (given that psychiatrists, as a first measure, administer drugs) without addressing their emotional distress. In the dreams about her patients, she sees herself and does not take notice of their pain, which is why she cannot treat them.

The psychiatrist appears in the film as an anxious woman who suffered harsh experiences in childhood but repressed them. The film opens with the psychiatrist's emotional collapse when she is flooded by her childhood experiences of abandonment, loss, educational cruelty, and self-inflicted aggression. Despite them, Jenny has never been in therapy. She is unaware of her difficulties and her unsuitability to the profession. She lives in dismal loneliness, estranged from her husband and daughter, and detached from her sexuality, but does not seek professional help.

Although the film's theme appears to show the psychiatrist's encounter "face to face" with herself after her psychotic breakdown (Avshalom 2018), it is also a sharp critique of her as a therapist. Her personality is unstable. She has never truly confronted herself and her wounds or tried to heal them, and, therefore, cannot truly meet her patients and be "the wounded healer" for them. Instead of a professional therapist, the film presents an option of humane therapy conducted by her friend Thomas, who enables her to undergo the process of therapeutic self-confrontation in his presence. Humane motives drive Thomas. He comes to her house to save her when she attempts suicide, sits long hours by her bedside, hugs her, and attentively contains her dreams and the self-psychodrama she undergoes in her intense encounter with figures from her past, with her harsh memories, her terrifying fears, and with other negative feelings she has hidden from herself throughout her life. He neither asks nor inquires and is mostly silent, allowing her to go through the process.

The friend who plays the therapist's role in a borderless mixture of friend and therapist, without time and place limits, emerges as possessing positive aspects but also questionable ones, such as his sudden desertion that betrays the patient's trust. We see the friend here rather than the professional therapist. The end of the film does not attest to any healing changes in the sick psychiatrist.

Man Facing Southeast, Equus, Persona, and *Face to Face* expose the risks of symbiotic over-involvement—loss of the therapist's separation and potential psychotic states. Borderless involvement can swallow up the therapist into the patient's madness. In *Man Facing Southeast*, the therapist takes the patient to the circus. We see both of them watching the tightrope walker as a symbol of their psyche hanging by a thread. Rantés tells the therapist: "What happened, doctor? You feel you're close to the border and fear going on?" Indeed, the therapist must protect himself from dangerous over-involvement. Is that why Thomas, Jenny's friend in *Face to Face*, suddenly deserts her and leaves for another country after sharing her harsh experiences?

Breaking boundaries is also a feature of films that relate to therapy indirectly rather than in its conventional contexts, such as *Julie Walking Home, Marnie, Intimate Strangers*, and *Face to Face*. The therapist in them is not a professional but someone who stumbled into the role—the magic healer, the husband who treats his wife, a clerk mistakenly considered a therapist, and the friend who acts as a therapist. The archetypes and complexes activated in psychotherapy, however, exist in every therapeutic situation. Consequently, they are also present in these films and others that do not deal with psychotherapy but with a couple's relationship where one is devoted to the other's assistance. One example is Hitchcock's detective film *Vertigo* (1958). The film tells the story of John Ferguson (James Stewart), a former police detective who suffers from fear of heights. He is hired by a friend to track the friend's wife (Kim Novak), who, as it were, has become possessed by the soul of her dead grandmother and vainly tries to save her from her suicidal urge. In an analogy to a therapeutic situation, such a position grants the therapist a sense of power and gratification derived from knowing that someone depends on him, which is perhaps addictive. Ferguson, the therapist, is drawn into identification and over-involvement and seeks to save the patient instead of saving himself so that his involvement is also a defense mechanism from his fears.

Later in the film, we find that the friend has hired a woman to play the role of his wife and fake her suicide. The detective is captivated by the woman's charm, falls in love with her, becomes distraught when she supposedly kills herself, and is hospitalized in a catatonic state. Like the detective in *Vertigo*, the therapist may become the victim of the patient's entrapping manipulation (even if unconscious) and mentally collapse.

Another example is Pedro Almodóvar's film *Talk to Her* (2002). A male nurse taking care of a girl in a coma is swallowed up in an all-consuming infatuation with her. His devotion answers his needs, and he has no life beyond his care for her—the treatment and the infatuation are inseparably entwined. He sleeps with her while she is unconscious, is sent to jail, and kills himself. In his death, he identifies with her coma, taking "therapy" to the brink, as it were, and up to death! In both these films, the "therapist" falls into an abyss from which he had sought to rescue the patient.

These films reaffirm the warnings of ancient myths not to look back at Hades, entering it when unallowed and unequipped.

The Therapist's Wounds and Emotional Difficulties

When therapists and patients meet, each becomes a mirror for the other, through which they become aware of themselves and their difficulties. Cinema brings therapists face-to-face with themselves, as in the film's name. I return now to *Good Will Hunting*. The young patient looks at a picture hanging on the consulting room wall where a man is rowing in a stormy sea and says that the painting portrays the therapist, who is in a storm and rows out of an inner turmoil. The patient sees the therapist's inner truth but, at the same time, he projects the picture of his stormy psyche on this painting, which thus becomes a mirror they both share. Recognition of this fact later enables the boy to enter the therapeutic process. The man rowing in the sea of the unconscious psyche symbolizes the therapeutic process where the ego is strengthened and learns to navigate without drowning in emotional floods. Therapy's role is to build a boat stable enough so that this rowing will bring them to a safe shore. Therapist and patient are partners in this rowing in the stormy sea and in the building of the boat, which is the therapeutic container that enables the process.

Yalom says about both therapists and patients what André Malraux said, quoting a country priest: "First of all, people are much more unhappy than one thinks . . . and there is no such thing as a grown-up person" (2002, 6). Yalom implied that there are no "grown-up" therapists who do not need therapy, noting that the idea of the "fully analyzed" therapist is mythic in its nature (ibid., 8). He refers to a Herman Hesse story about two healers who lived in different places. One fell into despair and went on a voyage to seek help from the other, whom he met on the way. It then turned out that the second healer had also been in distress and had gone out to seek help from the first. The second healer, however, does not tell this to the one who came to him seeking help and, instead, takes care of him and makes him his assistant. The patient thus helped the therapist to heal since healers, too, have pending problems that their patients help them solve.

The therapist is expected to be internally integrated and psychically mature, but Freud already knew this was not always true: "It cannot be disputed that analysts in their own personalities have not invariably come up to the standard of psychical normality to which they wish to educate their patients" (Freud 1964, 247). Yet, it is precisely the therapist's recognition of her difficulties and their implications for her work that allows her to be a therapist. Harry Stack Sullivan, a highly influential psychiatrist, went even further when he defined psychotherapy as a discussion of personal issues between two people, one of whom is more anxious than the other. Sullivan claimed that if the therapist's anxiety is greater than that of the patient, they reverse roles, boosting the patient's self-esteem by the very fact of helping the therapist (Yalom 2002, 108). *When Nietzsche Wept* rests on this perception, and many films do deal with the therapist's wounds, anxiety, and vulnerability.

Ronald Laing (1970) claimed that psychiatry describes patients through characteristics that fit the psychiatrists themselves—detachment, alienation, and relationship problems. He argued that psychiatrists deny their problems and see them in the patients, turning them into scapegoats and victims of their emotional conflicts. They can thus deny their difficulties and perpetuate those of the patients, as the therapists are portrayed in *Man Facing Southeast* and *Equus*.

Some films, as noted, show how the therapist's wound serves him and turns him into a wounded healer, as in *Good Will Hunting*. Still, many films portray the therapist as cold and detached, businesslike and uninspiring, brittle and depressed when these emotional difficulties affect his work.

The Son's Room shows the alienated therapist sitting behind the patient's back and unable to mourn his son, which leads him to stop being a therapist. In *Persona*, the psychiatrist herself collapses. In *Equus*, the therapist is emotionally detached and has a psychotic breakdown. In *Lantana*, the therapist is in a marriage crisis after her daughter's death. Her emotional estrangement from her husband is replicated in her alienation from her patients. The film script leads her to her death.

In *Shrink*, Kevin Spacey plays Henry Carter, the depressed psychiatrist of the big Beverly Hills stars, who has nothing left to give his patients. Carter earns money from treating people in the Hollywood film industry and writing best-sellers about happiness, health, and good living. In the film, we learn that he has lost his desire for happiness, health, and good living following a tragedy related to his wife. He is depressed and unable to bring meaning to his sessions with his patients, who pay him a great deal and to whom he gives little. A girl called Jemma, who pays little, is the one who will ultimately change Carter's life.

In some films, the problems confronting therapists in their couple and family ties lead them to turn therapy and therapeutic relationships into the content of their lives (*Equus, Man Facing Southeast, Zelig, K-Pax, The Prince of Tides*). The therapist in these films is revealed as a lonely person, for whom the asymmetric therapist-patient relationship and the exaggerated devotion to the patient substitute for mutual human connections and couple and family life. Therapists can then enjoy a measure of control and supremacy that allows them to avoid the genuine intimacy of an equal, dialogical, and reciprocal relationship.

This model fits the therapist of *Intimate Strangers*, who is depicted as a lonely man, failing in his relationships with women, stuck in his parents' home, clumsy and rigid, and affected by problems resembling the patient's. He is an accountant who, by chance and against his will, becomes the "therapist" of a young woman who mistakenly entered his office instead of the consulting room next door and talks to him about herself. Even after she realizes her mistake, she continues these therapeutic sessions where he mainly listens, and she talks until her problem is solved. This quasi-comic situation emerges as a critique of psychotherapy because the purported therapist, an accountant (meant as the antithesis of a psychologist), enables her therapeutic process merely by listening and posing commonsense questions. The "true" psychologist—the one with the diploma whom the accountant consults—is conceited and overconfident. His only explanation for the situation that developed is that the girl's story about her problems was perhaps made up, and her coming to his room was an intentional manipulation—everything is fantasy, as Freud had thought. This interpretation emerges as untrue and as the psychologist's fantasy.

Moreover, a patient of the neighboring psychologist is genuinely helped with his fear of elevators, not by his therapist-psychologist but by the patient who is the film's protagonist. She meets him when both are on their way to their therapists, persuades him to experience the elevator with her, hugs him when they are there, and allows him to scream out of fear.

We find, then, that her therapy with the accountant succeeded, and as a result, she changes her attitude. From despair, from a perception of the situation as lost, and from her inability to leave her despotic and pathological husband, she proceeds to separate from him and change her residence and her profession. Her ability to change is revealed as greater than that of the "therapist."

As in other films, boundaries are broken here too. The patient's husband drags the therapist into voyeurism of their sexuality when he makes love with his wife in a hotel room across from the therapist's window. The cinematic look at the therapist then presents him as stuck, helpless, and sustained by his voyeurism and by the patient's seductiveness. The therapist falls in love with her and, to remain in touch, relocates to the place she moved to when she left therapy. The therapy succeeds in changing him too, which is the positive part of the story. The lonely therapist is thus presented as one who needs the patient as much as the patient needs him. The therapist in the film needs the patient because she projects unto him the ethical figure, one possessing the required life skills. Unlike his ex-wife, who mocks him, she believes in him and sees his positive side; therefore, he needs her to solve his impasse. The therapist's excuse for a renewed meeting with the patient he fell in love with was the return of a lighter she had forgotten in his room that had belonged to her father, who was killed in her early childhood. Her forgetfulness could be seen as a "Freudian slip" on her part, leaving with him a libidinal drive of passion for the male/father (the lighter), thereby conveying her desire for him to replace the absent father as an object of love and sexuality. The therapist is thus unwittingly acquiescing to this wish, which is also his own. At the end, we see the therapist sitting beside her and speaking about himself, suggesting that a change process is beginning in him. We could say that the patient is his *anima*, his bridge to the emotional world—frightened, yearning, and daring all at the same time.

The patient came to therapy because she was caught in a trap. Accidentally, she had run over her husband and could not leave him. Fundamentally, she is reenacting her mother's life, who accidentally killed her father. Following the therapeutic intervention, she breaks the compulsive repetitive circle and leaves her husband. At the same time, the therapist also lives in a closed loop where he reenacts his father's life—he lives in the same house, works in the same office with the same secretary who had also worked with his father. Following the patient, he, too, manages to break this circle and begin a new voyage. Again, as in many films, the ultimate solution is to consummate the therapist-patient love.

Behind the therapist's emotional difficulties and blocks is his internal wound. At the beginning of *Man Facing Southeast*, a picture flashes twice through the therapist's consciousness—an image of two heads, each one wrapped in fabric, close to one another, and almost kissing but blocked by the fabric cover. When the image reappears the second time, blood pours from one of the covered heads. In my view, this image conveys the wish for closeness of both therapist and patient and of people in general, the blocks that prevent its realization, and the wound caused by the vulnerability we all bear and create around close relationships. Ultimately, intimacy and truly close relationships are the foundation of our human existence.

Wounds and difficulties do not in themselves disqualify a therapist. Change can begin when the wound behind the therapist's flaws and limitations is exposed. The wound is what therapist and patient have in common; only those who sense their own wounds can feel those of another.

Adolf Guggenbühl-Craig points to a potential problem when the archetype of the wounded healer is split—the therapist identifies with sane, conscious, and healing existence while projecting the unconscious, sick, and wounded one onto the patient. This split in the therapist's psyche pushes the patient to his wounded and unconscious side, obstructing his development. Only when the therapist acknowledges the wounded and the healing sides in both of them can the split close (Guggenbühl-Craig 1971, 197–208).

Films matter because they raise in therapists the awareness not only of the patient's wounds but of their own too. They also raise awareness in the public of their own and the therapist's wounds and of their contribution to the therapeutic process. In films that show the wounded therapist as questionable, the problem does not lie in the very existence of wounds and their emotional difficulties. Instead, the concern is their intensity, the therapist's unawareness of her difficulties, her inability to change, and the direct damage inflicted on patients when therapists unwittingly use the patients' difficulties to help themselves without helping the patients, as is the case in *Man Facing Southeast* and *Holy Smoke*.

The Shadow and the Evil of Patient and Therapist

The shadow is the inferior and undeveloped part of the personality, which includes qualities considered primal and negative. Because of these qualities' unsuitability to the attitudes of consciousness, the ego tends to deny their existence and repress them to the unconscious, from which they operate. When dealing with the shadow, the gap between the persona and the shadow needs to be addressed. The mask of the persona is a compromise between the individual and the world concerning the way we show ourselves—it both covers and reveals. Usually, the emphasis is on the aspect of the persona as a mask meant to show positive aspects and hide shadow ones.1 Whereas the persona is intended to conceal the shadow from the world, forgetfulness, and a split identity are meant to hide from the individual traumatic shadow experiences that occurred in the past. The extreme of the shadow archetype is evil.

Jung claims that individuals can acknowledge the relative shadow in their nature but find looking at absolute evil a disturbing and shattering experience (Jung 1978, 10). Indeed, the recurrent motif in films on therapy is that of a traumatic shadow event in the patient's life, as in *The Soul Keeper*, *Face to Face*, *K-Pax*, *Marnie*, *Spellbound*, *Three Faces of Eve* (sexual exploitation), and *Ordinary People* (the brother's drowning). In most films, the patient is the victim of a shadow event of evil, violence, or sexual exploitation, which leads to forgetfulness and a serious identity problem. The result is the extreme cases, such as those of patients Rantés and Prot, who identify with an altruistic humane mission and appear, as it were, without a shadow.

In other films, the patient suffers through his shadow's qualities, acts, and feelings. David's shadow (in *David and Lisa*) is unconscious murderous aggression; the shadow in *Marnie* is theft, manipulation, and a murder she committed in her childhood; *Zelig* is a chronic liar; in *State of Play*, the patient is a psychotic criminal; in an episode of *Colombo*, the patient seduces her therapists; in *K-Pax*, the patient murders the members of his family; and in *Equus*, the patient stabs and blinds the horse. In the last two examples, the patient's act is so cruel that the price is psychosis.

The therapist, like a father confessor, can purportedly contain the patient's terrifying shadow. French poet-writer Philippe Claudel, who was a devout Catholic, cites a priest who describes his role as the sewer man of those who confess to him:

> Men are strange. They commit the worst crimes without a second thought, but afterwards they cannot live with the memory of what they have done. They have to rid themselves of it. And so they come to me, because they know

> I'm the only person who can give them relief, and they tell me everything. . . . I'm the sewer-man. I'm the man into whose brain they pour all their filth, all their shit, and they feel relieved . . . When it's over, they go away as though nothing has happened. . . . They can sleep in peace, and . . . I am overflowing. I cannot take any more . . . I feel alone because I must absolve them.
>
> (Claudel 2009, 115–116)

The therapist's role, like that of a father confessor, is to contain the shadow of the other and be compassionate, going through a transformative process that will transmute the negative feelings evoked by the patient into compassion. But whether hostile or compassionate toward the patient's shadow, the therapist may fall into arrogant hubris if he forgets his own shadow. Many films deal with the shadow aspect of the therapeutic archetype and with the shadow side of the therapist.

The Jungian view has significantly contributed to awareness of the therapist's shadow, though other approaches have also begun focusing on it. Psychoanalyst Eliane Amado Lévy-Valensi removes the professional therapist's mask and sharply exposes the narcissistic "character neurosis" of a "very disappointing homo psychoanalyticus" (1971, 177), who slyly disregards reality, the other [the patient], and his own creative dimensions. "It is the psychoanalyst, then, who wastes his resources, or many of them, to protect appearances," "who cunningly pretends to set up the world on the dimensions of an analyzed ego" (ibid., 161). She argues that, often, "the exaggerated reserve in the analyst's behavior, his excessive silence, only convey the fear of taking risks, the fear of exposing to the patient that he had not understood or had not understood enough" (ibid., 168). In her view, the therapist "codifies his escape routes within the technique" and sees himself as "a small god who is sheltered from counter-transference" (ibid., 177), busy in conflicts with his colleagues.

Therapeutic relationships are not only relations of love, as we would wish. Often, the therapist's shadow is hidden from the therapist herself, who is identified with her positive professional stance and her good intentions. Sometimes, the shadow is misleading when it disguises itself as unconditional therapeutic love. Anne Sexton writes: "I begin again, Dr. Y.,/ this neverland journal,/ full of my own sense of filth./ Why else keep a journal, if not/ to examine your own filth?" (Sexton 1981, 564).

Suspicion about the shadow motivation of the therapist's love is conveyed in *Marnie* when the patient says to her husband-therapist-detective: "You're pathologically stuck on a criminal woman who screams when you come close to her. You're dying to play doctor." For her husband, thieving Marnie may represent his unconscious shadow side, which he projects onto her because, for some reason, her shadow does not threaten him, and something in her attracts him beyond her beauty. The way the husband forces her to live with him and the inquiry into her past is explicitly the shadow side of the detective and his own controlling and belligerent shadow.

One of the therapist's shadow aspects is the power to influence the patient, which can turn into control of the patient—a negative factor in therapy (Guggenbühl-Craig, 1971). Therapists who involve the patient in their symbiotic needs and their need for love influence patients in hidden ways. Another aspect of the therapist's shadow hastens the decoding of the patient's riddle and sometimes even coerces the patient into hypnosis at the risk of his psychic balance. So the therapist in *Equus* seduces the patient into revealing his secrets, deceitfully promising him that his pain will then pass, just as in *K-Pax*. A prominent instance is the husband-detective-therapist in *Marnie*, who forces her to marry him as a condition for not handing her over to the police and compels her to come with him to her mother's house to determine the source of her trauma. Drugs, electric shock, and a lobotomy are also coercive measures when adopted without the patient's consent, and all are present in films on therapy. Open and covert defiance of the therapist's power turns these films into political protest documents. An analogy emerges between the power of the therapist and that of the therapeutic establishment, which is equated with the power of the political establishment to destroy the freedom of the human spirit, as in *Man Facing Southeast* and *One Flew Over the Cuckoo's Nest*. The therapeutic establishment is revealed in these films as protecting bourgeois conservatism and condemning creative individuality in the name of the therapeutic norm, which turns into a Procrustean bed for all those who deviate from it. Dictatorial regimes are known to place dissidents in psychiatric hospitals and compel them to undergo destructive "treatment." In these films, the establishment is not concerned with the good of the individual patient but with the institutional order and aggressive control over patients.

In *A Clockwork Orange*, the patient is a vicious, brutal youth, and the behavioral therapy offered to him will lead him to be repelled by all forms of sex and violence. By comparison with the two previous films, the patient here is cruel, but so is his treatment. In all three films, the treatment is also meant to punish the patient and take revenge on him as society's scapegoat.

Sometimes, the therapist identifies with the aggressive shadow through a distorted ideological justification. When the nurse in *One Flew Over the Cuckoo's Nest* emerges as a self-righteous and moralistic character who cannot contain disorder and criticism, she projects onto the rebellious patient the chaos and evil threatening her psyche. Referring him for a lobotomy merely expresses her cruelty, which identifies with that of the establishment and has the theoretical backing of a medical procedure.

Parallel to the search and discovery of the crime/trauma/shadow that caused the patient's symptoms, in other films, the narrative focuses on the discovery of the crime/shadow of the therapist. In this context, Hitchcock's *Rear Window* is a film I see as a metaphor for therapy, and its protagonist as a metaphor for the voyeuristic detective therapist. The protagonist is a photographer. Photography, an act where consciousness observes and records reality, can therefore symbolize the process of consciousness. The protagonist is a voyeur photographer who looks into others' windows, and that is his shadow. Looking into the neighbors' rear windows, however, is not only the voyeur detective but also the audience. The fact that the spectator looks at the protagonist, who looks at the plot through a telescope analogous to the camera, enables the spectator some distance. This setting of an onlooker looking at an onlooker is reminiscent of the paintings of Caspar David Friedrich (1774–1840). In most of them, the picture's viewer sees the back of a lonely individual looking at a distant scene.

The film's protagonist is a voyeur of others' lives because he is in a wheelchair. His handicap is a metaphor for the weakness and disability of the therapist, which may lead him to deal not only with the lives of others instead of living his own life but also to "rear window" voyeurism. In his disability, he embodies the anti-hero aspects and the wounded healer. Interestingly, the neighbor in the apartment across who is exposed as a criminal is played by Raymond Burr, who, in *Ironside*, would play a detective in a wheelchair. A potential hint to the shadow of the detective-therapist is discernible here.

Discovering the truth about the dark mystery in the lives of others becomes increasingly the photographer's main pursuit. Instead of assuming a distant stance and reporting the suspicion of a crime to the authorities, he is actively involved in the detective inquiry into a crime he discovers in the rear window of the apartment across. This involvement reaches a peak when he sends his girlfriend to the crime scene to check data and gather evidence and is attacked by the criminal, who found out he is being tracked and enters the photographer's home. At times, the therapist goes through a similar experience when he is drawn into a potentially dangerous involvement from a distant observing stance. The criminal that the photographer-detective tracks sees the detective as patients see the therapists through their own radars. They see the therapist's shadow and vulnerability, which they sometimes experience as a crime against them even when at stake is merely a random failure of empathy. In such cases, the patient's shadow will attack the therapist. Lindner (1962) tells us of a patient who tried to strangle him, though this is an extreme case, and patients will usually limit themselves to active or passive anger reactions. The therapist, however, is attacked not only by the patient's shadow but by his own, which is activated by his shadow side (betrayal, aggression, erotic needs, and so forth).

The therapist's therapeutic shadow comprises the therapist's narcissistic needs—control-oppressiveness, aggression, fear of rejection, need for love or admiration or symbiotic neediness, seductiveness, envy of the patient, exploitation, charlatanism, needs for glorification, ambition, prestige and honor, power, as well as the shadow of exaggerated pride/hubris, and grandiosity.

In her comments (relevant also to therapists) on the shadow of the spiritual teacher, Maty Lieblich notes that images of the guru pose the greatest threat to him. The paradox is that, as the guru advances in his spiritual path, so does the danger of self-deceit and of falling into shadow temptations that become increasingly cunning, sophisticated, veiled, and powerful. Deeper insight is not an insurance against consciousness' growing talent for self-deception (Lieblich 2009, 279).

A certain dosage of the therapist's shadow is natural and inevitable, and consciousness of it can help the therapist neutralize its influence on behavior. The more flexible the ego, the more it can agree to acknowledge and absorb shadow aspects and control them, so they will not be expressed in behavior. Acknowledging the shadow's existence as a universal human archetype frees us from concern about its existence and eases our guilt for feeling it inside us.

The patient's encounter with his shadow is essential to every therapeutic process. This encounter is meant to expand consciousness, weaken the shadow, control it, and direct it toward building the whole personality within a moral setting. In analytic therapy, the therapist learns to contain both her shadow and the patient's without feeling hostile toward the parts of the patient's shadow she finds unbearable in her psyche. At the same time, the patient's ability to accept the therapist as including a shadow facilitates his acceptance of the "good enough" therapist—whose shadow and light complement one another in an integrative model of the self—and thus also acceptance of his own shadow.

When the therapist identifies with the Jesus archetype in the aspect of absolute devotion and shadow denial, the danger is that her shadow side or the patient's shadow will attack her and overwhelm her. For instance, when the therapist denies her own dependent neediness, she may encourage the patient's dependence on her, making it harder for him to eventually separate from her. Or, in another example, when the therapist denies the patient's aggression and wishes to see him as only kind and polite, she may be attacked by the resentments of the patient, who thereby demands that she acknowledge, accept, and contain his anger. He may require the therapist to confront her anger toward the patient without deceiving herself by claiming that she is invariably loving. Denying needs for love, erotism, power, and control can push the therapist into sexual-erotic exploitation of the patient.

In the story of the pied piper of Hamelin, the city's inhabitants lose-sacrifice their children, who were attracted by the piper and disappeared with him because they refused to pay him. One focus of the shadow in therapy is indeed payment. It touches on the needs and feelings of both therapist and patient around self-value, grandiosity, authority, neediness, exploitation, fear of poverty, greed, stinginess, generosity, fraud, and more. All these are shadow feelings that seldom come up in therapy and supervision (Toder-Goldin, 2012). One instance of the problem resulting from the therapist's denial of the significance of money and her need for suitable compensation is that she may refrain from collecting her fees on time and build up resentment against a patient who does not pay. Lévy-Valensi calls us to abandon the rigidity of the therapeutic stance, overcome the fear of life, and reexamine the issue of payment in therapy (1971, 171). Films dealing with therapist-patient relationships do not deal with this shadow issue. What is the shadow or the enormous complex of therapists and patients hiding behind this issue's repression in cinema? Possibly, the issue of money in these relationships is entirely ignored as a way of conveying the wish of the cinematic patient that the (pseudo-parental) therapist should give of herself without expecting a return.

In several of the films mentioned, what characterizes the therapists as humane is precisely their shadow, which is described as leading to the therapy's success. In *Good Will Hunting*, the young patient teases the therapist and guesses that his wife left him for another. The therapist, grieving his beloved wife's death, loses control, attacks the boy, and tries to choke him. When the therapist is revealed as an angry and vulnerable man, the boy can give up his defenses and the fear of exposing his weaknesses and aggression.

Films that present a love affair with the patient as part of a successful course of therapy (such as *Prince of Tides* and *Marnie*) relate to the therapist's shadow being valuable to the therapy.

Many more films, however, are concerned with the therapist's harsh shadow. To use the metaphor in Hitchcock's *Rear Window*, cinema itself is, in many films, the telescope looking through psychotherapy's "rear window" and discovering the "hidden crime"—the therapist's shadow. In *Equus*, we meet the therapist's shadow in his murderous dreams, his pugnacious invasion of the boy's psyche, and the dishonesty of his vain promise of recovery, which is close to a betrayal. In *Man Facing Southeast*, we also encountered the therapist's duplicity.

In *Persona*, the prolonged intimacy without time borders leads to the heavy shadow of therapist and patient breaking through the persona of them both. Elisabet's life as an actress is a persona (her social mask), but her prolonged muteness, covering inner violence, is also a persona. The nurse's persona is that of a devoted and loving caretaker. The two women do not truly see one another. Each one is in her nightmarish hidden world and uses the other for her needs. The shadow of envy, competitiveness, arrogance, betrayal, and aggression that burst into the relationship between them is the shadow that had existed from the start in each one's psyche.

Both live in the gap between their successful professional persona, which is a false pretension, and the violent and treacherous shadow feelings they hide. Both have severe problems with their partners and with motherhood. Alma, the nurse, who talks about herself and the pains of her life in a touching open way, breaks her persona mask and confesses her shadow parts.

Elisabet's hidden violence is hinted at in her collapse when playing Electra. In Greek mythology, Electra persuaded her brother Orestes to murder their mother, Clytemnestra, who had murdered their father, Agamemnon. The power of Electra's evil shadow probably led to Elisabet's collapse and silenced her. The all-or-nothing mechanism operates in Elisabet: either an admired actress on stage or absolute muteness and silence. Her violence, transmuted into muteness, becomes masochistic toward herself and sadistic toward Alma, who is meant to take care of her. The picture of the nail stuck on a hand, which opens the film, conveys the sadomasochistic violence already latent in the image of Jesus.

Is Bergman hinting that therapists in the classic psychoanalytic model are violent in their estranged silence with patients? Is this the violent aspect in the therapist who is purportedly a redeemer?

Elisabet, the patient, is a victim of her personality, her violent and treacherous shadow impulses, and the persona that covers them without consciousness and a chance of change. Perhaps Alma's wounds, which opened before Elisabet's, will later turn Alma into Elisabet's wounded healer. We do not find out by the end of the film. Or perhaps Alma—who is supposed to be the carer, who showed trust and spoke openly about herself, opened her wounds, cried, and expressed her direct resentments in speech and physical violence toward Elisabet—will be the one able to go through a healing process in the wake of their encounter.

Several other films focus on the therapist's shadow. In *State of Play*, the patient seduces the therapist into over-involvement to save him from economic disaster. In the end, she is drawn into the criminal world he lives in and falls in love with a criminal who had plotted the entire course from the start to entrap her and exploit her financially. She enters the betting hideout, where the criminals meet, persuaded by her hubris that she has the power to save. She descends to the underworld abyss, unaware of the seductive, deceitful, and destructive power of the dark shadow in the world of crime and in her psyche. Ultimately, she avenges herself on the criminal who seduced her into falling in love with him, robbed her, and artfully exploited her—she kills him. She is thus forced to discover the unethical criminal inside her. The criminal who used her was thus her guide, even if a deluding trickster, who reveals to her the criminal side within herself. At the end of the film, we see her in a light flowery dress, unlike the discreet, grey, bourgeois suit she had worn before and had fitted her professional, restrained, rigid, and distant persona. We see her stealing from another woman a lighter like the one her previous criminal companion had owned. Did the criminal experience awaken her to a more aware primal life, or did it turn her into a crime-addicted petty thief (like the addicts to obsessions she writes about in her book)? No proper integration appears to have taken place in her psyche.

In *Holy Smoke*, the therapist (Harvey Keitel) specializes in the treatment of addicts through an intensive therapeutic program of three consecutive days that he and the patient spend together alone in an isolated place. The patient in this film (Kate Winslet) is a woman addicted to a guru in India, and her parents force her into this withdrawal treatment. The starting point of the therapy in this film is the coercion and aggressive control of the therapist, who enhances his power by pretentiously quoting theories and writers. Finally, the therapist is revealed as lacking any sexual or moral borders. At a moment of total breakdown and weakness, the patient tries to call for help from outside by drawing a circle of stones where she writes, "Help!" calling for rescue from the therapist's shadow and possibly from her own. The breaking down of her defenses peels off from her the power persona that had so far enabled her to withstand the world. She now undresses and remains naked, as one who is ready to confront herself.

This moment involves a potential for change when she turns to the therapist, asking for a hug that conveys a call to be saved from collapse and her need to be contained physically and psychically, mixed with erotic seduction. At this moment, however, the therapist betrays his calling to protect her from herself and from translating her emotional needs into sexuality. He is a charismatic-narcissistic man who responds erotically, setting off the process of their joint decay. He is dragged into a sadomasochistic game with the patient when she dresses him in women's clothes, and he is carried away into a violent dependence on her, almost up to her murder. He had tried to wean her from dependence and submission to the Indian guru but is trying to create in her an identical dependence on him. Her discovery of the evil inside her, which comes to light in her approach toward the therapist, exposes the falseness of the goodness and light that had accompanied her admiration for the guru. But she lacks any option of working through and transforming the shadow revealed to her in her psyche because no therapeutic process is taking place in the encounter with the therapist, only a destructive power struggle. Both the patient and the therapist lack any consciousness from the beginning to the end of the film, and that is the shadow's victory. In this film, the enchanted charisma of the therapist is revealed as a persona hiding his heavy belligerent-narcissistic shadow as a magic charlatan and false messiah. The therapist encounters his own harsh shadow when doing therapy. His persona crumbles while his inadequately built personality falls apart, and he cannot resist being flooded by unconscious shadow powers (as we saw in *Equus*, in *Persona*, and in *Face to Face*).

In the satirical film *Happiness*, we meet miserable, depressive, ridiculous, disturbed, or perverse life in all the characters, including aggressive-murderous dreams in the therapist, who is himself a patient. He is an emotionally detached psychopath with the persona of an ordinary decent guy, and he is a pedophile who is steadily interested in his son's friends and sexually abuses one of them. Another satirical film is *Dr. Pomerantz*, a depressed therapist who seduces depressed patients visiting a public clinic into coming to his private consulting room and, for a reasonable fee, enables them to end their suffering by jumping off his balcony.

In *The Silence of the Lambs*, the sick shadow of the psychiatrist-therapist reaches a dreadful extreme of absolute evil. The story deals with a cannibalistic psychiatrist, a sadistic murderous psychopath who embodies the most terrifying archetypal evil.

One episode of the television series *Colombo* deals with a psychiatrist who seduces a patient. He treats her with hypnosis and gives her drugs that boost hypnosis, all as part of a study and the writing of a book researching the manipulation of human behavior. The situation describes the therapist as a devious man who uses the patient for his narcissistic needs and is uninterested in her welfare. She, however, also uses him as one of the several therapists she goes to bed with.

The situation where she lies on the couch and he administers drugs and does with her as he wishes resembles sexual intercourse. The patient tempts him into an erotic encounter in the beach house she owns with her husband. Her husband is suspicious of her relationship with the therapist and joins them at the beach house, and, in a struggle between the two men, the psychiatrist unintentionally kills him. Colombo immediately guesses what happened. Meanwhile, the psychiatrist hypnotizes the patient and, influenced by his suggestion and by hypnotic drugs, persuades her to jump into the pool from a height of five stories, as she had done in her childhood in front of her father. He means for her to kill herself so she will not denounce him in her police testimony, using information he had received from her to hurt her and save himself. The psychiatrist is a young, handsome, elegant man with a charismatic persona who is slippery, manipulative, characterized by psychopathic features, and abuses the therapeutic transference. The detective is his antithesis: he has no interest in a professional and individual persona, only in the truth. He dresses carelessly and seems crude, associative, and unfocused. But he, so we learn, is smarter and more humane.

The therapist's shadow revealed in these films is hard and frightening. This hard shadow, bordering on evil, is presented in most films without an option of therapeutic transformation. These films seem to condemn the therapist's shadow when they leave the entire situation at an impasse.

Concern with the hard shadow of therapists and patients is perhaps sharper in cinema due to its interest in dramatization, primal impulses, and extreme emotions that appeal to spectators. Erich Neumann discusses the dark allure of evil and the shadow and warns against the fascination with psychopathology and evil itself (1969, 84). Neumann's comments also fit the shadow revealed in films dealing with therapist-patient relationships and with psychotherapy.

The cinematic description of the therapist's heavy and pathological shadow in several films evokes many questions. It merits note that the harsh shadow of the murderous therapist had already appeared in two German silent films released in the interwar period. In *The Cabinet of Dr. Caligari* (1920) directed by Robert Wiene, one of the most famous films of the time, Caligari is the director of the local psychiatric hospital obsessed with the story of a previous Dr. Caligari, who had used a somnambulant patient to murder people. After Caligari breaks down and reveals his madness, he is hospitalized. We then learn, however, that this story had been a patient's delusion, and Caligari had been his therapist. After the patient's delusions are exposed, Caligari proclaims he will now be able to cure him. The spectators, however, do not know whether Caligari is a murderous psychopath or a psychiatrist trying to cure a patient who, in his delusions, identifies him as a murderer.

The second film, *The Last Will of Dr. Mabuse* (1933), was directed by Fritz Lang and released when Hitler was already in power. In this film, the director of a psychiatric institution also sends people to kill in his name, unable to control his murderous impulse. In both films, it is impossible to separate delusion from reality. In *From Caligari to Hitler*, Siegfried Kracauer suggests that Caligari is a premonition of Hitler in his use of hypnotic power, the "manipulation of the soul which Hitler was the first to practice on a gigantic scale" (Kracauer 2004, 73).

Trust in Therapy

In many films, cinema conveys distrust of therapy. The essential impediment to trust is the patients' unconscious anxiety about their own shadow, about the shadow and the deep sickness and perversion possibly hiding in the therapist's psyche behind the professional persona, or perhaps about the sickness and perversion hiding in everyone's psyche, as in their own, and projected onto the therapist.

In *Man Facing Southeast*, Rantés (the patient) says: "I don't believe that anyone cares about anyone on this planet," even though he does care about others. He cannot trust anyone, not even the therapist, who, at the end of the film, indeed shows that he is untrustworthy. In *Holy Smoke*, the therapist asks the patient: "What harm will come to your soul if you entrust it to the wrong person?" Several films convey patients' suspicions about the therapists' ability to love. In *Good Will Hunting*, the boy tells the therapist—"Your wife must have left you for a lover." The patient in *Don Juan DeMarco* says to the therapist—"What do you know about great love?" and the young patient in *Equus* says to the therapist about his wife, "I bet you never touch her." The patient's hidden question to the therapist is—Do you know how to love? Do you deserve love? Could you love me? Can you be trusted? Will you leave me and betray me?

But what happens when the therapist no longer trusts? "What do I do in the consulting room, who has answers? I cannot find my place," says the therapist in *Equus*. *K-Pax* and *Man Facing Southeast* also show the therapists' doubts about the possibility of therapeutic assistance and expose their helplessness rather than the trust in their profession, which should be guiding them. These therapists, who have many problems, hold a radical either-or view: primal psychosis or a banal life. They are unaware of the option of an enriching dialogue with the unconscious and a true interpersonal relationship with themselves and the patient.

The therapist in *Equus* tells the sleeping patient: "I'm lying to you. He [Equus] won't really go that easily. Just clap away from you like a nice old nag. Oh, no! When Equus leaves—if he leaves at all—it will be with your intestines in his teeth. And I don't stock replacements." Rantés' therapist wonders: "How will he react if I put my hand on his? It will be a kind and tender gesture, which he so much needs, but he cannot expect that from me, and neither can I, wretched idiot. He has not yet understood—that is his punishment, this long suffering. You will not be saved, my friend. Welcome to hell." Such a therapist is indeed unable to help.

Mistrust of the therapist in cinema reflects many people's mistrust of therapy. Cinema appears to be conveying here the known fear of many people from the psyche and from psychotherapy, which leads many to say they do not believe in therapy and to describe therapists and the therapist-patient relationship in negative terms. The catch is that cinema describes therapy as a cathartic dramatic event or a hypnotic trance with fast results. It does not address the patience required in therapy to go through a prolonged process of change, which includes many hours of dealing with day-to-day materials. The mistrust conveyed in cinema also reflects the general public's problematic image of therapy and the therapist, hence the significance of films describing the good healer, since they describe therapeutic success as resulting from love, commitment, and human and professional skills. These positive films convey the wish and the belief that therapy will accomplish its mission to heal the human psyche. The cinematic narrative becomes part of psychotherapy's theories-beliefs about life as leading to the integration of identity, the repair of fractures, the healing of wounds, and the realization of the self and parallels redemption theories that believe in mending a broken world and in the sparks in individual and collective life.

Note

1 Esther Harding distinguishes the dark shadow (the negative repressed aspects of the psyche) from the bright shadow (repressed positive aspects) (Harding 1970, 79). My focus in this book is on the usual meaning of this concept—a dark negative shadow.

References

Agnon, S. Y. (1985) *A Simple Story*, trans. Hillel Halkin (New York: Schocken Books).
Amado Lévy-Valensi, Eliane (1971) *Les voies et les pièges de la psychanalyse* (Paris: Éditions Universitaires).
Avshalom, Leah (2018) "Collapsing When Attacked by the Personal Self: On Ingmar Bergman's Film *Face to Face*" [Heb] http://www.Jung-Israel.org
Campbell, Joseph (1988) *The Power of Myth* (New York: Doubleday).
Claudel, Philippe (2009) *Brodeck's Report*, trans. John Cullen (London: Quercus).
Freud, Sigmund (1964) "Analysis Terminable and Interminable." In *The Standard Edition of the Complete Psychological Works of Sigmund Freud*, trans. James Strachey (London: Hogarth Press).
Guggenbühl-Craig, Adolf (1971) *Power in the Helping Professions* (New York: Spring).
Harding, Esther M. (1970) *The I and the Not-I: A Study in the Development of Consciousness* (Princeton, NJ: Princeton University Press).
Jung, C. G. (1978) *Aion, C. W. 9*, Part II, trans. R. F. C. Hull (Princeton, NJ: Princeton University Press).
Kracauer, Siegfried (2004) *From Caligari to Hitler: A Psychological History of the German Film* (Princeton, NJ: Princeton University Press).
Laing, R. D. and Aaron Esterson (1970) *Sanity, Madness, and the Family: Families of Schizophrenics* (Harmondsworth: Penguin).
Lieblich, Maty (2009) *At the Edge of Ego* (Jerusalem: Keter) [Heb].
Lindner, Robert (1962) *The Fifty-Minute Hour: A Collection of True Psychoanalytic Tales* (London: Transworld).
Neumann, Erich (1969) *Depth Psychology and a New Ethic*, trans. Eugene Rolfe (London: Hodder and Stoughton).
Sexton, Anne (1981) "Letters for Dr. Y." In *The Complete Poems*, ed. Linda Gray Sexton (Boston: Houghton Mifflin).
Schwartz-Salant, Nathan (1998) *The Mystery of Human Relationship: Alchemy and the Transformation of the Self* (London: Routledge).
Toder-Goldin, Miki (2012) "The Unheard Cry for Money." *Sihot/Dialogue: Israel Journal of Psychotherapy* 26 (3): 232–241 [Heb].
Yalom, Irvin D. (2002) *The Gift of Therapy: An Open Letter to a New Generation of Therapists and Their Patients* (New York: Harper).

Chapter 5

Cinema as a "Chief Supervisor" for Therapists

The American Psychological Association (APA) cooperated with film producers seeking to change the representation of therapists in the problematic terms endorsed in most films. Therapeutic norms are breached even in films that show therapists at their best. Too many films show therapists as even more disturbed than their patients and committing serious and dangerous ethical offenses. The APA noted that therapy is portrayed in dramatic terms and confused with hypnosis, and films present a shallow, ambitious, or caricaturist description of therapists. They were also bothered, however, by the representation of therapists as helpful and loving while violating professional norms and also as extremely successful, a description that could lead spectators to a distorted model of the therapist's work.

Contrary to the APA's approach, I suggest that therapists should approach films as a supervisor—at times severe and at times humoristic and satirical—who views both patient and therapist from an Archimedean meta-standpoint. My concern here is to understand why cinema portrays therapists and therapist-patient relationships as it does—what is the meaning and purpose of this depiction? In other words, what should we learn from cinema? If we take cinema as a collective dream, let us ask ourselves—what does this dream want from us?

At times, the omniscient standpoint offered in films permits a more comprehensive vision than that available to supervisors of therapists in reality. The supervisor sees what happens in the therapy only through the eyes of the supervised trainee. Indeed, the only place where supervisors can see the therapy beyond the trainee's subjective reporting of it is in the encounter with the patient's dreams. The cinema dealing with psychotherapy is thus a kind of model patient and a chief supervisor teaching us about ourselves.

The cinema's view of therapist-patient relations is also the way that transference and countertransference view therapy and includes the ways therapists and patients view one another across a broad range of objective and subjective perceptions, both accurate and distorted. Films can be the "patients" that will help therapists correct therapeutic errors. They show the qualities of suitable therapists and their unresolved problems, thereby serving as their instructors and therapists.

Glen Gabbard recounts that a patient who had just seen the film *Ordinary People* (1980) asked him to hug her as the psychologist had hugged the suicidal patient in the film, hoping that she could be helped as the patient in the film had been. Gabbard, however, noted that films differ from reality and therapy relies on words (Gabbard and Gabbard, 1989). I remember how touched I myself was by the warmth and humanity of that cinematic hug but my training led me to think, just like Gabbard, that the breaking of boundaries was wrong and unprofessional. Psychotherapy has since gone through many changes. One can understand Gabbard's embarrassment at being asked for a hug when the need and the capacity to hug that particular patient were not evoked in him. And yet, today, Gabbard's response appears condescending, short on empathy, and lacking proper attention to the messages of cinema.

At first glance, the striking fact about these films is that, almost without exception, they are based on therapist-patient relations that breach the borders of orthodox therapy. In that sense, these films turn cinema into a collective dream of transference, fulfilling the patient's wish for closer, friendlier, warmer, more intimate, loving, and involved relationships with the therapist. As noted, these wishes sometimes reflect a need for an enveloping motherly hug and a primary connectedness that knows no boundaries.

Some films convey the patient's fantasy that the therapist will need him (due to her failings or wounds), and he will then become the center of the therapist's world. In practice, the yearning to become the therapist's "chosen" patient is realized in all films through the script's focus on one personal story. The narrative that emerges shows the therapist, throughout the film, exclusively concerned with a single patient. Usually, we do not see therapists meeting with other patients or other aspects of their private life, but only those touching directly on the treatment of the specific patient. In other words, the cinema's narrative creates a situation of chosen patient and involved therapist.

Stephen Mitchell (1993) deals with the dilemma of how far to satisfy the patient's wishes by incorporating a dimension of mutuality into the therapeutic relationship. Will fulfilling the patient's wishes prove beneficial or the opposite? "The very nature of the analytic process necessitates that the analyst fails to meet all the patient's desires. The asymmetry of the analytic relationship is painful, inevitably for the analysand, often for the analyst" (Mitchell 1993, 194–195). Mitchell does not rule out gratifying some of the patient's wishes, just not all of them. "What is most crucial is neither gratification nor frustration [of the patient's wishes], but the process of negotiation itself" (ibid., 196).

We might view the wishes conveyed by these films as a justified refusal to accept the orthodox boundaries of psychotherapy, particularly of psychoanalysis, which imposes distance and a therapist-dominated hierarchy that perpetuates the patients' estrangement. The many films that rejected these alienating boundaries, which were typical of the early decades of psychoanalysis and psychotherapy, may have contributed to changing them. These rigid boundaries pretended to invest therapists with anonymity and neutrality, turning them, as it were, into a white screen and a mirror that merely reflects projections, and these films may have helped the current intersubjective approach to emerge.

In the early days of psychoanalysis and psychotherapy, fixed rules defined the asymmetric distance in the consulting room. The current relational and intersubjective approach has introduced flexibility and a new attentiveness to the patient's needs. Psychoanalyst Patrick Casement emphasizes that we must learn from the patient. When a patient tries to persuade the analyst to deviate from the classic technique (especially one who rigidly adheres to it), the request should not invariably be taken as seductive or manipulative. The patient may be seeking a different balance in the relationship, and this balance is an important factor (Casement 1985). Irvin Yalom (2002) goes even further. He urges therapists not to fear loving their patients, touching, hugging, and caressing them (within limits). The patient's desire, after all, is no different from that of the therapist's—to be loved by them. Yoel Hoffmann (2010), writing from the viewpoint of the patient, relates to therapists who refrain from any closeness while they do need a hug:

> If only the New Year would bring about a condition in which their souls would melt (as one melts lead) into the great form of the soul of the world, and there'd no longer be any separation between their eyes (behind glasses) and the eyes of the people they're looking into. And that the rule against hugging others might be dropped, and, above all, that someone would hug them.
>
> Because there is no loneliness greater than that of the psychologist. His thought is always doubled, as he's forced to consider thought upon thought, and sometimes thought upon thought upon thought.
>
> (152)
>
> This is also the answer to the Zen riddle about the sound of the one hand, and also the answer to the torments that Freud says a person endures. That is, that someone should touch someone, and so forth.
>
> (95)

In this light, the writing of these scripts and their execution in films may be attempts to wrest control from the orthodox therapeutic narrative in order to demolish it, attacking the conventionally accepted links between patient and therapist (Bion 1959). Alternatively, these scripts attempt to reshape the therapeutic narrative, dictate it, and "correct" it.

Belittling the therapist and changing the narrative is also an Oedipal rebellion against the therapist as an all-knowing, controlling parent who lays down the rules (in the consulting room) and charges for it. Often, the film seems intent on depriving the therapist of his special, exalted status as the bearer of archetypal projections—guide, repository of supreme knowledge and vision, possessor of high wisdom (the wise elder), omnipotent (magician), redeemer, and healer. Such films do not only set out to divest the therapist of this screen of idealization—an initial admiration important in the therapist-patient relationship—but also to draw attention to the therapist's shadow, exposing the vulnerability of therapists draping themselves in the mantle of the healer persona and at times trapped in the hubris of their professionalism. The aim is to reveal the therapists' weaknesses, flaws, and their frequently being no more than a mirror image of the patient. In that sense, the cinema is our therapist and helps us to refrain from professional self-aggrandizement.

But cinema goes too far. The strong need for closeness, and the anger at its frustration in reality due to therapeutic boundaries, forces the cinematic therapist to satisfy these needs. Cinema goes beyond voicing a desire—it creates narratives that fulfill it. We could say that cinema is itself the patient seducing the therapist into breaching the time and place boundaries of the consulting room—from a hand touch to an embrace, from empathic involvement to identification and blended identities, even as far as overpowering symbiosis and erotic fulfillment, or some other form of exploitation. Acting as the patient's agent, cinema tempts the therapist into ever closer entanglement to the edge of a perilous and forbidden surrender.

Sexual relations with the therapist in cinema fulfil a taboo-breaking fantasy of forbidden sexuality between therapist and patient, which also extends to the taboo on child-parent incest (Stein, 1973). Breaking such an absolute prohibition is exciting, arousing a mixture of fear and deep desires, and cinema wants its spectators to be excited. Exposing in films what happens in the consulting room breaks the taboo of therapeutic confidentiality, although, in the era of television reality series, this taboo has already been breached.

Cinema, however, not only seduces therapists into breaking boundaries but also punishes them for not resisting the temptation to do so. It thereby resembles the patient testing whether the therapist will cope with the experiences, the challenges, the expectations, and the temptations he sets before her and then "punishes" her for failing to do so by labeling the therapist as hopelessly disturbed. Thus, the patient figuratively destroys the therapist and takes revenge on her for his needing her, for failing to meet the patient's high expectations of precise empathic attunement, for failing to bestow the total primary involvement that many patients long for, and for failing to fit the archetypal idealized projections. This belittling and disparaging could also be intended to reduce the patient's envy of the therapist and the inferiority feelings accompanying the previous idealization. Once the chosen and admired one, the therapist is now exposed to the spectators as someone leading a trivial life, mentally ill or even criminal, destroyed while attempting to cure others.

In many films, this reviling of the therapist appears to convey feelings of hostility transferred from a primary aggression against parents or some other authority figure. In the Israeli television series *In Therapy* (2005), this aggressive deriding dimension is two-faced. On the one hand, they showed a reasonable therapist, well-intentioned and professionally skilled, who destructively crosses erotic boundaries. On the other, the filmmakers showed the audience the private life of the actor playing the therapist, the behind-the-scenes Assi Dayan (the notoriously wild-living son of the famous general, Moshe Dayan), in all his many failings. A dual shaming was thus displayed, seemingly suggesting that is what therapists are really like away from the consulting room, while Assi Dayan is not a therapist but an actor exposed in his sad decline.

Films showing the therapist as exploiter, psychopath, criminal, or mentally ill throw out the baby with the bathwater, as if eliminating the therapist's power in the cinema removes the need for therapy. Abel is thus murdered without fulfilling the wish—attaining the love of God-father-mother-therapist.

Ingmar Bergman's films seem free of this fierce stance against therapists. He deals with insanity and its hazards, considering whether being helped by another is possible. His films depict a descent into a psychic chasm holding a potential for both healing and madness. In *Through a Glass Darkly* (1961), a girl goes on holiday with her family, but their incapacity to give her love and support leads to a mental breakdown that culminates in a psychotic episode. The film describes the entry into a psychotic process but without a move toward healing. In *Persona* and *Face to Face*, Bergman shows people lacking any training acting as therapists. It is unclear whether his concern as an artist is to record and show the suffering in the encounter with the psyche's dark depths, regardless of its outcome, or whether he believes in the healing resulting from this process since neither film clarifies the result of this journey into the depths. Bergman may be offering a concealed critique of the therapeutic profession, perhaps thinking that it lacks the proper tools to treat people and that the encounter with the shadow and the other torments of the soul can be entrusted to anyone capable of devoted therapeutic loving. What beguiles him is the journey itself and the very process of the psyche's disintegration. Bergman is fascinated with the suffering and the compassion that can confront and contain it. He does not seem to believe in the recurrent happy-end Hollywood message (found in *Prince of Tides, Good Will Hunting, Ordinary People, The Three Faces of Eve, David and Lisa, Spellbound, Zelig, Intimate Strangers, Marnie*, and *Don Juan de Marco*). He knows that the descent to the depths is only the beginning of a long journey and is seemingly uninterested in—or perhaps doubtful about—the healing-integration process that is supposed to follow. The cinematic look sees the depths of the psyche as gripping and dramatic raw material or as an absorbing riddle awaiting solution, and is not necessarily driven by the concern to alleviate psychic anguish. Bergman's narrative, stating that we do not need an experienced therapist to accompany us in the descent to the psychic underworld, is mistaken. A century of psychotherapeutic experience attests that this journey is of necessity long and that professional accompaniment is indispensable. Goodwill, containment, and a warm hug will not suffice.

Films about psychotherapy show the range of archetypical processes, the many complexes at work in therapy and therapist-patient relations, and the many reflections of these relations in cinema. In Roberto Calasso's terms when speaking about Greek mythology, I would say that these films encompass all the versions of the therapeutic myth, which are as a "maze of mirrors in a hall deep in the sea" (an image in a dream of one of my patients). The image implies that in the depths of the unconscious are mirrors that reflect, miniaturize, magnify, or distort what is reflected in them. Looking at these mirrors from above will reveal a kaleidoscope resolving the entire systemic riddle into a single composite picture. Cinema does not explain the meaning or the solution of the riddle, only the interrelations between the mirrors' parts.

Shedding the Mask of the Persona

Patients sometimes share their insights about their therapists with them. Rantés, for example, in *Man Facing Southeast,* tells his therapist: "You're great but unhappy. You know that, but you don't care." Don Juan de Marco comments: "You're as great a lover as me, even if you've lost your way." The patient in *K-Pax*, noting the distance maintained by his therapist, advises him to relate to his children.

Many patients, like those in *Man Facing Southeast* and *K-Pax*, possess a superpowered sight—an ability to penetrate their therapist's mask. As the therapist says to the patient calling himself Don Juan de Marco, "You, my friend, have seen through all my masks." After his young patient tells him some home truths about his barren married life, the therapist in *Equus* says: "Advanced neurotics can be dazzling at that game. They aim unswervingly at your area of maximum vulnerability."

And here is an example from my practice: A young and special girl I treated a long time ago for three years took an interest in me and saw me as if she had subliminal vision. One day she asked: "Ruth, what about you, has life only been good? No pain? Surely there was pain. And how was it with your parents?"

Later, she wrote a kind of story about me: "Ruth would like to go on holiday to the seaside instead of being a psychologist and getting tired. She wants to see kites and butterflies. She wants lots of potted plants around. Ruth really wants to step into the sea and live in a cave by the sea, and she likes all sorts of shapes. She wants to go back to childhood and climb trees. What they didn't allow her to do as a child."

Like those patients on the border between sanity and madness, cinema has high-powered vision. It affords us a reflection of ourselves. It sees through the masks of the therapeutic persona, and gives us insights.

Cinema looks down on therapists condescendingly, critically, and maliciously reproving, but at times lovingly and admiringly, with compassion or humor. All this, as Elisabet, the patient, says in *Persona*, "for the right side of the psyche to come out," and to meet "the undiscovered self," like the title of the book that Marnie's husband urges her to read.

All patients confront therapists with questions about themselves, asking how they cope with their own problems when encountering them in the patient. These questions are meant to lead the therapist to self-awareness.

In the same way, the cinematic camera shows the "rear window" of both patient and therapist, with the therapist emerging as patient and the patient as therapist given that it is often the patient (in cinema and in reality) who, for good or ill, treats the therapist. Patients do this through the effect of their personality on the therapist, through their complexes, which compel therapists to see like complexes in themselves, through their inhibitions or lack of them, and through their openness or lack of it to the unconscious, to imagination, to the irrational and amoral in the world. Cinema shows the therapist's unsolved problems as the mirror image of the patient so that, in effect, it asks—who is the patient here, who is treating who, and whose treatment are we watching?

The cinema screen is like a mirror set up in front of us, the therapists. At times, it is a narcissistic mirror reflecting our beauty or the ideal of successful therapy (*David and Lisa, Sybil, Good Will Hunting, Ordinary People*). At other times, it is a mirror compelling us to see ourselves as we are—good and dedicated but also capable of hurting and being hurt, disabled, limping, and even ugly. The cinematic vision forces us to see the nakedness under the emperor's robes of the therapist, who is sometimes led astray by the weavers of our professional persona. Cinema exposes the shadows and the weaknesses that the mask of the therapeutic persona keeps under wraps—the grandiose, arrogant stance, omniscient, inflated with self-importance, driven by narcissistic needs. Cinema is a mirror pushing to self-criticism and self-awareness, shattering the persona and the self-deception of the one wearing it and the one looking at it. Smashing the narcissistic looking-glass allows us to dive through the shards into the waters of the swamp, where we will encounter the depths of our therapeutic psyche and its shadows.

Early psychoanalysis shaped the persona of the therapist as one that sees—from a distance— but is not seen. Greek mythology recounts how Perseus, in order to defeat the Medusa, was gifted by Hades, god of the underworld, with a helmet of darkness that made him invisible. When therapists appear in this seeing invisible persona, patients will know nothing about them, their life, and their feelings during the therapy. They will thus be shielded from emotional exposure and vulnerability and use their role as voyeurs who see without being seen.

Greek mythology tells us about Echo. She falls in love with Narcissus (Netzer 2011, 194–195), who is unable to love and relate to the other. In effect, he cannot "see" her and, ultimately, she fades away into bodilessness, her voice all that is left to her. Does not the therapist choose to be like Echo, seeing and unseen, in order to enable the patient to briefly be Narcissus, seeing only himself and relating to his legitimate narcissistic needs? Sometimes this is what the patient needs, but sometimes the therapist pays a price for doing this. If I turn into another's echo and annul my own self vis-à-vis the other, I may become invisible even to myself because I do not see my own needs. Echo suffers from being only a voice since she can only repeat Narcissus' words and not utter a word of her own. Therapists are liable to find themselves trapped in what I call the Echo complex, when their motivation to treat draws too largely on the need to please the other while neglecting their own needs. The Echo complex is, in fact, a narcissistic disorder in reverse, afflicting those who are not allowed to live their own narcissistic needs, take care of themselves, and preserve their well-being, having lent their needs to the other. This complex may also encourage the patient's aggressive behavior toward the therapist. When liberated from it, however, the therapist learns to protect himself and show the patient the offensive aspect of her behavior.

Today we know that this seeing and unseen persona is a therapist's illusion. The persona of invisibility is quite implausible. Many patients identify the therapist's feelings and even dream about the therapist's supposedly concealed emotional state and reactions. Postmodern intersubjective therapists are aware that they are not invisible. Indeed, they are interested in occasionally showing themselves so that an authentic rather than only a projective relationship can be established with the patient.

The Narcissus myth recounts that, having spent so much time gazing at his reflection in a pool, Narcissus fell into it and drowned. Yet, some say that Narcissus fell and drowned in the pool hoping to break through the beautiful image reflected in the water—to plunge into his true depths, inspired by the drive to self-knowledge. Joyce McDougall says that Narcissus implores us to rescue him (1989, 115). It was only for lack of other means of confronting himself that his drive to self-knowledge beyond what his enchanting reflection was telling him brought him to disaster. Fear of shedding one's mask, then, is justified. That is the story of the therapist in *Equus*. At first, Echo-like, he is rigid, distant, and detached from the patient because removing the mask, as described in his dream, means dismissing the persona of the skilled therapist and exposing his violent and alienated shadow. He cannot cope with that.

Equus, to my mind, is the most profound of all the films in its insights and in the complexity of the characters, which is not surprising given that the film is based on Peter Shaffer's play. The therapist, conscious of his difficulties and wounds following the encounter with the boy, undergoes a slight change. The rigid, remote, and controlling therapist we encounter at the film's beginning becomes more approachable. His voice softens, he sits next to the boy rather than across him during their conversations, and he even speaks about himself. The therapist is indeed breaching accepted consulting-room boundaries, but a process is also unfolding whereby the therapist's awareness of his own wounds enables him to descend from a patronizing position of authority to one of modesty and fellowship. Later, however, having shed the mask of defenses, he comes too close, enters the patient's psychotic bath, and stays there. He plunges into the hell-bath of his own self, melding with the boy's inner world. For the therapist in *Equus*, who admires the boy's cult of the horse, the horse becomes the voice of the depths of his soul, the voice, as it were, of the self.

> I can hear the creature's voice [Equus]. It's calling me out of the black cave of the Psyche. . . . He opens his great square teeth, and says "Why? . . . Why Me? . . . Why—ultimately—Me? . . . Do you really imagine you can account for Me? Totally, infallibly, inevitably account for Me? . . . Of course I've stared at such images before. Or been stared at by them, whichever way you look at it. And weirdly often now with me the feeling is that *they* are staring at *us*—that in some quite palpable way they precede us . . . this one is the most alarming yet. It asks questions I've avoided all my professional life."
>
> (63–64)

As a narcissist, he has no empathy for the boy or for himself and, therefore, cannot return from hell and be healed.

The patient who presents himself as Don Juan asks the therapist: "How would you feel if they took your mask away?" This is the anxious question of the cinematic patient who fears his psyche will be invaded, he will be prematurely deprived of his image, his persona, and his defenses, and he will be improperly treated.

The therapist in *Don Juan* says that removing the patient's mask will lead him to become irreversibly disturbed. In the end, however, the patient gives up his Don Juan mask and reveals who he is. Both *Equus* and *Don Juan* speak of a concrete object placed over the face symbolizing the psychic mask.

The masks of the therapist and the patient resonate against each other. In both films, the therapists' need to tear off their professional masks is identical to their felt need to escape the triviality of their existence.

The discussion of the two Bergman films, *Persona* and *Face to Face*, pointed to the tension between the mask of the persona and the shadow and wound concealed underneath it. The collapse of the therapist-patient persona is part of the broader collapse of boundaries and the mixing of their identities. Both films show the persona crumbling before a more fitting one has been built since the integrative self that would enable this building is yet to evolve.

Removing masks, however, does not necessarily imply that the therapist will talk about himself. Mainly, it means that the therapist, rather than identifying with his professional mask, will live the authentic truth of his selfhood and, accordingly, will be present with full empathy and with his inner truth in the therapeutic encounter.

Taking off the mask to draw closer to the patient is akin to undressing to enter the shared alchemical bath (Jung 1983, 85–96). It is also reminiscent of the Sumerian myth of Inanna, the proud queen who goes down to the underworld to meet her sister, who is mourning her husband. The queen is commanded to remove every badge of royalty and shed every clothing item until completely naked. Only due to the empathy and compassion that her emissaries show for her sister's suffering is she allowed to leave the underworld.

The words "mask" and "screen" share a linguistic root in Hebrew, and in English too, "to mask" and "to screen" can have similar meanings. The cinema screen is a mask through which we therapists seek to remove our own masks. The persona mask is also meant to screen the individual's intimate privacy from others and protect one's borders from encroachment by the world. At times, however, the mask becomes an inner screen, hiding from the person her wounds, her self, and her inner child.

The Inner Child

Fernando Pessoa writes: "I took off the mask and looked in the mirror./ I was the same child I was years ago./ I hadn't changed at all" (Pessoa 2006, 9 August 1934).

Removing the mask allows access to the inner child, a vulnerable child and yet one who sees the truth and for whom truth comes first and last, because the child is among the symbols of the true self. To join hands with our true self, we must join hands with our psyche's inner child. The therapist in *Equus* says he cuts parts of the children's personality, viewing their analysis as their sacrificial death. Yet, what he fears is that he has long ago sacrificed his inner child, who is the authentic symbol of the self and of renewal in the life he has renounced. The motif of the child features in several films, which should come as no surprise since many of them deal with the evolvement and the birth of the true identity and true self of the patient and, sometimes, also of the therapist.

The psyche's complexity comes forth in *Persona* through the metaphor of the child. Alma, the nurse-therapist, aborts the child she is carrying, and Elisabet, the patient, rips up the picture of the suffering child and is incapable of mothering her own child. In *Julie Walking Home*, the psyche's development comes forth in Julie's return to her husband and in her pregnancy. In *The Soul Keeper*, Sabina becomes a healer and develops methods for treating children. We see her healing a child who has, till then, sat paralyzed and dumb, the only survivor of the children's home she had set up. In *Man Facing Southeast*, the patient connects with his therapist's children, as in Jesus' dictum: "Truly, I say to you, unless you turn and become like children, you will never enter the kingdom of heaven" (Matthew 18:3).

The Anima

Behind the mask is also the anima. To sustain a proper dialogue with the depths of their unconscious and their psyche, therapists need the anima—the feminine-emotional-intuitive aspect of the psyche concerned with human relations and connection with the inner world. The anima is the emotional potential for empathy, compassion, and love that therapists will feel toward themselves and the patient.

Several films track a therapist's ability to feel empathy for their patient's psyche. As Rantés, the patient in *Man Facing Southeast*, says to his doctor: "I don't want you to treat me. I want you to understand me." He is looking for empathic understanding—being together while containing and accepting the patient.

In Hitchcock's *Rear Window*, the one who actively breaks into the apartment where the crime occurs is the detective's girlfriend, who represents his anima. It is impossible to be a therapist without the anima, which provides access to the truth, in the emotional sense, about the patient's psyche. The photographer-detective's masculine-logical perception of the truth does not suffice. This dynamic is also present in *Equus* and *Man Facing Southeast*, where the therapists are detached from relations with women and the anima and find it hard to empathize with their patients.

It is not maternal love but the anima that is the basis for therapy and proper therapeutic love. Men tend to project the anima onto women and are attracted to women who can connect them to the anima in their psyche. But connecting to the feminine element is a prolonged internal process that cannot be realized through a relationship with one concrete woman. Many infatuations, however, including therapeutic ones, are driven by the attraction to the anima symbolized by the patient or the therapist, potentially leading to the collapse of erotic boundaries and the breach of therapeutic limits.

Sabina in *The Soul Keeper* is Jung's anima, Julie is the anima of her son's healer in *Julie Walking Home*, the patient is the therapist's anima in *Intimate Strangers*, and Lisa is David's anima.

In *Equus*, the therapist initially adopts an aggressive, manipulative approach, using hypnosis to enter the boy's psyche before gradually building up his patient's psychic forces. He acts as the knife he uses in his dream to sacrifice the boys because he lacks the emotional warmth of the anima in his psyche, detached from his anima as he is from his wife. Over the course of a barren dialog with a woman friend he attempts and fails to connect to his anima. Sensing the boy's distress, the friend attempts to act as his anima and explain the boy's anguish, but she cannot surmount the wall of his alienation.

In *Equus* and *Man Facing Southeast*, the therapists' difficulty connecting to women expresses the problem of connecting to the depths of their own psyche, hence their failure to connect emotionally with patients and help them. Both these films expose the fear that some therapists live shallow inauthentic lives, detached from their anima and the depths of their souls. The therapist in *Equus* admits to the banality of his existence: "I shrank and chose to live my life pale and provincial, because I'm a coward." Don Juan's therapist makes a like admission to his wife: "We have sacrificed our lives on the altar of mediocrity. What happened to our divine fire?" And Don Juan tells him: "My perfect world is no less real than your world. Only in my world can you breathe . . . I know why you need me, for a blood transfusion because your blood has turned to dust and blocked up your heart. Your need for reality will stifle you until your life just fades away."

In *Man Facing Southeast* too the therapist is a lonely man without real relationships with women. Like Orpheus, he withdraws into his music and does not turn his longing to a concrete woman and, contrary to his patient, Rantés, does not use his music to draw closer to or help his patients. His impossible infatuation with Rantés' friend and sister, Beatriz, is his futile attempt to connect to the anima. Through his love for her, he tries to connect to the emotional element in his psyche and to the spiritual, human, and moral dimension of Rantés, her brother. The name Beatriz sends us to Beatrice, Dante's beloved and guide in the *Divina Commedia*. Dante's first guide is Virgil, but then Virgil leaves him, and the parting from him resembles leaving a therapist. Beatrice, who takes Virgil's place as a guide, represents revelation and intuition, according to Rollo May (1991, 163). May interprets Dante as arguing that reason can guide us so far but, to reach higher, intuition—a female principle— is needed. In Jungian terminology, Beatrice is anima. In psychotherapy, too, we need to be guided not only by the masculine-logical principle, used chiefly for interpretation, but also by the feminine principle, which has recourse mainly to feelings, intuition, and the connection to the unconscious. Psychotherapy has, with time, shifted its emphasis from the male to the female principle. Having begun its course relying on the father principle— interpretation, emotional distance, uncompromising principles—it moved on to the mother principle—the containing and transformative mother who enables development—and thence to the female principle, the anima, derived from the mother and comprising empathy, containment, attention, presence, compassion, intuition, and a connection to the depths of the psyche.

Interpretation v. Emotional Experience

Most films about therapists and patients do not deal with psychological interpretations but strive for the experiential truth of repressed feelings, given that cinema is not a medium of rational insights but rather of emotional and sensual experiences. Hence, it seeks the emotional truth that is the true story behind the symptom, the truth behind the persona of therapist and patient, the truth behind the colorless, banal, and tamed life, the truth that is a corrective experience. In addition to positive feelings, cinema looks for the experiential truth expressed in the catharsis of painful emotions from the past and the painful feelings that arise in the therapist-patient relationship.

Some of the films discussed revolved around the therapist-detective genre and hinge on the uncovering of a repressed truth that will provide the great redeeming insight. But even in them, it is the released emotional experience, not the new interpretation, that is described as healing the psyche. One example is *Intimate Strangers*, where the "therapy" succeeds only by dint of the containment and attention of a "therapist" who never trained to be one.

I would venture that therapy films preceded psychotherapy itself in favoring the emotional-experiential aspect over interpretation. Yalom notes: "Therapists place a far higher value than patients on interpretation and insight" (2002, 174). He holds that intellectual insight has no importance, and what matters is the very process of the search for it: "Patients bask in the attention paid to the most minute details of their life, and the therapist is entranced by the process of solving the riddle of a life. The beauty of it is that it keeps patient and therapist tightly connected while the real agent of change — the therapeutic relationship — is germinating" (ibid., 176). Many of the interpretations are directly concerned with the therapist-patient relationship. Yalom notes that patients remember the gestures and conduct of the therapist towards them and how the therapist-patient relationship felt, not intellectual interpretations. This approach matches the current trend in psychoanalysis and psychotherapy, emphasizing the subjective presence of therapist and patient: "The core is the mode of the therapist's presence and involvement, not the interpretation as a final product" (Lazar 2003, 134).

Dreams in Films About Psychotherapy

Cinema's lack of interest in interpretation in general extends to the interpretation of dreams. Its focus is instead on therapist-patient relationships. Ruth Sarig writes: "Every film looks like a dream or could have been a dream but, surprisingly, dreams seldom appear in films" (2008). Although psychotherapy has dealt with the interpretation of dreams since the days of Freud, even films that deal with psychotherapy hardly do so. Only six of the films mentioned here include a dream; in two, it is the therapist's dream. In *David and Lisa*, the dream about the threatening clock hands exposes the young man's aggression and fears. In S*pellbound*, the dream of the amnesiac patient, a doctor, is a critical element of the therapy and the narrative of the entire film, when the detective's pursuit of the dream's meaning overlaps the detective's pursuit of the lost memory and the meaning of the guilt. The detective inquiry, the psychic inquiry, and the dream inquiry join together. In *Equus*, the dream is the therapist's, revealing his doubts about himself and his professional skills. In *Happiness*, the dreams are the therapist's, who is also a patient. In *Face to Face*, the female psychiatrist who suffers a psychotic breakdown has four bleak dreams describing her life's hardships. In *Marnie*, the "patient" has nightmares related to her past. In these films, the dream presents the essence of the dreamer's problem and is like the first dream a patient brings to the therapy that, according to Jung, expresses the patient's diagnosis and prognosis, as the films indeed show.

The role of dreams is to bring the dreamer to awareness of a problem and its associated emotions. Sometimes, the dream's role is to inform the therapist about the patient's emotional state and ego resources. In films, however, as in literature, dreams play a further role—to update the audience on the essence of the unconscious problem by showing the character's deeper psyche and its activating force. Even if we do not understand it, the dream is a starting point for the dreamer's psychic processes. An added role is to deepen the cinematic emotional experience as a story within a story. Thus, like a dream in literature, the dream in cinema ultimately serves the work.

In literature, the dream usually appears without any explanation; the same is true of films. The unconscious materials of the dreaming character, however, speak to and resonate in the unconscious of the reader/spectator. The absence of dream interpretation in cinema is a way of connecting to the sense of mystery and riddle. The character's dream infuses a tense silence while we wait for something to happen, though we do not know what it will be since the narrative is built toward the future and related to the character's inner processes. The tension arises from the wish to solve the meaning of the riddle. Hitchcock deployed the characters' dreams in his films as paths to the causes of their pain, as in *Marnie* and *Spellbound*. Rather than the cinematic therapist, the spectator becomes the potential intuitive interpreter of the dream. The therapist's role in the film, and in the film as a whole, is to contain and sense the dream experience rather than interpret it. *David and Lisa* stresses the fear evoked by the dream of the clock, which is also a guillotine, and the film then deals with David's recovery following the relationship he develops with his therapist and with Lisa, not with the interpretation of his dream.

In *Face to Face*, the emphasis is again on the presentation of the sick psychiatrist's harrowing dream experiences and the containment-attention of the friend-therapist. The weight is on her very exposure to the dreams, to the delusions and awful memories from her childhood.

Dreams can be healing even when uninterpreted. Jung said that dream images and symbols have healing powers by virtue of being unconscious contents that have assumed a form potentially intelligible to consciousness. Sometimes, the very experience the dream raises constitutes its meaning, and the restoration of the dream as pictures in a film can be the essence of the films discussed. Cinema has the impossible power to patently "photograph" dreams and set them before us. The sight of the dream on the screen enables the dreamer, the therapist, and the spectator to share the dream experience. In my view, however, dreams rarely appear in films (and, when they do, they do not focus on the patient and on interpretation) because films about therapy are mainly concerned with the therapist-patient relationship.

Whose Dream Is This?

Film director Emir Kusturica said that the artist who directs films is "the objective dreamer," who dreams one dream for all of us, implying that the cinema is itself the objective dream. Jung argued that the collective unconscious is the objective psyche. In that spirit, I have come to see the body of therapist-patient films as a shared dream in the cinema's collective unconscious, which looks at therapy and the therapist from the perspective of the patient and of transference. In that sense, cinema is a kind of corrective, compensatory dream that, by reflecting the current state of affairs and introducing a new awareness, acts as a counterbalance to the collective consciousness of the therapeutic profession and each of its practitioners. Cinema is not merely a wish fulfillment dream gratifying the love and aggression needs of the patients, but also a warning to the therapists-spectators regarding all the therapeutic pitfalls as well as a dream guide to them.

On second thoughts, however, it crossed my mind that this representation of cinema as expressing the transference of cinematic patients to their therapists is no longer valid today, when psychotherapy is viewed as an intersubjective process where therapist *and* patient respond to the two-way transference between them.

The picture before us, then, is more complex. Ultimately, it is more accurate to see the films as conveying the full range of the collective unconscious of both patients and therapists, who dream the therapy and the therapeutic field that is the arena of their therapeutic interactions. After all, many patients dream about their therapy and their therapists, as therapists tend to dream about their patients and the therapy.

Jung describes the therapeutic relationship as resting on a unified subconscious field of the collective unconscious where counter-crossing takes place, with therapist and patient representing unconscious contents they have projected onto one another (Jung, 1983: 59). Beginning in the 1990s, relational psychoanalysis started viewing patients' dreams not only as their own creations and as solely representing their intrapsychic processes but also as a joint endeavor, related to interpersonal processes taking place between the dreaming patient and the therapist.

Support for this approach is found in the fact that the motif of breaching boundaries is prominent not only in patients' dreams about their therapists but also vice-versa. A study by Kron and Avni (2003) showed that breaching boundaries features in most therapists' dreams about patients. Therapists' dreams also included negative feelings of aggression, betrayal by the patient, vulnerability, sexuality, encroachment on their personal space, and role exchange—all of which feature in films. Kron and Avni concluded that therapists' dreams about their patients are also interpersonal events that play a critical role in the tangled and complex web of the therapeutic relationship.

The breaking of boundaries is present from the start in films in the very presentation of therapists as mirror images of their patients and suffering from similar problems, eroding the distinction between them. As Denis, the psychiatrist in *Man Facing Southeast* puts it in the film's closing scene: "We are all the stupid or mad children of the same father." Indeed, we all have a personal father with problems and "scratches" of one kind or another, and we all have an archetypal father who embodies virtues and weaknesses, strengths and failings, as is also true of the mother.

Images of redemption, aggression, betrayal, breaking borders, involvement bordering on infatuation and sexual fulfilment, together with other motifs considered in the films, can be viewed as expressing the yearnings and anxieties of both therapists and patients, when dreams are one of their expressions. Most people working in the cinema medium are part of a social group that has experience with psychotherapy and views it as fashionable. It is plausible that many scriptwriters were or are patients, and many scripts were written as a cooperative project of scriptwriters with therapists and patients (such as the Israeli series *In Therapy*, for instance).

Thus, the body of films about therapy is a kind of shared dream taking place in a shared field—the transferential space between therapist and patient and between reality and imagination. It is a space composed of transference and countertransference, which is the totality of intersubjective connections between the conscious and the unconscious of therapist and patient. It is an entity in its own right ("the third"), and also the alchemical container for the meeting of psychic materials, where the alchemical exchange of the therapist's and the patient's psyche will purportedly occur, together with the mixture and transformation of psychotherapeutic theories.

My initial claim, then, that the cinema is the patient seducing the therapist into over-involvement resembles Eve accusing the serpent for tempting her to eat of the apple. God obviously declines to accept this evasion of responsibility and expels her from the consciousless Garden of Eden, forcing humans to an endless confrontation with the need to draw a distinction between good and evil. Like Eve and like their patients, therapists must forever remain aware and responsible for their part in the therapeutic relationship. So who is the seducer between therapist and patient?

What can save therapists from the pitfalls and obstacles pointed out by cinema is their obligation to maintain self-awareness of the archetypes and complexes that drive them and their patients. They will thereby gain a better understanding of their patients and of themselves in the therapeutic situation. They will be less affected by the negative projections and claims cast at them, and be prudently aware of the trap posed by the false images held by their patients and by themselves.

The therapist's awareness of the redeemer archetype (the rescue fantasy) that seduces into over-involvement, of the magician archetype that lures into swift solutions, of the narcissistic reward ensuing from such involvement, of the fascination with the patient—all can help the therapist to moderate and regulate the connection, using the archetypes' energy in the service of the therapy rather than at its expense. The therapists' acknowledgment of their wound and shadow is also crucial for resisting an inflated over-identification with the archetype projected on them—the redeemer, Jesus, the shaman, the magician, the omnipotent. This awareness enables therapists to use their wound and their shadow for life instead of death.

Awareness is also required of the way that patients perceive therapists, of the anxieties and desires of patients and therapists alike, of the risks lurking in the path of attempts to gratify those desires, especially of wishes for closer involvement and for breaking down therapeutic boundaries, of the patient's expectation of a devoted, all-encompassing love. Above all, therapists must be aware of their unresolved personal problems, which can negatively affect their professional skills.

Cinema as Trickster

The look of cinema as the look of truth plays the role of the wise fool, the court jester charged with exposing the truth behind the pretensions, the subversive mocking trickster who breaches norms and boundaries to enable a new perspective and challenges us to accept change and a new awareness (Netzer 2008, 233). As a jester-fool, cinema highlights the need to slacken the stranglehold of therapeutic conventions and reexamine therapeutic boundaries. As a subversive figure, cinema guides therapists when it points to their shadow to effect a positive transformation in the therapy (the shadow and the jester are the trickster's two faces). As a jester, cinema uses humor (*Zelig, Don Juan, Analyze This, Happiness*) to break through the terrible seriousness and political correctness of discussions on psychotherapy. Relying on humor, it challenges and rereads fundamental assumptions about madness, mental disturbances, and therapy. For example, Zelig, who has a very "fluid" personality, flies a plane across the Atlantic upside down and receives a hero's welcome in the United States. Americans forgive his many deceptions and pin on him a medal for courage. And Zelig notes: "It shows you what a man can achieve when he's totally psychotic," "His illness is the very source of his deliverance," and "It is his very disturbance that made him a hero."

Man Facing Southeast challenges our notions of consciousness and the normative boundaries defining it. It exposes us to the possibility that borderline mental states are not only doorways to the unconscious but also stops or relay points to other worlds, to other states of consciousness, and to the option that some people possess ultraviolet sight not only in a physical sense, like the patient in *K-Pax*, but also in a spiritual sense.

Given the postmodern openness to various truths, it would be appropriate to welcome these films and learn from them as we learn from patients, as Casement (1985) recommends. Furthermore, it would be appropriate to let cinema treat us in the spirit of Ferenczi's old idea that the patient treats the therapist.

The implication is not that all the patient's wishes must be fulfilled. The cinema as jester-fool enables, in humor's tricky indirect way, to skip past the psychotherapeutic establishment's conservative objections to criticism, holding up to ridicule the patient's desire for totality and the readiness of some therapists to submit to it or even to suggest it themselves (for example *Zelig*). *Zelig* and *Analyze This* illustrate the patients' longing for total parental giving, as that of a mother to a child at all times. The patient in *Analyze This* is a mafioso who suffers from anxiety, breaks into his therapist's home, overpowers him, and demands that he remain constantly beside him.

On the one hand, it sometimes seems that cinema is attempting to overpower therapists, commanding them to fulfill unrealistic childish fantasies. On the other, cinema itself appears to be ridiculing these wishes. These two films are comedies that disparage not only the therapists swept into such fulfillment but also the desires themselves.

Cinema as a Negative Trickster

In this section, I deal with six other films, five of them produced after the publication of the original Hebrew version of this book in 2013. These films present therapy misleadingly and even negatively. They thereby illustrate the negative aspect of the trickster archetype, the liar who is by nature confusing, although initially, as noted, it had been meant to serve developmental processes.

1. *Bagdad Cafe* (Percy Adlon, 1987) is described as a comic surrealist drama. The plot takes place at a truck station and motel in the Mojave Desert in California. At the beginning of the film, Jasmin, a tourist, has a fight with her husband, leaves the car, and arrives at the Bagdad Cafe. At the same time, Brenda, the café owner, has a fight with her husband and kicks him out. Jasmin stays at the café and meets its colorful patrons, who include a Hollywood sets painter and a tattoo artist. Jasmin cleans and polishes the neglected building and turns it into a friendly site. She also listens to the clients' troubles and entertains them with magic tricks, helping them and herself. The film shows two women, each one busy with her own problems, who are transformed by their encounter. The Jungian thought underlying the plot comes forth in the theme song accompanying the film from the start—"Calling You," a text suggesting awareness that this change had been meant to happen and that the two women had been fated to meet and change.

Both women are ruled by a negative, controlling, rigid, and aggressive animus (the masculine element). Both of them soften and become friends in the course of the plot, which stresses the tricks that Jasmin performs as an amateur magician. Using these skills, she attracts a large audience to the café, which becomes a thriving entertainment venue and brings joy to all. The film emphasizes the magic tricks as a change factor in the plot and the process the women undergo, implying that magic plays a part in the psychic transformation beyond conscious insight.

What bothered me in the film is the extensive and pronounced emphasis on magic tricks as change factors in the plot and as affecting the women's development. The god, or the archetype in charge of the psychic changes, is Hermes-Mercury, known as Hermes Trismegistus, "thrice greatest" in his magic power. Unquestionably, in antiquity, when knowledge of psychological and physiological processes was limited, every change was experienced as miraculous or magic. Today, we know that psychic change is mainly the result of prolonged work, not miracles. Philemon, described in *The Red Book* as Jung's inner guide, refuses Jung's request to teach him magic and points out that he must tend to his psyche as he tends to his garden, investing in it daily. Only continued attention enables occasional magic and miraculous moments when archetypal materials spontaneously burst out, bringing a message into the process and promoting it through coincidences and high experiences.

But the film emphasizes magic tricks and, consequently, I found its description of the women's change process unpersuasive. Performing these tricks would not have been possible without the technical resources available to the cinema. The film thus turns into an *ars poetica* statement about cinema itself, about the cinematic magic that enchants the spectator with its technological potential, just like cinema can also show dreams as reality and mix sanity and madness. In this sense, in its positive aspect, cinema opens us to a fictitious reality, as to a different consciousness, in order to expand the spectrum of our experiences. Cinema, however, has a narcissistic dimension in its creators (that can also reflect this aspect in the therapist), which will impress us as do its magic stunts. Cinema sells experiences, which is why it leans toward extremism and, generally, does not demand from itself faithfulness to the psychic reality. The negative trickster component of cinema enters here. The emphasis on magic becomes an emphasis on the shadow side of magic, enabling the creation of an imposing and seductive persona. Here, the film "treats us" in the sense that it indeed seduces us into quick magic changes. But is this the psychic truth? I can imagine a different continuation of this plot when Jasmin influences people at the café by offering them new songs or drawings or talking to them. But then we would not have been impressed, and the process would have taken much longer...

2. *Silver Linings Playbook* (David O. Russell, 2012). I begin by noting that I did not like the film, which deals with an important subject—recovery from mental illness. This supposedly comic film addresses this motif superficially, in extreme and exaggerated terms, and the humor turns into a ridiculous farce.

Many characteristics of therapy films are found in this movie, which presents the problems of medical judgment, the medical establishment, and doctors, as noted above. As for the equation of who is healthy and who is sick, the healthy ones in *Silver Linings Playbook* (like the father of the patient, whose life is organized around betting and magic thinking, and his friend, who submits to his dominant wife) lack any adaptation skills and tend toward uncontrollable rage outbursts.

The medical establishment is presented as helpless. The patient throws away the pills he was prescribed and decides to overcome his illness through addictive running. Moreover, the doctor interferes in the patient's life and breaches all the rules about therapeutic boundaries without reason, meeting him at a football field and a dance hall. He looks foolish when he shouts like the other football fans, paints himself in the team's colors, and fails to utter even one sensible statement.

The film's problem is that it ridicules everything and resorts to a hackneyed cliché stating that love cures all. The two most difficult characters, psychiatric patients, supposedly heal one another through their love. *Silver Linings Playbook* uses another worn-out and unreliable New Age formula and turns, in a way, into a parody of positive psychology.

The film is based on a mistaken claim stating that bipolar illness and a borderline personality disorder can be cured through alternative medicine. Were I to compare it to other deep and carefully crafted films on mental illness and therapy relations (produced in the second half of the twentieth century and offering a significant critique of current therapy that merits attention), I would say it is a dull mold that emptied of any meaning the statements it could have made. It is a pity that an actor like Robert De Niro stars in a foolish role. Instead of treating us, this film harms us.

3. *Side Effects* (Steven Soderbergh, 2013). I disliked this film too. It presents psychiatrists as people whose motivations are mostly money, sex, and power.

The patient, the lead character, is sexually seduced by a psychiatrist and driven by her to kill her husband so the psychiatrist can gain from it. Another psychiatrist, who from the start had been driven by care and good will to help the patient, accepts financing from a drug company that exploits his economic distress and leads him to cooperate by giving his patients a new drug. Ultimately, the patient who had faked her illness and ostensibly killed her husband due to the drug's side effects pays the price when she is indicted for murder. She now has a choice—psychiatric hospitalization or a murder trial. But then everything is reversed, and the "good" therapist, who had appeared as a victim of the system and of the two women, labels the patient as schizophrenic and hospitalizes her to save himself. The patient is the victim of both of them. The anger and the frustration I felt are also due to identification with the patient, the victim of this script, involuntarily committed as a mental patient when she is not. I resented the presentation of the therapists as lying abusers with dark motivations, even though the patient is also presented as an impostor who cheats everyone. I also felt exploited as a spectator. Almost to the end of the film, the script makes me empathize with the patient and her doctor, both seeming victims of the patient's severe condition and the drug's side effects, only to reveal their manipulative aspect.

I was disappointed that such a film was produced for financial gain at the expense of destroying the spectators' trust in therapists. This film is not interested in the truth of the psyche, nor in therapeutic relationships in this highly demanding profession, but in the script's manipulation of all the characters, including the spectators. The patient is a fake patient, and the therapist is a fake therapist. The film fakes concern with psychic issues, but is not interested in the psyche.

I later understood that the film is built as a *film noir*—a style of thriller with dark content where characters manipulate one another, usually starring a *femme fatale* who entraps the protagonist. In this film, two *femmes fatales*, a patient and a therapist, ensnare the good and caring therapist, leading him to become devious, oppressive, and corrupt like them. Therapy serves as a kind of excuse for making a thriller, in a cynical manipulation that presents therapists as corrupt when the end of creating a successful thriller justifies the means.

The film is also problematic because it does not seek to expose issues we deny, as I discussed above, showing how the shadow aspect affects therapists. Instead, it projects from the world of cinema (which deals with motivations of profit, control, power, and exploitation) onto the world of therapy, as if the therapeutic profession, too, is, essentially, only like that. Possibly, what is even more insulting is that what happens in therapy is of no interest to the scriptwriters.

4. Exploitation also plays a role in *The Best Offer* (Giuseppe Tornatore, 2013). I felt the script in this film had used me as it used the protagonist, who is tricked by a network of forgers. We both fell into the trap when we believed that the girl who refused to leave her parents' castle was agoraphobic and needed help.

The protagonist, aptly named Virgil Oldman, is a man in his seventies who suffers from the same anxieties as the girl. He, however, has learned to control his fears by using gloves that protect him from infection and by aggressively dominating his assistants, who attend to his needs for prestige and assets. He is the managing director of an auction house dealing with works of art, lives alone in his opulent home, and has never had a relationship with a woman.

In a cynical world where feelings do not count and the other turns into a means for accumulating wealth, as Oldman relates to his assistants, a reverse process ultimately takes place—he becomes a target for others accumulating wealth at his expense.

The script could be said to be psychopathic: people whose identity we do not know lead a man to come out of his alienated, hostile, homophobic shield when he succeeds in trusting the imprisoned girl, who seduces him into believing that she is helpless and in need of his protection and assistance. The hero entrapped in his isolating shield is seized by the archetype of the hero who rescues the captive maiden, and she plays with him at will under cover of her, as it were, fearful vulnerability.

Although the forgers want to steal Oldman's vast assets, as they indeed do, he returns to life, cured of the neurosis that had imprisoned him. But when he discovers at the end of the film that he has lost everything, his fundamental belief is affirmed: trust no one, neither one who feigned to be a poor girl in need of chivalrous protection nor the faithful assistant who, for years, cooperated with him in the forging of works of art.

The cinema that had pretended to be "our therapist," seduced us into believing that the film shows how two patients help one another to leave their panicked hiding place and let love heal everything, as in *David and Lisa*. However, this cinema is instead exposed as a fake of the good, humane, and loving therapist when it does not love its protagonists or its audience. Its interest is to profit from us, the spectators.

As the director of *Cinema Paradiso*, Tornatore sang an ode to the love of cinema, whereas in this film, he shows cinema's shadow side. Oldman's assistant says to him, "Everything can be forged. Feelings too, and even love." And the film indeed proves this—the girl's love for Oldman was false. Oldman has a saying of his own: in every forgery is a trace of truth.

We pitied Oldman, whose sole experience of love had been looking at countless portraits of women hanging close together on the walls of his secret room and believing that they loved him, and we are ultimately left pondering: what is truth and what is false?

Most of the film enables us to acknowledge the ability of the frightened and reclusive individual to be healed. But when it is clear that the girl had faked agoraphobia to exploit Oldman, we find that we, too, were misled. Such a film, like the film *Side Effects*, is exasperating in its debasement of the therapeutic profession and the human psyche, which is exposed here only in its dark sides.

5. The film *Double Lover* (François Ozon, 2017) pretends to be a cinematic masterpiece but is an almost demonic and cynical manipulation of the suffering experienced by both therapists and patients. The film is driven by the wish to profit from the patient's pain and by the ugly and blatant slander of the therapist, who is described as a pervert and a psychopath.

The plot deals with the sexual and therapeutic relationship between a young woman who goes for treatment and two psychologists who are twins. Each has a different therapeutic style but both ignore therapeutic boundaries, and sexual power relations develop on the couch.

The film is a cheap and perverse-violent manipulation that dresses up as a psychological thriller to build a captivating mystery. Yet, it is also unfounded and surrealistic, a mixture of fantasy and reality bordering on psychosis. It uses the psyche's fundamental pains—loneliness, rejection, desertion, the grasping of every love seemingly offered to the suffering person—as well as the distrust that urges the breakup of the relationship, the search for fraternity-twinhood, brothers' envy, the inner splits between good and evil that turn into splits projected onto people, psychosomatic pains, dominance, belligerence, lies, violence, therapeutic incest, and the patient's exploitation by the therapists. All of them radically breach all the therapeutic rules for the sake of the omnipotent sadomasochistic rules of the film's producers. A film of this type is a negative trickster, delighting in the powers of the shadow and destroying trust in the therapeutic profession.

6. The film *The Son* (Florian Zeller, 2022) describes the marriage of Peter and Beth, who confront a crisis when Nicholas, Peter's seventeen-year-old son from his previous marriage to Kate, has a breakdown and needs therapy. We see one therapy session, with the boy sitting across the therapist for an hour of silence. The boy does not attend other sessions, as he had not attended school, without the therapist informing the parents. We do not see a therapeutic session with the parents. The drama ends with the psychiatric hospitalization of the boy following a failed suicide attempt. After his release, he kills himself. The film successfully transmits the parents' helplessness and lack of understanding in dealing with their son. However, between the lines, it comes across as a veiled critique of the therapeutic

establishment's inability to help the boy. The scriptwriter presented the therapists as unskilled, lacking insight, and as helpless as the parents. The choice not to devote screen time to the therapeutic process is an a priori erasure of the therapeutic potential. This choice delivers a grim message to the spectators, whose children may one day require support from a profession that has helped many.

In sum, these films deal with therapists who, in many ways, are problematic. I was pained by the contempt and the unbearable lightness that characterized the radically negative presentation of the therapists.

After about forty films dealing with therapy, most of them based on quality scripts, why persist in devoting attention to the topic if there is nothing new to say, if there is no significant statement about therapy and its clients, and if no complex or deep perception emerges from which to learn about the human psyche? Why create a lucrative cinema based on a cheap attitude toward therapy and the psyche and on an insulting approach toward the original essence of cinema as therapist? Possibly, when the powers of the shadowy trickster (motives of profit and publicity) are the main drives for making films, the shadow forces are also more strongly evident among the film protagonists. In such films, cinema does not fulfill its role as therapist.

References

Bion, Wilfred (1959) "Attacks on Linking." *International Journal of Psycho-Analysis*, 40: 308–315.
Casement, Patrick (1985) *On Learning from the Patient* (London: Tavistock).
Gabbard, Krin, and Glen Gabbard (1989) *Psychiatry and the Cinema*, second edn. (American Psychiatric Press).
Jung, C. G. (1983) *The Psychology of the Transference*, trans. R. F. C. Hull (London: Routledge & Kegan Paul).
Kron, Tamar, and Nadav Avni (2003) "Psychotherapists Dream About Their Patients." *The Journal of Analytical Psychology* 48, 3: 317–339.
Lazar, Rina (2003) "Schools and Trends in Psychoanalysis: The Relational Trend." *Sihot/ Dialogue: Israel Journal of Psychotherapy* 17 (2): 131–135 [Heb].
May, Rollo (1991) *The Cry for Myth* (New York: Norton).
McDougall, Joyce (1989) *Theaters of the Body: A Psychoanalytic Approach to Psychosomatic Illness* (New York: W. W. Norton).
Mitchell, Stephen A. (1993) *Hope and Dread in Psychoanalysis* (New York: Basic Books).
Netzer, Ruth (2008) *The Magician, the Fool, and the Empress: Tarot Cards in the Circle of Life and in Therapy* (Tel Aviv: Modan) [Heb].
Netzer, Ruth (2011) *A Hero's Journey* (Tel Aviv: Modan) [Heb].
Pessoa, Fernando (2006) *A Little Larger Than the Entire Universe: Selected Poems*, trans. Richard Zenith (London: Penguin Classics).
Sarig, Ruth (2008) "Dreams and Films." Website of The Israeli Jungian New Association— http://www.israjung.co.il [Heb].
Shaffer, Peter (1974) *Equus* (New York: Avon).
Stein, Robert (1973) *Incest and Human Love* (Dallas: Spring Publications).
Yalom, Irvin D. (2002) *The Gift of Therapy: An Open Letter to a New Generation of Therapists and Their Patients* (New York: Harper).

Chapter 6
Cinema, Madness, and Anti-psychiatry

In *History of Madness*, Michel Foucault studied society's attitude toward madness and noted that, from the Middle Ages to the Renaissance, madness was allowed free expression because it was viewed as part of the divine plan (Foucault 2006). Madness appeared as a theme in works of art and was viewed as a riddle storing the world's hidden powers. From the seventeenth century onward, the mad replaced the leper as a boundary marker between the normal and the deviant. They then began hospitalizing the "deviants" that threatened the prevailing social order—marginal elements whose presence in a healthy society was viewed as scandalous—among them criminals, prostitutes, the poor, the unemployed, and, of course, the mad. Rather than attempting to cure them, the adopted policy involved separation and isolation to release society from the "scourge" growing within it. Madness became an object of imprisonment and concealment in an attempt to prevent scandal and avoid shame. Patients' outbreaks of violence in institutions were dealt with cruelly and without any effort to impose discipline because the mad were thought incapable of improvement, and treatment involved mainly restrictions, like restraints on aggressive beasts. The mad were not approached as human beings and were not viewed as sick people since they were deprived of the rational power that is the very essence of humanity. Hence, they were also considered immoral. Foucault shows that society has consistently used scapegoats to define the "normality" of others. His book was published parallel to the mid-twentieth century emergence of the anti-psychiatry movement, whose spokesperson and leading source of inspiration was R. D. Laing.

Laing (1970) held that modern society shuts individuals within walls of conformity that hinder their potential and destroy their personality. In Laing's view, "madness" may merely result from the individual's inability to repress his normal senses and adapt to an abnormal society, a view conveyed by the therapist in *Equus*. Peter Shaffer wrote the play in 1974, a few years after the publication of Laing's book. The recognition of the sanity in madness was introduced into the therapeutic establishment as part of Laing's anti-psychiatry movement in the 1960s–1970s, which argued that people who bother the family are labeled as mad and distanced from society. Laing contributed to the change in the attitude toward madness and acted to undermine the therapist-patient hierarchy. The influence of the anti-psychiatry trend on cinema is evident in films dealing with therapy. One example is *King of Hearts* (1966), an anti-war parody where Alan Bates plays a Scottish soldier in WWI who is sent to defuse a bomb left by the retreating Germans in a small French town. He discovers that the area is deserted except for the inmates of the local asylum who take over the town and crown the soldier their "king of hearts." The question of sanity and madness arises in *K-Pax*, *Equus*, *Man Facing Southeast*, and *One Flew Over the Cuckoo's Nest*, all affected by the anti-psychiatry stance.

In the circus scene in *Man Facing Southeast*, the tightrope walker seemingly symbolizes the dangerous seamline between sanity and madness and the risk entailed by this walking if it were attempted by Rantés, the therapist, and the spectators.

The difference between madness and sanity is progressively eroded, with the growing appreciation of the psychic depths of the patient who crosses the borders of consciousness. The patient's madness is experienced by the therapist and the spectator as the psyche's authentic truth: "We all have contour lines separating the credible and incredible. But what is objectively incredible is *often* experienced as actual. I suggest that this is even the normal case" (Laing 1982, 44). Laing argues that our culture (in the early and mid-twentieth century) represses not only the instincts and sexuality but all forms of individuals going beyond themselves. In a society of one-dimensional individuals, it is unsurprising that anyone experiencing other dimensions and who is unable to deny them or dismiss them will be at risk of destruction by others or of betrayal of what he knows. In Laing's view, in the current circumstances of madness spreading over everything we call normality, sanity, and freedom—all our criteria are equivocal and dubious.

The therapists in *Equus*, *Man Facing Southeast*, and *K-Pax* represent this position, which romanticizes madness. These films (especially *Man Facing Southeast* and *One Flew Over the Cuckoo's Nest*) protest against the psychiatric establishment whose clear-cut stance is that madness is madness is madness.

This view is endorsed by Patrick White, who describes Theodora, the protagonist of his book *The Aunt's Story* (White 1948), and most of the protagonists of his other books as victims of a mediocre world that ostracizes them and fails to understand their unique mystical depth. Theodora is endowed with unusual poetic sensitivity and telepathic spiritual and mystical insight, which hinder her integration in society. As a result, she breaks down. This depth perception parallels the patient's ultraviolet sight in *K-Pax*. White ascribes to psychotherapy the power to acknowledge that "madness is sanity," in Laing's terms. The therapist's recognition that madness is sanity collapses the hierarchic dichotomy of therapist-patient and sane-mad, joining the questions posed in many films about who is mad and who is sane.

Contrary to the pattern of excluding the mad that began in the seventeenth century, the recognition of the authenticity present in madness is currently returning. Giora Shoham conveys this fascination with madness in reference to Van Gogh, admiringly describing how, in his bravery, Van Gogh tested the boundaries of his sanity and thereby expanded our experience of transcendence (Shoham 2003, 174).

Shoham also quotes Norman Brown, who says: "It is not schizophrenia but normality that is split-minded in schizophrenia. The false boundaries are disintegrating. Schizophrenics are suffering from the truth" (ibid., 178). The fascination of the cinematic therapist and of films in general with madness as divine was evident in *Man Facing Southeast*, *K-Pax*, and *Equus*.

Another approach argues that therapy will heal the individual's madness and make life banal. We find echoes of this idea in White when Holstious suggests to Theodora, who is breaking apart, that she should follow the therapist and submit to his expectations: "It is part of the deference one pays to those who prescribe the reasonable life. They are admirable people really, though limited" (White 1948, 283). The therapist in *Man Facing Southeast* thinks to himself: "We can drug him [the patient], and he will be like everyone," "What can I say to help him? It would be better for him to go to a priest. I will drug him, and he will never get rid of these pictures."

The therapist in *Don Juan de Marco* opposes giving drugs to his patient, who is diagnosed as psychotic (a diagnosis that later proves mistaken) because "if I drug him, I will not be able to enter his wonderful world." In *K-Pax*, the therapist successfully persuades the patient to be hypnotized to save him from a closed ward where "he will get an injection every day and sit smiling like a fool all his life." The therapist in *Equus* is impressed by the patient, who loves horses and is against tying them, whipping them, and using them for work and in the circus.

The dilemma between drug treatments that prevent acute psychosis but harm creativity as opposed to psychotherapy without drugs, which sustains the psyche's authenticity, is a familiar quandary in the therapy world, even though drugs are currently less harmful than in the past. Indeed, the psychotic hallucination has been claimed to be healing, relying on metaphors of redemption. John Perry describes the psychic processes in madness. In his view, the alchemic process of collapse and reorganization occurs in the hallucinations of psychotics, which include ideas of death and of return to a primal place where opposite forces clash. Out of the destructive struggle, the redeemer figure and the idea of the sacred marriage emerge, and the redeemer creates a new, fair, and harmonious society. Hence, claims Perry, if we refrain from giving drugs and allow the psychotic hallucination to run its course, the process will lead to healing, restoration, and the rebuilding of the self through the symbolism of redemption. The psychotic fantasy thereby acquires meaning: it records destructive processes, and the very occurrence of the hallucination enables the healing and rebirth of the newly structured psyche (Perry 1976). Perry, however, a contemporary of Laing, appears to be beguiled by the wealth of the fantasy's contents, ignoring the depth of anxiety and pain experienced by psychotic patients. Moreover, there is no guarantee that the patient will emerge from the psychosis, which may leave permanent damage behind. Jung notes: "We must not underestimate the devastating effect of getting lost in the chaos, even if we know that it is the *sine qua non* of any regeneration of the spirit and the personality" (Jung 1974, 148). Perry, following Jung, assumes the existence of a purposive restorative movement during the hallucinations. Jung, however, warns: "I must own that I use the word 'purposive' with some hesitation. This word needs to be used cautiously and with reserve. For in mental cases we come across dream-sequences, and in neurotics fantasy-sequences, which run on in themselves with no apparent aim or purpose" (Jung 1972, 231). Given that the consciousness of people with a mental health condition is precisely the one that cannot actively participate in the hallucination process, they are at risk of remaining within the chaos since return is impossible from some regressions. Hence, in almost all psychotic situations, only anti-psychotic drugs enable the alchemic process, and they are the grail of compassion and healing (Netzer 2004, 206). Whoever favors the independent process of a self-healing psychotic hallucination has no compassion for its victim's pain.

In the films considered, the therapeutic dilemma concerning the use of drugs joins another quandary confronting the therapist, who is unwilling to give up her own gain from the psychotic episode. Cinema is identified with the will to preserve the fascinating psychosis and with the therapist who draws on the patient's creative suffering to yield her creation from it: the film. The therapists' solution in *Equus* and *K-Pax*—to discover the unconscious truth through hypnosis—also serves the need of the cinematic medium to enrich itself with materials representing an exciting drama and "sacrifices" the patient undergoing destructive treatment to satisfy the therapist's needs. Thus, by leaning toward the sensational, cinema sometimes sacrifices the truth of the psyche, the patient, and the spectator.

The therapist, in reality and in the cinema, can project the sick pole within him onto the patient, thus identifying himself with sanity and healing and strengthening the sense of his own resilience. In that sense, he "sacrifices" the patient, who is pushed further and further toward the pole of illness and serves the therapist as a scapegoat. In that sense, the cinema enables the spectators too to feel sane when their sickness is projected onto the patient on the screen.

The cinematic therapist often uses the patient to return the energetic spark to his life. In *Intimate Strangers*, the therapist finds the lighter the patient had lost, and in *The Name of the Game*, the therapist steals from the criminal the lighter that she wanted as if she were stealing a new primal-shadow life energy. In these films, the therapeutic meeting enables the therapist-patient to bring back the energetic spark missing from their lives. In *Don Juan*, the patient's spark is the "divine fire" of love, which kindles the therapist. In *Equus* and *Man Facing Southeast*, the therapist senses the patient's energetic spark, which derives from the power of the archetypes floating in the world of madness. When the patient gives the therapist this spark, mutual healing takes place.

What the therapist encounters in the patient's psyche parallels what all of us, as spectators, encounter in characters appearing in films that do not deal with therapy: to meet the parts of our psyche—the sane and the mad, the good and the bad shadow, the primal-spiritual-creative-female/male part, our greatness, and our defeat. Like the therapist and cinema itself, the spectator draws on the patient's stormy emotional world and inner resources, which are inseparable from his pain and merciless exposure. Cinema, like literature, strives to remove the mask from its protagonists. We, as spectators, may then learn to remove our masks, override the defenses that split us off from ourselves, and feel our pain and the yearning for love and the transcendent.

References

Foucault, Michel (2006) *History of Madness*, trans. Jonathan Murphy and Jean Khalfa (London: Routledge).
Jung, C. G. (1972) *Two Essays on Analytical Psychology, C. W. 7*, trans. R. F. C. Hull (Princeton, NJ: Princeton University Press).
Jung, C. G. (1974) *Dreams*, trans. R. F. C. Hull (Princeton, NJ: Princeton University Press).
Laing, R. D. and Aaron Esterson (1970) *Sanity, Madness, and the Family: Families of Schizophrenics* (Harmondsworth: Penguin).
Laing R. D. (1982) *The Voice of Experience* (New York: Pantheon Books).
Netzer, Ruth (2004) *Journey to the Self: The Alchemy of the Psyche—Symbols and Myths* (Ben Shemen, Israel: Modan) [Heb].
Perry, John Weir (1976). *Roots of Renewal in Myth and Madness: The Meaning of Psychotic Episodes* (London: Jossey-Bass).
Shaffer, Peter (1974) *Equus* (New York: Avon).
Shoham, S. Giora (2003). *Art, Crime and Madness: Gesualdo, Caravaggio, Genet, Van Gogh, Artaud* (Portland, OR: Sussex Academic Press).
White, Patrick (1948) *The Aunt's Story* (Penguin Books).

Chapter 7

Therapy and Redemption
Myth, Healing, and Religious Symbolism

Ingmar Bergman writes about the religious aspect of cinema. In his view, once art was separated from worship, it lost its main creative drive. In the past, artists had been anonymous, their work was performed for the glory of God, and talent was a divine gift. Today, the individual's life has become the most sublime form of artistic creation, and subjectivity has become almost sacred.

> We stand and bleat about our loneliness without listening to each other ... Thus if I am asked what I would like the general purpose of my films to be, I would reply that I want to be one of the artists in the cathedral on the great plain. ... Regardless of whether I believe or not, whether I am a Christian or not, I would play my part in the collective building of the cathedral.
> (Bergman 1960, 9)

Walter Benjamin (2015) describes the loss of the religious dimension in photography. He considers the possibility that photography and cinema will make art shallow. The era of technical reproduction shifts art from a ritualized-religious-magic context to a ritualized-secularized context at whose center is the representational (aesthetic) beauty of art and the artist. Notwithstanding Benjamin's concerns in the mid-twentieth century, however, the religious dimension persists in the cinematic experience. Director Bruno Dumont claims that the overt/covert presence/absence tension embodied by God characterizes the art of cinema as well:

> This tension is what interests me more than anything when making films. A powerful link ties cinema to religion, and I do not mean this in the superficial sense that people worship stars and so forth. I mean that in cinema too, to plunge into the experience when watching a film you have to believe in the presence of what is absent. I think that the beauty and power of cinema stem from this aspect. In the cinema, you have to believe.
> (Klein 2010, 2)

Religious faith, art, myth, and healing were intertwined from their very start. Art served in the creation of temples, while myths and sculptures of the gods were the basis for healing rituals that included prayers to the gods. Thus, for example, the art of cave paintings was a religious ritual describing the hunting of animals, when the painting was assigned magic powers of influence on the hunter's success.

The myth, consistently sustained within a religious world, describes the relationship between humans and the gods. It functioned as a tool of tribal therapy by expressing harsh feelings and conflicts while simultaneously suggesting how to cope with them by describing the paths of heroes when dealing with obstacles. Rollo May notes that the myth's healing power lies in raising unconscious impulses, terrors, and longings to consciousness while revealing new goals, ethical insights, and possibilities. The myth is thus a way of working through the problem at a higher level of integration (May 1991, 86).

In antiquity, healing processes were tied to divinity. Its representatives—the shaman, the spiritual leader, the priest, the rabbi—were religious authorities to whom healing powers had been delegated as mediators between humans and the divine. The therapist, too, acts as a substitute, and the metaphors of the healing god shifted to the therapist.

The healing archetypes of the redeemer and the shaman latent in the archetype of the therapist are originally religious. The term *Therapeutae*, referring to an ancient Greek sect, meant "servants of god." Therapists serve the god that is in their psyche and in the psyche of those who turn to them. The archetype of the wounded healer, which exists in the therapist's psyche, appeared in the religious world in the shape of the wounded Jesus, the shaman, and the Jewish messiah, who are described as injured.

The dreams that serve psychotherapy today were ascribed in the past to the gods, who sent dreams to humans. Thus, for example, healing through the interpretation of dreams occurred in Greece in the temple of Aesculapius, the god of medicine. Today, cinema channels to itself anew aspects of art, religious belief, myth, dream, and healing.

North American Navajos have a healing myth whereby people who had been sick or wounded went on a journey to the gods, who healed them. These people then returned, taught the healing rites to others, and vanished into the realm of the gods. In this myth, healing is a divine undertaking. Therapy films are, in a way, collective rites of shamanic healing witnessed by the entire tribe. The music of the films is healing music.

Religion dealt with evil, sin, and guilt, while God was a source of confession, forgiveness, atonement, love, and redemption from sin and evil. The confession prayer in Judaism (on the Day of Atonement) and the confession to the priest in Catholicism are therapeutic rituals under the aegis of God and institutionalized religion. Healing occurred by listening to the confession, granting a pardon, and in magic rituals and ceremonies of exorcising demons conducted by the religious authorities.

Terril Gibson says that the cinema is now the most visited cathedral, inspiring the hope once bestowed in houses of prayer (Gibson 2005). Cinema fulfils the therapeutic role that in the past had been fulfilled solely by myth and religion, expressing the hidden emotional world of humans and their sins, that is, their shadow parts. This applies even more to films that deal with psychotherapy, which mean to show us various ways of coping with complex feelings, sins, and guilt in the therapeutic process and in life. Raising the repressed then serves the role of the forgiving healing confessor, not only for the cinematic patient but also for the spectator. We saw in *Marnie* that the therapeutic process leads her to the discovery that she had killed her mother's lover in her childhood. In *Spellbound*, the patient represses an event that made him think he is guilty of murder. *Ordinary People* describes a family's breakdown after the accidental death of the eldest son and the therapeutic process of the various characters, among them the second son who feels guilty for his brother's death. The therapist (Donald Sutherland) helps his young patient understand that his guilty feelings are unfounded—he is not to blame for his brother's death and could not have rescued him.

With the collapse of religion in the early twentieth century, the search for healing and the wholeness of the psyche shifted from religion to sexuality, love, mysticism, drugs, art, psychotherapy, and the art of cinema. Myths and healing rituals endorsed by religion shifted to the secular establishment, and we will rediscover them in the cinema.

Max Weber argues that every culture or religion develops some norm or model of salvation when it tells humans how they must behave to appease and please the gods in the context of their religion. Mordechai Rotenberg, who cites Weber, adds that some theology is behind every psychology in the popular normative sense. The salvation pattern is later secularized and percolates into psychotherapy, which replaces religion. The Protestant claim is that salvation is attained through hard work and worldly success. Psychiatry and psychotherapy are related to this achieving individualism, evident in psychotherapy in the investment of concentrated efforts in psychic processes. Rotenberg says that psychology did not develop in laboratories but in religious settings, drawing primarily on encrypted meta-codes or religious and cultural indicators transformed through secularization (Rotenberg 1994, 10–15). Erich Fromm (1950) also addresses the relationship between theology-religion and psychotherapy.

The mythological narrative that religion, literature, cinema, psychotherapy, and the psyche in general offer is the archetypal-mythical model of the hero (who struggles with the monster of life's difficulties and overcomes it) and, simultaneously, the narrative of religious redemption. This mythological-religious narrative has consistently included the entanglement of conflict and its solution, anguish and its release, repression and its exposure, ignorance and knowledge, evil-sin-guilt and their atonement, descent into the abyss and exit into the light, sickness and recovery, break and repair, wounding and healing, exile and redemption. This narrative, which is also the therapeutic narrative, is present in every myth, legend, and story, including the contemporary one. We expect a happy ending, where some form of personal providence comes forth and helps the positive hero to triumph. This narrative, which is undermined in the modern literature prevalent in the secular world, recurs not only in mystery books, in cinematic thrillers, and in bionic films but also in many other stories.

The happy, redemptive ending results in the emotional catharsis of the reader-spectator. In fact, the story is examined in light of the success or failure of the redemption narrative, which has a religious source. Like the myth, psychotherapy and the cinema are pervaded by the redemption narrative. Pier Paolo Pasolini's *Theorem*, Andrei Tarkovsky's *The Sacrifice*, and Clint Eastwood's *Gran Torino* are examples of the yearning for redemption and the redeemer in the cinema.

The cinema dealing with psychotherapy is suffused with a religious symbolism found in the concealed archetypal basis of healing (Netzer 2004, 310). In myth, religion, and psychotherapy, we all need faith. The presence or absence of faith enables perseverance and the mustering of resources for the inner and outer voyage. Faith in the power to undertake the voyage leads to outer and inner achievements and to development in its course, denoting faith in the search processes, in the significance of the voyage as a constant engagement, in its necessity, and in its very meaning. In religion, it is faith in God. In psychotherapy, according to Jung, it is faith in the meaning of the psychic-spiritual voyage and in the psyche's commitment to its mission—the realization of the self, denoting faith in the ego's power to achieve its aims and in the healing power at the core of the self that exists in God's image.

For therapists who are fully confident in their task and in the healing power of the self, faith in therapy substitutes for faith in God. A patient who has faith in the therapist projects onto him her needs for worship and faith in God.

Common to religion and psychotherapy is also the worship of the guide. Against people who need to be admired and worshipped, there is the human need to admire and worship. The need to admire and to be admired are two sides of the same coin, two faces of the same archetype. When the parent's admiring mirror look does not help to build in the child's ego the essential positive narcissistic confidence, he will seek affirmation of his existence by admiring others or in their admiration of him. This need is often transferred to the therapist as admirer-admired and as one who can be worshipped. However, there is admiration beyond the ego's narcissistic aspect: the ego's admiration and worship of a power greater than itself, a numinous power, constitutive, absolute, and certain, which is the core of the self that is experienced as divine or as a reflection of the divine.

The religious stance includes worshiping a spiritual entity greater than the ego. The therapist in *Equus* says: "Can you think of anything worse one can do to anybody than take away their worship?" The young patient worships the horse, as prehistoric people had worshipped the totem animal whose power protected the tribe. The totem was the ancestral father who became the tribe's god, and the god-totem symbolizes a tribal self that is projected onto the animal and unites the tribe like a great parent-god. Later, personal totem animals were created that symbolized to the tribe members their individual self as anchored in supernal knowledge and in the power ascribed to the animal. For the patient in *Equus*, whose strict father is absent from his life, the horse is not only Jesus but a father substitute. He is the horse-father whose look makes the boy feel castrated and impotent and leads him to seek revenge. The father and Jesus are mixed here, and the totem of the father turns into the totem of the god. This mixture applies in situations where the father-god replaces the actual father, who is absent.

Jungian analyst Marie Von Franz writes that no healing is possible without contact with the numinous, which can be experienced in the encounter with archetypal symbols that appear in dreams and creative pursuits. Without the numinous, the best that can be expected of psychotherapy is some relief or social adaptation. However, the numinous, like any healing element, can, in her view, become dangerous when the ego is weak and shows no humility vis-à-vis what is greater (Von Franz 1993, 45). Archetypal contents may become possessed by images of omnipotence and identification with them, like the patients in *Man Facing Southeast* and *K-Pax* and the therapist in *Equus*.

The patient's dangerous worship of the horse in *Equus* derives from an unconscious fascination that surrenders to a large archetypal force and is controlled by it. The therapist in *Equus* does not expect the patient to redirect to him the admiration and worship of the alternative father-god role he plays, nor does he feel he deserves this, given his doubts about himself as a therapist. He knows that the terrible implication of healing him is to deprive him of his worshiping the power of the horse-Jesus when the boy is not anchored in the core of the mysterious numinous power of his own self.

Freud forgot-abandoned the spiritual aspect and the search for redemption that concern both dreams and films. Cinema was born in a godless secular era; henceforth, cinema is like a creator of the universe. The unconscious of the secular person and of twentieth-century cinema believes in the individual who assumed divine greatness after the death of God. Nietzsche proclaimed the death of God, and Jung said that, since the death of God, humans have enthroned themselves in his place. That is the foundation for the grandiosity of political leaders and dictators—there is no God in their hearts, and they impose their inflated, capricious, pugnacious ego on the world. People transferred their need to trust a supreme power to their leaders.

Contrary to the enthronement of the ego is the Jungian approach, which places the self at the center of the psyche. In Jung's approach, faith in the numinous core of the self could be viewed as a substitute, as it were, for faith in God when God turned into the archetype of the self. Jung claims that religious feeling is, by nature, the basic human feeling. Modern individuals who have detached themselves from religious feeling and thereby lost the fundamental ground of their spiritual existence pay for it with mental disturbances. The patient's worship and idealization of the therapist, therefore, should be respected as a stage where the patient learns to sense the religious dimension in his own psyche by experiencing the numinous powers that guide him from the inside. On the one hand, the therapist should be ready to accept the patient's admiration and, on the other, give up the patient's worship as well as his own narcissistic need for it. The patient may then ultimately direct his worship to the numinous-transcendent core of his own self.

According to Jung, religious feeling enables us to recognize the core of the self as the meeting place of the divine and the human, thus acknowledging the self's core as our existential foundation. Perhaps Rantés identifies with this view when he experiences himself as a relay station for powers in outer space. He plays in the church and tells Denis, his therapist: "If God is in you, you kill God every day within each of you." Denis says that only a priest will be able to help his patient. In the closing scene, as noted, Denis also says: "We are all the stupid or mad children of the same father." We might say that the father is not only prehistoric man or the archetypal father but the transcendent father, the source of our psyche, whose religious foundation is acknowledged by both Rantés and Denis. Rantés translates the divine into a concrete spatial entity, while Denis seems to lack faith in God as he lacks faith in therapy. Perhaps because of this, we see him several times in the film with the white curtain opening up in the wind as if it were asking him to receive the new spirit seeking to enter his soul. The wind symbolizes the spiritual, irrational, esoteric, numinous world that cannot be perceived with the senses and the ordinary consciousness that hesitates to open up to it. At one point, Denis stands up and closes the window.

The title of Bergman's film *Face to Face* is taken from the description of the face-to-face encounter with God in the apocalyptic vision: "For now we see in a mirror dimly, but then face to face. Now I know in part; then I shall understand fully, even as I have been fully understood" (1 Corinthians 13:12). The title hints at the possibility that a face-to-face encounter with ourselves is an encounter with the divine element inside us, though nothing attests to it in the film. Indeed, the face-to-face encounter with ourselves seems like a disappointing replacement for the face-to-face encounter with God.

In the old world, where God and religious feelings had a place in life, God was identified with love. Secular cinema believes in the therapist as a substitute and an emissary of God, an agent of healing, redemption, and love. This view is behind the patient's desperate resolve to be loved by the therapist, in a replication of divine love that contains parental and erotic-romantic love, as if that were the only path to healing and redemption.

Jung cites an example of a patient who developed a strong dependence on him. Most of her dreams touched on the doctor's personality, but his appearance in the dream seldom resembled him. At times he was unnaturally big. Other times, he looked old or resembled her father, but he was curiously woven into nature, as in the following dream:

> Her father (who in reality was of small stature) was standing with her on a hill that was covered with wheat-fields. She was quite tiny beside him, and he seemed to her like a giant. He lifted her from the ground and held her in his arms like a little child. The wind swept over the wheat-fields, and as the wheat swayed in the wind, he rocked her in his arms.
>
> (Jung 1972, 132)

Jung concludes that "the unconscious placed a special emphasis on the supernatural, almost 'divine' nature of the father-lover, thus accentuating still further the over-valuation occasioned by the transference" (ibid.). He sees a purpose in these dreams: to elevate the therapist to godlike rank, to discover in the doctor the superior entity that the psyche longs for, inferring that the unconscious impulse, though seemingly focused on the doctor, seeks a god.

> Could the longing for a god be a *passion* welling up from our darkest, instinctual nature, a passion unswayed by any outside influences, deeper and stronger perhaps than the love for a human person? Or was perhaps the highest and truest meaning of that inappropriate love we call "transference," a little bit of real *Gottesminne*, that has been lost to consciousness ever since the fifteenth century?
> (Ibid., 133).

The patient was not religious, and the father-god in the dream, rather than as a traditional godlike character, appeared as a nature demon when the god-nature is the blowing wind, "stronger and mightier than man, an invisible breath-spirit" (ibid., 135), like an archaic god who surfaced from the depths of the unconscious psyche.

In *Through a Glass Darkly*, Bergman describes a young mental patient unloved by her dead mother and her alienated father. The girl seeks her redemption in hallucinations about visits from God. Instead of God, however, a terrifying spider threatens to climb on her. Even in her psychosis, she fails to create the loving God she needs. Instead of a God symbolizing a redeeming healing force, the spider appears as a regressive devouring power.

The collective unconscious of the cinema is thus a mirror image of the modern individual who has lost God as an object of worship. Secular individuals can worship their own grandiose identity, charismatic spiritual leaders, God substitutes, or a therapist. We find this pattern of therapist worship in *Julie Walking Home*.

The danger is in the transfer of the worship to dictators who assume the charisma of the absolute God and exploit it to activate murderous demonic powers against humanity, in a variation of God turning into a spider trapping believers in its web.

Worshiping a therapist obviously entails a problematic aspect. Identifying the therapist as the sole source of redemption is idolatry, which the critique of the therapist in films is intended to prevent.

Jung pointed to an inner balance in the psyche—when one pole of the archetype is taken to an extreme, the unconscious will bring up its opposite (Jung 1976, 375). Thus, when the archetypal image of the good-loving-redeeming-healing god is projected onto the therapist, so is its opposite—the evil god Satan. Hence, contrary to the descriptions of the therapist as loving, understanding, totally devoted, and a stand-in for the healing redeeming God, monstrous images of therapists appear, for example, in *The Silence of the Lambs*, where the psychiatrist is a cannibalistic sadist, and in an episode of *Colombo*, where he is a sexual predator and a murderer. This balancing act is the only explanation for the emergence of such terrifying psychopathic images of therapists: In the cinema, we meet face-to-face not only the shadow of God but also the human shadow.

The mythical religious power of cinema conveys the source of the human longing for a face-to-face encounter. God's face remains invisible—as God says to

Moses, "You shall see my back, but my face shall not be seen" (Exodus 33:23)—but cinema presents the human face and the face of the universe, where God is fully reflected. However sublime and terrifying, God's face is the source of cinema's power.

Youssef Ishaghpour and Jean-Luc Godard write: "But here it's the images that are looking at us, that's why it's our absence, it's the absence we see there and it's the gaze of the Void on us . . . the cinema image as that which shows, as revelation, fullness before interpretation, redemption and resurrection of the real" (Godard and Ishaghpour 2005, 106–107). In this formulation, the cinema concretizes a reality as if in a delusion, or a vision, or, in fact, as in a divine revelation. We see it and cannot touch it or, in the theological terms of André Bazin, "cinema is the revelation and epiphany of presence" (ibid., 131).

References

Benjamin, Walter (2015). "The Work of Art in the Age of Mechanical Reproduction." In *Illuminations*, trans. Harry Zorn, 211–244 (London: The Bodley Head).
Bergman, Ingmar (1960) "Why I Make Movies." *Horizon* (3), September, 6–9.
Fromm, Erich (1950) *Psychoanalysis and Religion* (New Haven, CT: Yale University Press).
Gibson, L. Terrill (2005) "Cin-Imago Dei: Jungian Psychology and Images of the Soul in Contemporary Cinema." *Cinema and Psyche* 73: 71–89.
Godard, Jean-Luc and Youssef Ishaghpour, *The Archeology of Film and the Memory of a Century*, trans. John Howe (Oxford: Berg, 2005).
Jung, C. G. (1972) *Two Essays on Analytical Psychology*, C. W. 7, trans. R. F. C. Hull (Princeton, NJ: Princeton University Press).
Jung, C. G. (1976) *Symbols of Transformation*, C. W. 5, trans. R. F. C. Hull (Princeton, NJ: Princeton University Press).
Klein, Uri (2010) "The Faith of Cinema." *Haaretz*, November 11, 2 [Heb].
May, Rollo (1991) *The Cry for Myth* (New York: Norton).
Netzer, Ruth (2004) *Journey to the Self: The Alchemy of the Psyche—Symbols and Myths* (Ben Shemen, Israel: Modan) [Heb].
Rotenberg, Mordechai (1994). *Christianity and Psychiatry: The Theology Behind Psychology* (Tel Aviv: Broadcast University Series) [Heb].
Von Franz, Marie (1993) *Psychotherapy* (London: Shambhala).

Chapter 8

Therapy in Cinema
The Wholeness of the Self, the Union of Opposites

Jung views the goal of individuation, of psychic development with therapy (as well as without it), as the realization of the true self. Indeed, in many films, the therapist and the patient go through a journey to reach the true self behind the masks. The archetypes at work in the therapist-patient relationship act to promote individuation and the realization of the self.

The archetype of the self is an archetype of the psyche's totality that contains all its opposites, and the contrasts within it become a fruitful and dynamic source of constant evolvement. From the self's viewpoint, in all its films about therapy and its contrasting outlooks, cinema conveys the full range of perspectives—the conscious and unconscious perceptions, the longings, and the fears of both therapist and patient. From this mosaic, cinema creates the overall picture of therapist-patient relationships.

Cinema, as noted, leans toward dramatic extremes. The psyche's oscillations from one pole to another express imbalance but yield fascinating cinematic results. Therapy, however, aims for the contrary—to find a balance between opposites, to moderate and regulate them, which means renouncing extreme archetypal images that confuse us and betray us and acknowledge that both of us, therapists and patients, are humans who cannot be more than good enough.

The psyche's aim to balance and reconcile its opposites and reach one self-identity features in many therapy films where the protagonist goes through a journey aiming to unify a split soul, connect the known to the forgotten that returned to memory (Lisa in *David and Lisa*, the patients in *K-Pax*, *The Three Faces of Eve*, *Sybil*, *Marnie*, and *Don Juan*) and merge the ego and the other. The attempt to unite the psyche's opposites is sustained in all therapeutic processes and visible in cinema. Alain Resnais says: "The characters in my films include contradictions, as it appears to me true to life as we know it." He seeks "to create an encounter between images, sound, and dialogues in films, leading to a work of art as stable as a statue. I believe that, in cinema, feeling flows when the film has a precise form." Resnais notes the importance of a "coherent tone," which follows "from the merging of all the film's parts into one" (in Klein 2010b, 2). Resnais tries to create a synthesis of the psyche's contradictions, the film's parts, the images, dialogues, feelings, and form, and of various aspects of filmmaking. The search for the unification of opposites in the psyche and art converges here.

DOI: 10.4324/9781003460688-9

Tracking the repressed story to return it to consciousness seeks to unite the patient's conscious and unconscious opposites. As Holstius, the therapist, says to Theodora in *The Aunt's Story* (White 1963, 277): "I expect you to accept the two irreconcilable halves. Come." Holstius proposes coexistence between her infinite, mystical, inner life and external, limited human life. He suggests the possibility of living in a time realm that contains both the inside and the outside, divine time, and clock time. This union of opposites is "true permanence" that, according to Holstius, is "a state of multiplication and division." His words spread peace throughout her body, and she then felt "there was no end to . . . [her] lives . . . These met and parted, met and parted, movingly. They entered into each other . . . were the same and understandable" (ibid., 284).

Cinema's description of the therapist's wounds and shadows is meant to prevent the therapist-patient split as one between healer and wounded. We can now see these two aspects in both of them as a dialectical union of opposites taking place in everyone's psyche. Overall, films show the good and the bad in the therapist as inevitable aspects of the psyche that compel us to be aware of their existence and to limit denial as far as possible. Cinema is thus a mirror of the totality of opposites seeking to unite in the psyche of the spectator.

I suggest that we therapists see films dealing with therapist-patient relationships as a series that acts as a compensatory dream sent to us to become better acquainted with the patients' psyche and more aware of ourselves, the therapeutic processes, and the therapist-patient relationships. We will then be able to learn from our mistakes and become better therapists. I do not mean wonderful therapists but good enough therapists—knowledgeable, empathic, attentive to our own selves, and allowing patients to grow out of and into their own selves.

I conclude with the words of Robert Lindner, who writes in his foreword to his book *The Fifty-Minute Hour* about the self of the therapist—the agent of the therapy:

> The common element in all the tales that follow is the self of the analyst. Each story, while it tells of a specific "case," deals finally with the deployment of that self in the therapeutic enterprise . . . That this agent is a mere human, just another person with his own hopes and fears, goals and anxieties, prejudices and pretensions, weaknesses and strengths, is really the heart of the matter.
>
> (Lindner 1962)

References

Klein, Uri (2010b) "The Statue of Cinema: Interview with Alain Resnais." *Haaretz*, July 23, 2 [Heb].

Lindner, Robert (1962) *The Fifty-Minute Hour: A Collection of True Psychoanalytic Tales* (London: Transworld).

White, Patrick (1963) *The Aunt's Story* (London: Penguin Books).

Glossary

Alchemy The study of chemical compounds in the pre-scientific era that attempted to produce precious metals from inferior materials. Jung used alchemic symbols as the basis for his theory of the psyche and the individuation processes, which are the psyche's alchemy.

Alchemical Bath A concept taken from an alchemical text, *The Rosarium*. It symbolizes the unconscious field shared by its two participants—the king and the queen, the brother and the sister, the therapist and the patient—when the two, naked, draw closer until they become one in copulation, and the separation that follows. This copulation is part of the patient's alchemical-transformative process.

Anima The feminine element in the male's psyche, which is also a bridge to his depths, to the unconscious, to feeling, intuition, nature, the senses, and the element that enables intimacy in interpersonal relations. Jung identifies the feminine with Eros.

Animus The masculine element in the woman's psyche, which is also a bridge to her unconscious, enabling expression of her masculine qualities and the development of consciousness; critical thinking, practicality, achieving goals, ambition, assertiveness, initiative, and inner authority. Jung identifies the masculine with Logos.

Archetype The archetypes are the building blocks of the collective unconscious. They are the primary templates of perception, imagination, feeling, and thinking, common to humanity at all times, a form of inborn psychic instincts existing objectively. Jung stated that the central archetypes are the father, the mother, the child, the wise old man, rebirth, the trickster, transformation, the spirit, death, and God. The archetypes embody the full repertoire of human experience and appear in symbols, which is the language through which the unconscious reveals itself to the conscious.

Compensation The self acts to repair the one-sided position of consciousness and, from the unconscious, sends the knowledge required to create a complementary compensation to consciousness. Through the unconscious and the language of the dream, the self acts as a compensatory function.

Complex The complex is an intricate set of emotions, thoughts and perceptions centering around one archetypal content. It is built from an archetypal core and the experiential contents originating from the person's experience that gather around it. For example, a "mother complex" comprises the encounter between the archetypal mother and the range of experiences with the personal mother. Like all archetypes, all complexes can become manifest in positive and negative qualities. The personal unconscious is made up of complexes rooted in the archetypes of the collective unconscious. The complex is a natural structure that, rather than expressing a problematic complication and mental disorder, conveys the sophistication of the psyche.

Eros Freud relates to Eros as life-love and as the opposite of Thanatos-death. Jung relates to Eros as a feminine element concerned with interpersonal relations and the opposite of the rational masculine Logos.

Hubris Boasting, excessive individual pride. According to Greek mythology, it is a provocation of the gods for which Moira, the goddess of fortune, metes out punishment.

Individuation The developmental process where the individual strives for wholeness and the unification of opposites toward self-realization. This process gradually intensifies in the second half of life. Jung identifies the alchemical opus with the individuation process. (See also *Repair*).

Inflation A swelling of the ego by an unconscious archetypal content that takes control of the ego.

Initiation The process of entering and joining a more developed stage or a membership group. A transitional and ritual development process, through learning and experiencing processes designed to strengthen and develop the psyche.

Libido The life energy found in instincts, emotions, and the spiritual and creative world. This definition contrasts with Freud's, who views the libido solely as sexual energy and the source of all others.

Liminality A point at the threshold of psychic states, transitional processes, and rituals, a mid-central stage detached from what was and will be and open to change processes.

Logos The word the world was created by, according to the myth. Jung views Logos as the rational, which is identified with the masculine and the objective, as opposed to the Eros that is identified with the feminine.

Numinous/Numinosity The direct, sublime, mysterious experience of elevation imbued with splendor and terror ascribed to the transcendent, the sacred, and the divine.

Participation Mystique A term coined by the anthropologist Claude Levi Brühl, referring to the psyche's initial sense of identity and shared connection with the world. It is an equivalent concept to *Unus Mundus* and *Anima Mundi*.

Persona-Mask The psychic system of adaptation to the outside world. The mask simultaneously represents and hides the person, mediating between the individual and the surroundings. The persona is shaped by the roles of individuals, who are known according to her persona.

Repair A kabbalistic term (*tikkun*) that refers to the repair of the broken vessels. The repair parallels the individuation process of unifying the opposites and fractures that split up the psyche. Repair, individuation, and self-realization deal with the simultaneous integration and containment of the psyche's conflicts.

Self The central archetype that symbolizes the totality of the psyche and contains both the conscious and the unconscious, the dynamics and the dialogue between them in the service of the individuation process and the relations with the world and others. The self is a structure and an evolving process, the scope and the unifying center of the psyche, with this synthesis corresponding to the biological level of coordination between the actions of the organism. It is the development process' source and aim, the archetype of order, organization, self-regulation, integration, centering, unification of opposites and wholeness, regulation, repair, and healing. It is also the archetype of the divine image and the divine spark in the human psyche: the soul. It is the experiential meeting point with the divine-eternal-transcendent. The self exists from the beginning and yet comes into being, and its aim is the individuation process that leads people to full realization of their consciousness, essence, and uniqueness. The self as personal providence sends individuals to realize their fate.

Self-Ego The center of consciousness and the activator of the self's potential. The development and actualization of the self occur mainly during the early years of life.

Shadow The inferior and underdeveloped part of the personality, which includes qualities considered negative. Because of their incompatibility with the psyche's attitudes, the self tends to deny the existence of shadow qualities and repress them to the unconscious, from where they operate. The role of awareness is to raise the shadow to consciousness, release the energies latent in the shadow to enable their regulation and transformation, and discover their value for development. The shadow also includes the positive parts of the self that were denied realization because of the negating attitude of consciousness.

Transcendent Everything that is beyond our consciousness and experience, usually referring to the mysterious, the divine, and the sublime.

Transformation A change that is an internal transformation of the essence, not simply a substitution.

Transcendental functioning The process taking place on the I/self axis of raising unconscious contents to consciousness, connecting and synthesizing various psychic opposites, and assimilating their integration for development and individuation. Jung considered this function to be the most important of all psychic processes. The transcendent function is not identical to the transcendent, which is the sublime, the divine beyond consciousness.

Trickster The cunning, clever, subversive prankster described in myths as the creator of the universe and the hero's servant. It uses creative deception to bypass resistance, thus enabling the breakthrough of new knowledge into personal and social consciousness. It is the sacred deceiver who allows the shadow to serve individuation.

Unconscious The part of the psyche that is not controlled by consciousness. A small part of it is the *personal unconscious* that Freud spoke of, where forgotten and repressed memories and experiences (especially those whose remembrance causes pain, guilt, censure, and mental suffering) are preserved. The larger and deeper part of the unconscious is the collective unconscious. The *collective unconscious* is the primordial, universal, inborn psychic layer comprising pivotal archetypes and mythical models, which are archetypal stories. The individual self emerges from the collective unconscious.

Index

abandonment 79
aggression 16–17, 88, 99–100
aggressive-murderous dreams 92
Agnon, S. Y. 52
alchemic bath 12
alchemy 47–48
Alexandri, Rabbi 53
alienation 82
Allen, Woody 10
Almodóvar, Pedro 81
alternative super-personality 51
Amarcord (1973) 19
ambition 88
American Psychological Association (APA) 96
Analyze This 78, 112
anima 16, 105–107
anima mundi 13, 15–16
animus 32, 112
anti-psychiatry movement 118–119
anti-psychiatry trend 119
anti-psychotic drugs 121
anti-psychotic injections 55–56
anxieties 10–11, 79
archetypes/archetypical 4, 49–61; cinematic images 9; identification and its fascination 72–78; -mythical model 125; parental figures 38; and personal existence 54; processes 100
Armstrong, Karen 12–13
art of temptation 5
As Good as It Gets 41
Aunt's Story, The 119, 132
authority 89
autobiography 14
avant-garde experimental cinema 24
awareness 7–8, 84–85, 111; of evil 11

Bagdad Cafe 112–113
Barthes, Roland 14
Bates, Alan 119
Baxter, Tom 10
Benjamin, Walter 123
Bergman, Ingmar 19, 56–57, 60, 100, 123
Bernhard, Ernst 9
Best Offer, The 115–116
betrayal archetype 51
Bialik, Haim Nachman 15
bibliotherapy 21–22
Bion, Wilfred 5
blue blood 75
borders of privacy and expression of feelings 69
boundaries in therapy 69–70
Brando, Marlon 73–74
breaking boundaries 80
Brecht, Bertolt 17
Brothers Karamazov, The 64
Brown, Norman 120
Buber, Martin 15
Buñuel, Luis 10
Burton, Richard 59

Cabinet of Dr. Caligari, The 93
Calasso, Roberto 59, 100–101
Camera Lucida (1988) 17
camera obscura 9
Campbell, Joseph 23
Canemaker, John 20
Carotenuto, Aldo 51–52, 60–61
Casement, Patrick 98
Castellanos, Rosario 23
charlatanism 88
Chesler, Phillys 46
child-parent incest 99

cinema: as bridge to the creator's true self and as self-healing 19–21; as "chief supervisor" for therapists 96–117; definition 19; as dream, unconscious and consciousness 8–12; gaze and knowledge 4–6; identification, separation and emotional element 12–17; metaphor 11; mirror and consciousness 6–8; myth and ritual 21–24; mythical religious power of 129–130; as a negative trickster 112–117; ritual and psychotherapy ritual 24–27; spectators 24; as trickster 111–112; wounding and healing cinema-spectator encounter 17–19
cinematic creativity 16
cinematic gaze 6
cinematographer 7; gaze 4–5
Claudel, Philippe 85
Clockwork Orange, A 87
Close Encounters of the Third Kind (1977) 58
'coincident love-hate' 49
collective consciousness 7, 109
collective spirit 22
collective unconscious 9
Colombo 92
committed suicide 52
communal partnership 13
compassion 11
compensation 51, 71, 89
complex 45, 75, 77, 80, 101–102
concealment 10
consciousness 7, 39, 77, 89; of self 7, 11
contact borders 69
containment-salvation 50
control-oppressiveness 88
countertransference 35
Crime and Punishment 30–31
Cupid 44

Dangerous Method, A (2011) 32
David and Lisa 67–69
day-to-day anxiety 79
death: and annihilation 34; of consciousness 67–68
defamiliarization 17
Deren, Maya 24
detachment 82
detective archetype 39
detective-researcher therapist 39
dim consciousness 12

Divina Commedia 106
divinity 67
Don Juan 65
Don Juan De-Marco 73–74, 94
Donnersmarck, Henckel von 5
Double Lover 116
dreaming consciousness 9
dreams 11, 109–111
Dr. Pomerantz 92
drug treatments 120
Dumont, Bruno 123
Durkheim, Emil 22

Eastwood, Clint 126
economic and sexual compensation 71
economic distress 114
educational cruelty 79
ego 51; consciousness 56; personality 63; -self 39
Eliade, Mircea 61
embryonic psyche 37–38
emotions/emotional: attitude 39; catharsis 125–126; closeness 41; conflicts 82; distress 79; drowning 20; -erotic love relationship 33; excitement 18; -feminine element 16; gaze 18; identification 12; and mental deadness 70; paralysis 20; provocation 13; return 71; wounding 18
empathic dialogic attention 41
envy of the patient 88
Equus 58–59, 67, 72–73, 75–76, 80, 82, 101, 105, 119–120, 126
Eros 5–6
erotic: boundaries 99–100; consummation 34; countertransference 35–36; infatuation 73; seduction 70
erotic-sexual archetype 47
erotic-sexual infatuation 45
experiential-fusing influence 13–14
exploitation 88–89

Face to Face 56–57, 79–80, 103, 128
faith in self 56
Fanny and Alexander (1982) 19
fascination 73
father archetype 32, 38
fear 10–11; of poverty 89; of rejection 88
feelings: of aggression 110; of love 42
Fellini, Federico 8, 19
female/feminine: archetype 38; -emotional bridge 74–75; -emotional element

16; -emotional-intuitive aspect 105; psyche's afflictions 44
femmes fatales 115
Ferenczi, Sandor 46
Ferguson, John 80
fictitious reality 113
Fifty-Minute Hour, The 132
film making 19
Folman, Ari 20
Foucault, Michel 118
Franz, Marie Von 127
fraud 89
Fredericksen, Don 23
Friedrich, Caspar David 88
friendly emotional-spiritual 75–76
frigidity 71
From Caligari to Hitler 93
Fromm, Erich 125

Gabbard, Glen 96–97
Garden of Eden 110
Geldman, Mordechai 12
generosity 89
Gibson, Terrill 13, 22, 124–125
glorification 88
Godard, Jean-Luc 130
god of individuation 37
Gogh, Van 119–120
Good Will Hunting 43, 67, 69, 81–82, 90, 94
Gospel According to Jesus Christ, The 60
Gottesminne 129
grandiosity 89
Gran Torino 126
gratification and transition 44
greed 89
Greek mythology 102
group-collective initiation processes 23
Guggenbühl-Craig, Adolf 84
guilt 11; for her sexual needs 31

hallucinations of psychotics 120
Haneke, Michael 11
Happiness 92
Hassidic rabbi-*zaddiq* 61
hate 48–49
healing 69; -integration process 100; processes 124; *punctum* 18
hero archetype 39
Hesse, Herman 81
Hidden (2005) 11
History of Madness 118

Hoffmann, Yoel 98
Holy Smoke 85, 91, 94
hubris 5, 43, 77, 86, 88, 91, 99
human/humaneness 11; betrayal 56; consciousness 6, 8, 67; spirit 87
humanity 8; into empathy 13; sympathy and 13
husband-therapist-detective 86

impersonal archetypes 72
In America (2002) 19
Indian shamanic rituals 22
individual consciousness 8
individuation 25, 27, 37, 60, 131
infatuation 110
inflation 59–60, 72–74
initiation 13, 23, 26
inner child 104–105
inner psyche 11
inquiry 69
intentional manipulation 83
Interpretation of Dreams, The 10
interpretation *vs.* emotional experience 107
In Therapy (2005) 99–100
Intimate Strangers 73, 80, 83, 106, 121
Ironside 88
Iscariot, Judas 55
Ishaghpour, Youssef 130
Israel-Lebanon War 20

Jesus-messiah-redeemer 49
Jesus-redeemer archetype 58
Jewish-kabbalistic myth 53
Julie Walking Home 31–33, 54, 63, 72, 80, 106, 129
Jungian approach 127
Jungian therapy 15

Kahane, Baruch 61
King of Hearts 119
Kohut, Heinz 41
Kornfield, Jack 24
K-Pax 57–58, 65, 67, 72–73, 75, 87, 101, 119–120

Lacan, Jacques 6–7
Laing, Ronald 82, 118
language of pictures 6–7
Lantana 82
Last Will of Dr. Mabuse, The (1933) 93
Lévy-Valensi, Eliane Amado 86, 89
libido 51

Lieblich, Maty 88
liminality 23, 27, 61
Lindner, Robert 57, 73, 88
Lisbon Story (1994) 5
literature and myth 8
logos 16
Lorca, Federico García 18
loss of separation and identity 78–81
love 40–48; compassion 42–43; components of 42; emotional and ethical aspects 43; erotic-sexual archetype 47; erotic-sexual infatuation 45; gratification and transition 44; lack of 42; primary-symbiotic fusion 43–44; psychotherapy 48; romantic-erotic realization 47–48; romantic-erotic yearnings 45; romantic infatuation 44; romantic love and psychotherapy 45; sexual feelings 45; and sexuality 32; sexual transgression 46–47; and sexual yearnings 32; spiritual-psychic complement 47; therapeutic 43; therapeutic reality 44
love-hate relationship 49

madness and sanity 119
Malraux, André 81
Mamet, David 24
Man Facing Southeast 31, 53–54, 57–58, 65, 67, 72–74, 80, 82, 84–85, 90, 94, 101, 105–106, 110, 119–120, 127
Maoz, Gadi 35
Marnie 40, 71, 80, 87
masking 10
materialistic collective consciousness 55–56
May, Rollo 21
McDougall, Joyce 103
medical establishment 60
megalomanic omnipotent power 61
mental health condition 121
metonymy 10
Middle Ages to the Renaissance 118
Miłosz, Czesław 15–16
mistrust 94–95
Mitchell, Stephen A. 6, 39, 41, 97
Monk and the Philosopher, The 42
Moon and the Son, The (2005) 20
mother archetype 37–38
Murch, Walter 22
mysticism 6
mythological-religious narrative 125

myths/mythology 6; ancestral human ritual 22; ancient bibliotherapy 21–22; cinema as 22; collective constitutive foundation 22; communal-tribal collective 21; constructs of humanity 22–23; definition 21; dramatization 21–22; entry and exit 23; film-watching ritual, triangular structure 23; -maker 14; psychic depths 23; and ritual 21–24; and sculptures 123–124; social and religious 21

Name of the Game, The 121
narcissistic-childish-primary fantasy 71
narcissistic gaze 7
narcissistic love 42
Narcissus myth 103
natural modesty 6
neediness 79, 89
negative self-image 51
Neumann, Erich 38, 93
Nicholson, Jack 41
numinous 126–128

Oedipal myth 14, 21
Oedipal rebellion 98
Oedipus' hubris 5
Ogden, Thomas 41
Oldman, Virgil 115
omnipotent: archetype 51; divinity 72; ego 51; magician archetype 63–65
One Flew Over the Cuckoo's Nest 56, 75
Ordinary People (1980) 67, 96–97, 125
over-identification 50, 111
Oz, Amos 30–31

parental archetypes 37–38
parents' archetypes 38
participation mystique 62
Pasolini, Pier Paolo 9, 126
patient's: entrapping manipulation 81; fantasy 97; seductiveness 83; -therapist dyad 53
payment in therapy 89
Perera, Silvia 11, 22
Perry, John 50–51, 120
Persona 60, 73, 80, 90, 100, 103
personality 79–80
personal neurosis 22
personal parental figures 37
persona-mask 90, 104
photographer-detective tracks 88
photography 14–15

physical: contact 33; -psychic space 23–24
pictorial-sound reality 12
place borders 69
pornography 6
post-Buñuel avantgarde 10
postmodern intersubjective therapists 103
pre-digital cinematography 9
prestige and honor 88
pre-verbal languages 15
primary archetypes in therapy 37–38
primary-symbiotic fusion 43–44
Prince of Tides, The 70
privacy and intimacy boundaries 5–6
problematic-shadowy aspects 42
psyche 8, 11, 14
psychiatry/psychiatric 82; hospitalization 114, 116–117; and psychotherapy 125; treatment 56
psychic/psychical: balance 87; normality 82; reality 12; -spiritual category of people 62; -spiritual voyage 126; transformation 112
psychoanalysis 10, 21; and psychotherapy 97–98; of vision 5
psychological identification 62
psychotherapy 5, 7, 18, 37, 41; in Buddhist therapy 27; cinema dealing with 126; conscious and unconscious 26; dreams in films about 107–109; ego and nuclear self 26; insecurity and uncertainty 25; love 48; mythical story 27; ordinary rituals 25; as a profession 26; psychotherapeutic process 27; recurring activity 25; ritual and cinema ritual 24–27; theories 110; therapeutic contract 25; therapist-patient relationships 27; transition rituals 26; in tribal cultures 27
psychotic breakdown 79–80
psychotic-catatonic collapse 75
psychotic criminal 85
psychotic fantasy 120
psychotic hallucination 120
punctum 17–18
Purple Rose of Cairo, The (1985) 10

quasi-comic situation 83
quasi-dream surrealistic dimension 10

Racker, Heinrich 46
real-time cinematography 19–20
Rear View 5
Rear Window 87–88, 90, 105

Red Book, The 113
redeemer: archetype 111; -savior archetype 50; -shaman archetype 63; -sufferer-victim 56
relational psychoanalysis 109
relationship problems 82
religion/religious 6; authorities 124; -medical rituals 61; and psychotherapy 126; ritual 124; symbolism 126
repair 68, 125
responsibility 11
romantic: -erotic realization 47–48; -erotic yearnings 45; infatuation 44; love and psychotherapy 45; sexless love 71; -sexual involvement 70–72; -sexual relationships 44
Rosarium 79
Rotenberg, Mordechai 125

Sacrifice, The 126
sanity and madness 101
schizophrenics 120
Schulz, Bruno 13
Schwartz-Salant, Nathan 70
Sechehaye, Marguerite 46
secular cinema 128
secularization 125
seducer of women 74
seductiveness 88
Segal, Robert 14
self: -aggrandizement 99; -awareness 8, 11, 13, 63, 69, 101, 110; -conscious 7; -consciousness 11; -deception 88; -ego 25; -esteem 82; -hatred 31; healing aspect 52; -healing psychotic hallucination 121; -identity 23, 131; -image 51; -importance 101; -inflicted aggression 79; -knowledge 7, 11, 103; -psychodrama 80; -sacrifice 34; -starvation 31; -value 59, 89
sensorial concreteness 18
sensorial fullness 12
sex/sexual 83, 110; consummation 70; contact 75–76; and death 5–6; ecstasy 58; -erotic exploitation 89; exploitation 85; feelings 45; fulfilment 110; knowledge 43; -pagan creature 73; relations 99; relationship 33; and therapeutic relationship 116; transgression 46–47; union 79; and violence 10–11; yearnings 32
Sexton, Anne 86

shadow 11, 30, 42, 48, 50, 85–87, 129
Shaman archetype 61–63
shamanism 61–63
Shem, Samuel 48
Shoham, Giora 119–120
Shrink 82
Side Effects 114–115
Siegelman, Ellen 41, 43
Silence of the Lambs, The 92, 129
Silver Linings Playbook 113–114
social consciousness 56
socialization process 16
Son, The 116–117
Son's Room, The 82
Sopranos, The 47, 67
sorrow 11
Soul Keeper, The 31–32, 46, 57, 73
spectator-observed relationship 12
Spellbound 40, 70–71
spiritual/spirituality 59–60; cinema 10; entity 126; -psychic complement 47; redemption 57–58
State of Mind 70
State of Play 91
Stein, Murray 62
stinginess 89
Stourdzé, Sam 9
Strenger, Carlo 41
suicide/suicidal 16–17; attempts 31; drowning 71; self-destruction 31; weakness 72
Sullivan, Harry Stack 82
super-consciousness 62
surrealism 67–68
Sybil 67
symbiotic neediness 88
symbiotic over-involvement 80
symbolic expressions 56
symbolization 10
sympathy and humanity 13

Talk to Her (2002) 81
Tarkovsky, Andrei 126
techno-shamanic ritual 24
Thanatos 5–6
theathron 22
theology-religion and psychotherapy 125
Theorem 126
Therapeutae 124
therapist-dominated hierarchy 97

therapist-patient relationships 12, 14, 18, 30–36; archetypes activated in 37–65; cinema's view of 96; description 67–69; equation 57; films, frequent in 44; hierarchy 118–119; split 132
therapist's: consciousness 84; wounds and emotional difficulties 81–85; wounds and shadows 132
therapy/therapeutic: in cinema 131–132; errors 96; infatuation 33; love 32, 42, 100; narrative 98; reality 44; and redemption 123–130; relationships 86; and romantic love 71; self-confrontation 80; and supervision 89
Through a Glass Darkly (1961) 100, 129
time borders 69
timelessness of death 67
Touch, The (1971) 17
traditional cinematic realism 12
transcendent 25–26, 47–50, 127–128
transformation 13, 16, 24, 93, 110–112
tribal myths 7
trickster, cinema as 111–117
Trier, Lars von 13
trust in therapy 93–95
truth-loving 7
two-way transference 109

Ullmann, Liv 79
unconscious: anxiety 93–94; murderous aggression 85; seduction 32; territory 67
Unger, Henry 5, 17

Vertigo (1958) 80
videotapes 11–12
violence 60
violent aggression 79
virtual identity 57
virtual representations 10
voyeurism 5, 83
vulnerabilities 110; of therapists 70

wakeful consciousness 9
Waltz with Bashir (2008) 20
Weber, Max 125
Wenders, Wim 5, 7
Western psychology 24
Western psychotherapy 27
When Nietzsche Wept (1992) 46, 82

White, Patrick 119
Whitmont, Edward 11, 22
Winnicott, Donald 4, 48–49
Wizard of Oz, The 64
wounded healer 18
wounded philosopher 53

Yalom, Irvin 45–46, 64, 98
yearnings 10–11; romantic-erotic 45; sex/sexual 32

Zelig 72, 112
Zentropa (1991) 13

Printed in the USA
CPSIA information can be obtained
at www.ICGtesting.com
LVHW021736041124
795688LV00040B/1268